DATE DUE			

The
United States Army

IN PEACETIME

ESSAYS IN HONOR
OF THE BICENTENNIAL,
1775-1975

ROBIN HIGHAM and CAROL BRANDT,
Editors

Published for the Freedom Park Foundation by

Military Affairs/Aerospace Historian Publishing
Eisenhower Hall, Kansas State University,
Manhattan, KS 66506, USA

Cover design by Robin Higham and Carol Brandt.

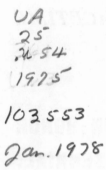

ISBN 0-89126-018-8 (hardback)

ISBN 0-89126-019-6 (paperback)

Printed in the United States of America
by
Ag Press
Manhattan, KS 66502

This book is sponsored by the Freedom Park Foundation, Inc., Junction City, KS 66441.

The Contributors

Richard A. Bartlett was born in Boulder, Colorado, in 1920. He was educated in the Boulder public schools and holds a B.A. and Ph.D. from the University of Colorado. His special field of history is the American West. His first book, *Great Surveys of the American West* (Norman, Oklahoma: 1962) won the Spur Award of the Western Writers of America. His two most recent books are *The New Country: A Social History of the American Frontier, 1776-1890* (New York: 1974) and *Nature's Yellowstone* (Albuquerque, New Mexico: 1974). He is presently working on a second Yellowstone history, *Wonderland: The Yellowstone Park in a Changing America*. Dr. Bartlett is professor of history at Florida State University, Tallahassee.

James Otis Breeden was born in 1936 at Morrisville, Virginia, and was educated at the University of Virginia and at Tulane. His special field is the history of medicine. His first book, *Joseph Jones, M.D. Scientist of the Old South* has just been published by the University Press of Kentucky. He is presently associate professor of the history of medicine at Southern Methodist University, Dallas.

B. Franklin Cooling was born in 1938 in New Brunswick, New Jersey. He graduated from Rutgers and obtained his Ph.D. from the University of Pennsylvania. He served for some years as Book Review Editor for *Military Affairs* before becoming Assistant Director for Research Services at the U.S. Army Military History Research Collection at Carlisle Barracks. He is the author of *Benjamin Franklin Tracy: Father of the Modern American Fighting Navy* (1973) and of *Symbol, Sword and Shield: Defending Washington, 1861-1865* (1975).

Marvin E. Fletcher was born December 1941 in San Francisco, California. He attended public schools there, and in 1959 received his B.A. from the University of California, Berkeley. He received his Ph.D. in 1968 from the University of Wisconsin. Since then he has been teaching at Ohio University, Athens, Ohio. Among the courses taught have been those in Black History, American Military History, and Jews in American History. He has published articles in *Military Affairs* and *Arizona and the West*. In 1974 the University of Missouri Press published his *The Black Soldier and Officer in the United States Army, 1891-1917*. He is presently at work on a biography of Brigadier General Benjamin O. Davis and on a study of enlistees in the army in the 1870s.

Martin and Joan Kyre, a husband-and-wife writing team, hold degrees from Ohio Wesleyan University. They are recognized authorities in the field of military occupation policy. Martin Kyre (Ph.D., University of Washington) is currently an Associate Professor of Political Science at Texas Technological University. His firsthand involvement with U.S. Army civil affairs includes civic action work during the Korean conflict and a variety of USAR assignments with both the Army Civil Affairs School and the Civil Affairs Division in the Pentagon. Joan Kyre's academic background is in sociology with a special concern for social theory.

Their first jointly authored book, *Military Occupation and National Security* (Washington: Public Affairs Press, 1968), was published following their field research on Okinawa. In 1972 they returned to the Ryukyus to study the termination of the American occupation and were guests of the Japanese Government at the 15 May Okinawan Reversion Ceremony held in Tokyo. A related project has since taken them to the Middle East. Their forthcoming book, *Military Occupation in Linkage Politics: Israel on the West Bank — United States on Okinawa*, reflects their continuing concern with the political issues that arise when a foreign army is charged with implementing a civil administration.

Donald J. Mrozek is Assistant Professor of History at Kansas State University. He received his Ph.D. from Rutgers University in 1972. His major research and teaching are in the area of United States military history, emphasizing the origins and development of major changes in defense poliScy. His publications include articles on colonial history in *The Journal of the Rutgers University Library* and on defense policy in *The Business History Review* and *Military Affairs*. He is currently working on a study of the transformation of American military institutions during the period from the Spanish-American War to the creation of the all-volunteer Army.

Leo E. Oliva was born in Kansas in 1937. After receiving his Ph.D. from the University of Denver, he moved to Fort Hays State College, where he is now Chairman of the Department of History. His publications include

Soldiers on the Santa Fe Trail, a number of articles on the Army on the Frontier in such journals as *Military Affairs*, as well as research interests in the American Indian and western literature.

Theodore Ropp was born in Illinois in 1911. He graduated from Oberlin College and received his Ph. D. from Harvard in 1937. He taught there and then moved to Duke University in 1938 with occasional years at the Naval War College and the Army War College. From 1966 to 1970 he was President of the American Military Institute of which he was made a Fellow in 1974. He is best known for his book *War in the Modern World* (1959).

James J. Stokesberry is an author and consultant in Washington, D.C. He served as staff historian for the National Armed Forces Museum Advisory Board in the Smithsonian Institution from 1965 to 1973 and conducted intensive research into mid-Nineteenth Century naval technology.

Alvin R. Sunseri is a Professor of History at Northern Iowa University in Cedar Falls. He received his Ph. D. from Louisiana State University. He has taught at colleges and universities in the United States, and is the author of numerous articles dealing with military matters and ethnic conflict. A book on relations between Anglos and Mexican-Americans in the Southwest entitled *Seeds of Discord: New Mexico in the Aftermath of the Anglo Conquest, 1848-1861*, is scheduled to be published by Nelson-Hall Publishers later this year.

Colonel William L. Hauser graduated from West Point in 1954 and has served tours with field artillery units in the United States, Germany, Korea, and Vietnam. In 1968-1969 he commanded a combat battalion in the Mekong Delta. He is a graduate of both the General Staff College and the War College and holds a M.A. in history from the University of Southern California and a certificate in Southeast Asian Studies from the University of Singapore. He wrote *America's Army in Crisis* (1973) while a Research Associate of John Hopkins University's Washington Center for Foreign Policy Research.

Robin Higham is the Editor and **Carol Brandt** is the Managing Editor of *Military Affairs*, Department of History, Kansas State University.

Contents

Note on Map and Photo Sources

Maps are by Bill Schroeder, Audio-Visual Center, Arts and Sciences, Kansas State University.

Except for a few photographs for which special credit is given, all pictures are keyed for the following sources, to which thanks are given for permission to reproduce:

FR   Photo Branch, Training Aids Office, Fort Riley, KS

LVN   Fort Leavenworth Museum, KS

KSU   Kansas State University Archives and the Military Science Department

NARS National Archives, Washington, D.C.

USA   U.S. Army Still Photo Library, Washington, D.C.

Foreword

Sponsored by the Freedom Park Foundation of Junction City, Kansas, this book honors the U.S. Army on its bicentennial.

The theme chosen was not the glorious wars of the past, but rather the contributions of the Army to and its relations with American society in peacetime. As the noted military historian Professor Theodore Ropp has said over the years, peace is the norm and war is the exception. The long quiet years of the Nineteenth Century were those during which the Army surveyed the country, saved the National Parks, and began to control the waterways as the people desired. In the Twentieth Century, the Army has benefitted American society not only as protector, but through its various activities ranging from medical advances and aid to disaster victims to its direct involvement in the welfare of the voters in many states. And its peacetime role has not been limited to the United States, but has included occupations of foreign lands with all the cultural implications which have come from intermarriage. In the present century, then, the Army has played a multitude of roles, not all of which have been covered in this book, which can only devote its pages to some of the most praiseworthy of the Army's activities.

The Army in peacetime, outside of the unusual Cold War period, has been much smaller than many other professions and trades. Yet as Kipling said about that ubiquitous British private, Tommy Atkins, its critics have been many, and they have overlooked the many quiet contributions made in favor of those that can be beaten with a publicity stick.

We hope this book acts as a corrective to those actions and a tribute to the men in Army green.

Robin Higham
Kansas State University

The Army today has forgotten its heritage. Modern officers may wonder what Army this infantry sergeant was in. He was, in fact, at Fort Leavenworth in the late Nineteenth Century, but reflects the Prussian influence after the victories of 1870-1871. (LVN)

Chapter 1

INTRODUCTION—

ARMIES IN PEACETIME

Theodore Ropp

The Historical Setting

Essays on peacetime contributions of armies may smack of public relations, so this introduction must first recall some home truths of U.S. Army history. The roles of war and the Army in making Americans the wealthiest and most powerful people in the world were episodic. Professional soldiers made major military decisions and invented or adopted some key military techniques. They shared in, but did little to formulate, the civic ideals and mystiques that accompanied national political, economic, technological, and military success.

Our peacetime regular Army was a guild of specialists. When the frontier disappeared and a century of "free security" ended in 1890, there were 28 times as many physicians (104,805) in the United States as active-duty armed service officers (3,718). The latter's numbers doubled in 1910 (7,562), and tripled again by 1938 (26,103), but were still far behind physicians (169,169). This compared with over 30,000 active-duty German officers in 1910—one for every 2,000 individuals—as against one for every 13,500 in the U.S. But in our global role, the 1950 figures were 181,465 officers, one for every 839 persons. Colonel Hauser's concluding chapter is concerned with the future of our—by previous peacetime standards— wildly inflated Cold War officers corps. More important, his essay reminds us that, to a greater degree than many other democratic peoples, we have obtained the government and the army we wanted. Hauser's "quaint old Army" of 1937 was still the guild proposed by George Washington in 1783. Its garrisons protected "us at least from surprise." It insured "similarity" in the militia's "Establishment,

Maneuvers, Exercise and Arms." It procured "Military Stores" for its "Magazines," and kept alive "Instruction" and the "Branches of the Art Military."

Thus these essays cannot claim that the peacetime U.S. Army before World War II was a major or dominant force in most areas of American life. What they do show is that in certain areas such as exploration, medicine, the handling of minorities, sports, and even the local economy—if not also in occupations abroad—the Army has been far more influential than its size would warrant, being in some cases actually the leader charting the course others would follow in far greater numbers. A comparative study would show that American soldiers have had few chances for glory either on or off the battlefield. For them, peacetime has been the norm and war the exception. Certainly, when American soldiers have entered politics, they have done so not as scheming leaders of a national faction, as in so many other countries, but as babes in the woods. Those generals who became presidents were as often amateur soldiers as professionals, whereas the professional soldiers were amateur politicians. Thus Washington and Jackson, both amateurs, as compared to Grant and Eisenhower, both professionals—with Harrison and Taylor zeroing out—were the most significant.

This may be only the historian's firm grasp of the obvious, but it would be hard to write a volume on the peacetime French or Russian armies since 1775, for example, without considering the Army in politics. Here, as Ronald Spector notes in his study of 1898's instant military hero, George Dewey (*Admiral of the New Empire*, 1974), an officer's political ideas most often simply reflected those of his age, as in an advertisement showing Dewey using Pears' Soap: "The first step toward lightening 'The White Man's Burden' is through teaching the virtues of cleanliness." Most of what every schoolboy has been told about the American soldier's subordination to civilian government and values—by such civilian scholars as Marcus Cunliffe and Samuel P. Huntington—happens to be true.

It is not only that we have seen our unprofessional military presidents as uniquely subordinate to a cherished perception of the system, it is that we have seen much that the Army has done as uniquely American. Commonly, when Americans have considered the roles of the Army at all, they have seen it as performing special services in the expansion of the United States. But the authors in this work do not say this. Although it is true that, for instance, as Leo Oliva points out, the Army explored the West and helped with the establishment of the great trails, in the past, in far distant lands, the Roman, the British, the French, the Russian, and the Chinese armies did the same, though at times with greater force and

The military problems that most interested Alexis de Tocqueville, the early Nineteenth Century observer of *Democracy in America* (1835-1840), had little to do with our regular Army. Why are "democratic nations ... naturally desirous of peace and democratic armies, of war?" "Which is the most warlike and most revolutionary class in democratic armies?" Why are "democratic armies weaker than other armies at the outset of a campaign and more formidable in protracted warfare?" The answers to such questions lay in the militia and volunteers, forces that these essays hardly consider. Tocqueville did not ask how the Industrial Revolution would affect war and armies. But the British sociologist Herbert Spencer (*Principles of Sociology*, 1896) saw such societies as less militant and less easily regimented. "On contrasting the characters of our ancestors during more warlike periods with our own characters, we see that, with an increasing ratio of industrialism to militancy, have come a growing independence, a less marked loyalty, a smaller faith in governments, and a more qualified patriotism," along with "a growing respect for the individualities of others, as is implied by ... the multiplication of efforts for their welfare."

But this trend was not universal. Germany's combination of feudalism, nationalism, and industrialism had led to "increases of armaments and of aggressive activities" and regression "toward the militant social type." Like the questions raised in the American psychologist William James' "The Moral Equivalent of War" (1910), such problems underlie current fears both of American military decline and of a peacetime Army increasingly isolated in a "marshmallow" society. But such questions were seldom asked while the peacetime Army of the early Twentieth Century was training, commanding, and stiffening those popular armies that carried the two World Wars to their more militant enemies. Now these questions are being raised again in conflicting proposals for universal training in either Asian nonresistance or in Asian martial arts. And they are related to the concept of an army whose goal is not victory, but, in Hauser's words, "deterrence by prolonged destructability," an idea not unlike Singapore's concept of national training to make that shrimp too poisonous for sharks to swallow.

Meanwhile, the violence of the early Twentieth Century had led many Americans to define peacetime much as Hauser defines it: the absence of war "in a small and dangerous world." Because "civilian society depends on the U.S. Army for its protection in this dangerous world," it must support an Army ready for immediate action. As Hauser notes, this is a major change from 1937, but, we might add, an even greater change from 1890. These questions of readiness—and for what tasks—make hard to compare our Army's peacetime roles with those of other armi

with apparently greater purpose. Richard Bartlett talks abo
saving Yellowstone, and thus may be talking about a unique.
experience, as is Marvin Fletcher in his look at the Arn
breaking down the walls around minorities—though many a
had to do this when their manpower needs have exceeded or
their prejudices. All of the authors suggest that further study
undertaken before we can reliably talk about the uniquei
American Army.

Of course what has biased our views is that the Army was
position for so many years during the Nineteenth and early
Centuries; it enjoyed "free security." After the War of 1812,
States was never in danger of external invasion. The Royal Nav
seaborne attackers already deterred by the Monroe Doctrine, a
the Canadians nor the Mexicans were in a position to mount an
Thus, after 1893, when the frontier was declared closed by t
Bureau, the Army was free—and was indeed forced—to
organizational and technological demands of the late Nineteent
round of European military developments, not to mention the
Russo-Japanese War of 1904-1905, to which it had sent observers.

How sharply our demands on the peacetime Army changed d
next 60 years is suggested by the Kyres' essay on the Army and
Affairs. "America as a nation has traditionally seen its Army'
actual or potential battlefields as being the primary reasor
existence." This is tradition in the American sense of tl
Traditional Due West Hog Calling. Colonel Hauser wisely sugg
even this "tradition" of overseas battlefields could be sharply mo
the post-Vietnam era. We can wonder how far—shorn of its
terminology—Hauser's analysis of the peacetime Army's roles
sumer, employer, and social catalyst would have been acceptec
jingoistic American population of the late Nineteenth Century? I
that the Army's major theorist, Emory Upton, did see the pea
Army as a social catalyst, but his proposals to make it such t
compulsory military service got nowhere because the nation of
believe that it needed a large European-style army at that time.
mid-Twentieth Century, however, we did need one, though this m
be true any more. Thus, the task of assessing the social role of one
time army during these two centuries in world civilization of demo(
industrial, technological, and social revolution involves elements th
at times either clearly national, time-related, or, as the Kyre:
Hauser note, connected to our perceptions of "peacetime" in a l
competitive international system which was severely strained by
same revolutions.

in "our" hemisphere, in that process by which, as Alfred de Vigny, a French officer who had been too young to win glory in the Napoleonic Wars, put it, "a modern army, as soon as it ceases to be at war, becomes a kind of constabulary, ... knowing neither its duty nor its status, ... searching in vain for its own soul" (*The Military Necessity*, 1835, trans. Humphrey Hare, 1953). In their "free security" situation, some Canadians fear that their army will disappear. Many Latin American "constabularies" long ago evolved into what Stanislas Andreski in *Military Organization and Society* (1968) calls "militocracies," whether their proclaimed political programs are conservative or revolutionary.

Vigny hoped that glory and personal loyalty to the sovereign—he had lived under three dynasties—would be replaced by the virtues of the Romans, for whom "peace was more laborious than war. They embellished their native soil with monuments, drove the great roads, [and] mixed the cement for the Roman aqueducts." The Prussians spent their "detrimental and sterile" periods of peace in organizing more than Napoleonic conscript armies and in equipping them with the new weapons of the Industrial Revolution. Our American Army found its outlets in continental expansion, in the concept of war as a science, and in similar "Roman" concepts of public service. After 1890, the demands of military science and foreign policy increasingly forced Americans to think of mass armies that could meet those compulsorily trained ones, which made even backward Russia and polyglot Austria-Hungary ready for instant mobilization and a war of great nations in arms such as broke out in 1914.

Among the most obvious areas that have not been covered in this book are the Army and education and the Army and internal order. The small size of our old Army and our early interest in public schools made the U.S. Army's role in elementary education marginal by comparison with army efforts in Tsarist and Soviet Russia, Communist China, and many developing nations. Many wartime Army testing and educational projects have been studied as well as some of the efforts to compensate veterans for the time "lost" in service. But earlier efforts to "upgrade" enlisted men, small and sporadic as they were, deserve attention, especially in connection with studies of long-service veterans. The Army's role in keeping internal order is more familiar. As we have noted, this role was often filled by the militia, or by vigilantes who might be described as *ad hoc* volunteers. This left the Army a few, by European standards, "civil disturbances," and a Rebellion which turned into a Civil War. There are some indications of what remains to be done in Jim Dan Hill's and Higham's essays in the latter's *Bayonets in the Streets* (1969) and *Civil Wars in the Twentieth Century* (1972).

Russian cavalry on their Siberian ponies encountered by U.S. troops during the march to Pekin. (NARS 111-SC-75112)

What will happen to the many long-service Army veterans who "reenter" American society in the next decade or so? Some may fit the Eighteenth Century pattern of the alcoholic misfit. Many more may fit that of the Nineteenth Century French or German postman, customs guard, or inn keeper, a person of some standing in a village or garrison town. Will American long-service veterans tend to settle near military bases, or move laterally into the bureaucracy or defense-related industrial jobs? Will they tend to form that hereditary guild of soldiers, once as familiar as the hereditary guild of officers? Or will the range of allegedly marketable skills for which they are trained make this as unlikely as an hereditary guild of television repairmen? In any case, though the sample of earlier American "lifers" is small, there may be quite a bit of information about them as yet unexploited.

Memoir writers have stressed continuity and tradition, not change, in the "quaint old" Army's subcultures. This is also true of those conflicts with civilian subcultures which have also helped to form the public image of the Army. "Too great a degree of separation," Hauser fears, may again increase "mutual suspicion and hostility." Thus it may be important to trace changes in the Army's subcultures and the degrees of separation from civilian subcultures. Here one gets the impression that the enlisted man's subculture has increasingly mirrored that of his officers, which has increasingly reflected that which Huntington sees as "the tiresome monotony and small town commercialism" of Main Street, Highland Falls, N.Y. Why the Army has moved from a small town to suburbia rather than to Detroit may be a manageable historical question. Its contemporary Little League-Rotarian life styles are not those, in any case, of Hauser's stable sergeant, polo playing officers, and ladies of the garrison. But these changes have been little studied, except for recent Army efforts to adjust to urban ghetto subcultures.

Some of these changes are also related to the Army's self-proclaimed role of "remedial social catalyst." Myths of its reforming or corrupting influence may not mirror reality, but there have been few studies of its earlier successes or failures to shape people up before returning them to society. Here, again, existing records might show something about social deviants' relations with the military and civilian judicial systems, and about the maturing effects of life in the old peacetime Army.

Researchers may have to look hard at small samples, but many peacetime Army problems were like those of Canadian-American relations, the flea in bed with the elephant. Almost every question—from the clout of the Congressmen on the armed services' committees to the easy spread of Spam by a wartime Army—involves this problem of scale. Its fluctuations are among the factors which make comparisons so difficult,

Foreign peacekeeping expeditions were broadening experiences. Here an American officer talks to a British officer of the Indian Army cavalry on the road to Pekin during the Boxer Rebellion, August 1900. (NARS 111-SC-88803)

even with the U.S. Army's British or Canadian relatives. For many reasons—common language, views of civil-military relations, unreadiness, and strategic functions—we have seen the peacetime U.S. and British armies as members of the same genus and most other European armies as different because of their size, readiness, and greater political influence. These relations have changed, and we might learn more about the relations of the peacetime Army and the people if, instead of repeating comparisons of the Anglo-American and European great power armies, with the Swiss as a small-power, militia variant, we examined some other small-power armies—such as those of Belgium, the Netherlands, and interwar Czechoslovakia—in less defensible strategic situations.

European military historians also have looked for practical lessons and at big historical questions: staff work, decision making, civil-military relations, weapons development, etc. Some of their resulting works came to such contradictory or obvious conclusions that booby traps are as obvious as opportunities for comparative research. So we can tentatively suggest comparative studies, without recommending particular methodologies. Some of the most promising areas, such as that of peace-time armies and elementary, technical, and civic education, in which, for instance, the Turks and Iranians are modern leaders, were militarily peripheral in the Nineteenth Century. Thus, although records are fairly abundant, previous researchers have not preempted or dug up the field.

Preliminary studies of some topics, such as the comparative costs of Nineteenth Century conscript and volunteer armies, indicate that these probably cannot be studied statistically. The tables of Average Annual Military Personnel per Million Population by Decades, 1816-1965, Average Annual Full-Time Conscripts, and Compulsiveness and Size of Military, and an Empirical Analysis of the Conscription Tax prepared for the President's Commission on an All Volunteer Armed Force (1970) are only indicative. To take some cases from these tables, the methods now used for estimating Gross National Products, Total Civilian Earnings Foregone against Total Military Compensation, and the educational and medical benefits which may accrue to the conscript, can hardly be used for Russia or a divided Germany in 1816-1825, Italy in 1846-1855, or Greece in 1866-1875.

The major historical problems of a Nineteenth Century military-industrial complex or militarism are just as hard to treat statistically. Herbert Spencer knew and was alarmed by the influence of arms makers and users in Imperial Germany. But an explanation of one of Germany's major peacetime military mistakes, the decision to build a High Seas Fleet, solely in terms of economic, political, and military interest groups,

Colorful and interesting were the Italian troops at Pekin in 1900. These are Bersaglieri (sharpshooters). (NARS 111-SC-75055)

is nonsense. This is equally true of Neo-Marxist views of late Nineteenth Century American imperialism. We know that peacetime armies were more influential in all of the other great powers of that era, Britain included, than in the United States. But many other facets of their influence—such as the frequently suggested relationship between conscription and factory discipline—have not been thoroughly studied. In the course of his comparisons, the historian may get new insights into the workings of these societies. In the 1880s, for example, workers in the French naval arsenals were still much closer in outlook to protected mercantile guildsmen than to freely competitive workers in a British dockyard, though the French workers were just as efficient, partly because their tools were more modern than those in the Royal ship factories.

Finally, earlier military historians' interests in weaponry and mechanization may have led us to overestimate the factory's role in homogenizing 1914 armies. By contrast with Herodotus' description of the forces serving Xerxes (VII, 60-87), 1918 armies were amazingly uniform, with the same weapons, management systems, grays, greens, and khakis. A Martian observer would have noticed some differences in helmets, collar tabs, foods, and footgear. But industrialization and war are only two of the forces that have standardized modern armies and peoples. Charles de Gaulle's *France and Her Army* (trans., 1942) listed "universal suffrage, compulsory education, the equality of rights and obligations, ... industrialization and city life, ... mass-produced goods, ... the press, ... political parties, trade unions, and sport, ... transportation, travel, and public hygiene," in short, a considerable number of those topics that these essays consider as important in the influence of the peacetime Army in American life. Many of these same topics can surely be studied comparatively, though not necessarily empirically or statistically.

Some General Comments

These essays cannot cover every aspect of two centuries of the history of armies in peacetime; they neither attempt this nor even try to look at every aspect of the U.S. Army in those long, quiet days. They do suggest some of our Army's contributions "to the growth of America" and some of "the institutional and organizational relationships" that have grown up between the Army and the people. By arranging the essays in something of a chronological order, the Editor has chosen to lead the reader from both large and small problems to the more general topics which today's peacetime Army faces in integrating itself into society. On the other hand, the essays for practical reasons do not try to cover every aspect of the two-way relationship between the Army and American society. Thus, these essays do not include—because so many studies are already available or because the influence was largely from the society to the Army—studies of the influence of Army organization on American business or civil-military relations. As already has been noted, our Army's subordination to civilian control and ideals is a highly successful example of political indoctrination. There is no essay on our Army's relation with the "popular" forces (the volunteers, the militia, the National Guard and the Reserve), except as Alvin Sunseri touches upon the economic influence of the Guard and the Reserve in Iowa. The old Army was too small and too busy to make them over, and contempt was often mutual.

Japanese soldiers were of considerable interest since they were obviously much more prepared for a modern entrenched war than were the troops of other nations in the mixed force in China in 1900. (NARS 111-SC-75033)

Our essays start with the story of one of the constant duties of all colonial armies—exploration. In most cases of European expansion around the world, the invaders needed to know what they were getting into. Leo Oliva thus tells in small compass of the valuable role that Army teams played in opening up the West by mapping it both for the benefit of distant politicians haggling about boundaries and for the immediate needs of the immigrants and their escort of soldiers. Oliva's chapter might have been linked to the other essays by a chapter on the First American Empire, but that story has been too often told, with rather variable results. Insofar as the Army's influence at this stage upon the economy was concerned, its "soldier-laborers" were too few to do more than house and partly feed themselves. Richard Bartlett shows in

Chapter 3, to borrow the title of Duane Hampton's book, *How the Army Saved Our National Parks* (1973) using the specific example of Yellowstone. Though not touched upon in the book, this was a forerunner of what the Army-led Civilian Conservation Corps did under the New Deal when it took young men into the Parks to build roads, undertake conservation measures, and promote the general welfare.

The Editor omitted the much overstudied "military-industrial-complex" as a specific theme from the book. Recent works have tended to distort wildly the role of the Army in the "MIC." As the essays by Alvin Sunseri and James Stokesberry show, the Army has been involved and has had a relationship with the economy and industry, but it has rarely been a dominant one. More often than not, civilians have for their own reasons demanded the military's presence either physically or financially for their own benefit. And in Nineteenth Century weapons development, the Navy was much more significant in terms of I.B. Holley's chicken-or-the-egg concept of the relationship between ideas and weapons.

The chapters on the relations of the peacetime Army, the Economy, and Technology bring up another problem, already noted as particularly difficult for the British and American armies, and especially for our American Army during its century of "free security." Continental European armies were always ready for mobilization, if not for war. Demands for British and U.S. Army services were concentrated in three periods; the Crimean and American Civil Wars, World War I, and World War II, with brief peaks for "imperial" operations. This inhibited the peacetime adoption of Army general staffs and concentrated weapons procurement, research, and development in crash wartime programs. Here, we might note in passing, Major David Armstrong's dissertation on *The Endless Experiment: The United States Army and the Machine Gun, 1861-1865* (1975) will shed much light on the effects of these demand fluctuations, because it covers so much time for a weapon which was not as brand new as the airplane, but did not clearly belong to either the infantry or the artillery. Armstrong's work also helps to answer one of Fuller's questions. Why had that "extraordinary inventiveness" which was "the main characteristic" of the American Civil War, an inventiveness which had developed both "a magazine-loading rifle and a machine-gun," only ended in Liddell Hart's "signpost that was missed?"

Armstrong's story begins with the standpat conservatism of the aged U.S. Army Chief of Ordnance, James A. Ripley. His eventual successor, the able Alexander N. Dyer, had chosen to finish his reorganization of production at the Springfield Arsenal before becoming Chief of Ordnance, a decision more important to the war effort than any speedup of testing or

*This well-equipped pony belonged to a Japanese Army engineer company
at Pekin. (NARS 111-SC-75032)*

production for a still technologically defective machine gun would have
been. But time had passed. The guns that were bought at the close of the
war were then used as cavalry weapons in the West, rather than infantry
or artillery weapons. Machine guns were used in the War with Spain, but
the new and undermanned General Staff then saw mobilization planning
as immediately more important than the development of new weapons
and doctrine.

The morals of this and other recent studies in the peacetime relations of
the Army, the Economy, and Technology before World War I may be: (1)
British and American experiences were never quite analagous because of
the larger size of the British Army, its more frequent tests against well-
armed opponents, and its earlier commitment to a possible Continental
European War; (2) the defeat of the U.S. Army's bureau chiefs did not

immediately mean a new attitude toward technological change; (3) small groups of officers and civilians eventually modernized the U.S. Army; and (4) this modernization mainly came after there was an effective demand for it just before the Great War.

Some More Limited Problems

Such successful excursions into some rather general areas of peacetime military history suggested similar ventures into areas where the Army's peacetime contributions were less striking or harder to evaluate. What is highly significant for the Army may be insignificant for the people. The essay on the Army and Minority Groups, for example, notes that the Army was significant for some minorities at certain times. But it did not attract many Eastern and Southern European immigrants, partly, it might be noted, because many of them were fleeing compulsory military service. The number of Army enlisted men in 1910 was 76,000. If 45 percent were foreign born, these 34,000 men were a small fraction of the 7,524,000 foreign-born white males, or the 9,425,000 white males with one foreign-born parent. Here, as in the case of the Army and Popular Culture, service in the wartime armies was surely more important, though some of the popular attitudes which resulted from those experiences were negative. Few members of minority groups, it might be added, served in the militia, and popular attitudes towards strike-breaking or disaster-relieving soldiers were as often formed by the militia as by the regulars.

Disaster Relief, Conservation and Ecology, and Public Health were not primary peacetime tasks for the Army. Its achievements in those fields show what "a few good men" can do. The story of the Army's National Park assignments, as its author would recognize, does not cover all of the Army's work in conservation and ecology. Flood and Disaster Relief are also fields in which the roles of the militia and civilian volunteers are important, though the cases cited here may restore the historical balance for those Army engineers whom Arthur E. Morgan sees as a main source of *Dams and Other Disasters* (1971). The Army's contributions to Public Health were also partly dependent on doctors who, like S. Weir Mitchell, would now be classified as reservists. The story is rather like that of the U.S. Public Health Service, from its modest beginning in federal care for merchant seamen and the efforts of its physicians to cooperate with local authorities to enforce quarantines and check epidemics to, eventually, its use of new scientific principles in the study of disease.

What these essays also indicate is the wealth of the Army's peacetime records, and the variety of its contributions to American life. They also

German Regular Artillerymen, Pekin, 1900. (NARS 111-SC-74930)

suggest how American some of these contributions were, as the Army responded to the changing demands of society and its own changing perceptions of its roles. During this century these roles became increasingly "military." But the ways in which the old Army had responded to peacetime "civilian" demands reminds us of Vigny's romantic notions of the Roman citizen army. These experiences also have some bearing on William James' idea—he was paraphrasing H. G. Wells—"that the conceptions of order and discipline, the tradition of service and devotion, of physical fitness, unstinted exertion, and universal responsibility, which universal military duty is now teaching European nations, will remain a permanent acquisition when the last ammunition has been used in the fireworks that celebrate the final peace."

The continuation of military deterrence under changing nuclear and/or conventional force balances may throw more light on how people come to feel secure. James felt that it would be "preposterous if the only force that could work ideals of honor and standards of efficiency into English or American natures should be the fear of being killed by the Germans or the Japanese. Great indeed is fear, but it is not ... the only stimulus known for awakening the higher ranges of man's spiritual energy." This question may be more closely related to the morale of a "prolonged destructability" Army than the peacetime Army's contributions to American life. But some other less speculative areas for thought—most of them still too broad for very specific ideas about methods or materials—are quickly apparent.

Peacetime Armies, Their Records, and Historians

Modern armies have inevitably become paper-shuffling bureaucracies. The blame lies in part with the armies themselves, in part with their size and the complexity of their needs, and in part with modern administrative concepts and democratic demands for accountability. But no matter what the cause, they create many kinds of records.

The chroniclers and memoir and adventure writers first filled the shelves with Western and Northwestern frontier and camel operas which were as far from the realities of peacetime service at Ft. Vancouver, Quetta, or Pau, where Vigny had found an English heiress and left the Army, as they were from those of combat. But these piles of regimental chitchat do show the obsessive interest of Nineteenth Century American and British soldiers in the distant rumblings and gossip which might mean a war, a promotion, or more pay, and the continued interest of American soldiers in European military organizational, scientific, and technological developments.

Many of the officers of the "quaint old" late Nineteenth Century armies were highly literate. Written orders were the foundation of Germany's "scientific" command and staff system, and for fixing responsibility in democratic armies, where officers could be less easily saved for their mistakes by powerful patrons or relatives. Written dispatches cemented the far-flung American and British services. Written reports were the chief product of exploring expeditions. Regimental and family ties were looser in the smaller U.S. Army; branch ties were stronger. Ideas, as well as gossip, were more likely to be published than in Eighteenth Century armies, less likely to be in Pentagon jargon than in the Twentieth Century. Perhaps these Nineteenth Century armies had simpler ideas than their descendants; in any case, their language was closer to English. In spite of clichés about no promotions for officers who read or wrote books, there is intellectual, as well as bureaucratic, history in the old Army's records. The military advantages of literacy are no more provable than those of training in sketching rather than photography. But one factor which may have facilitated the relatively rapid modernization of the U.S. armed forces about 1890 was the ability of many officers, in spite of their lack of formal scientific or managerial training, to communicate in writing, not only with each other, but also with interested citizens.

Historians first studied these peacetime records for policy and organizational and technological decisions which had contributed to success or failure in the World Wars. New *Ideas and Weapons* (1953), to use the title of I. B. Holley, Jr.'s classic study, had usually been pushed by small groups of officers and civilians, rather often in literary touch with each other, against what had often seemed to them to be the dead bureaucratic hands of underfinanced peacetime services. Holley dealt with the early air weapon and Robin Higham's *Armed Forces in Peacetime* (1962) with interwar Britain. Both showed that modernization was a more complex process than it had understandably appeared to be to the proponents of mechanized warfare, J.F.C. Fuller and B. H. Liddell Hart. Higham and Holley had seen penury, military conservatism, and opposition to a new B.E.F. hand the lead to Germany, while the Royal Navy's staffs, to quote Higham, were absorbed in "minutiae, machinery, and timetables" (which they had badly needed in 1914). The R.A.F. went in for "strategical speculations which lacked a sound operational basis."

Holley and Higham (in the latter's *British Rigid Airship*, 1961) studied "brand new" weapons and the institutions which formulated doctrines for their use. In his USAF Academy Harmon lecture, *An Enduring Challenge: The Problem of Air Force Doctrine* (1974), Holley sees doctrine as "a compass bearing" which gives "the general direction of our course.... A small error ... may place us many miles from the target." If those "who distill doctrine from experience or devise it by logical inference fail to exercise the utmost rigor in their thinking, the whole service suffers. As the old Scot preacher put it, 'A mist in the pulpit is a fog in the pews.'" Holley lays some of the earlier Air Service's troubles to its lack of an agency solely "devoted to the development of doctrine and its implementation or defense within the War Department." And the Air Corps agency which finally evolved at its Tactical School still lacked the "authority to promulgate doctrine officially ... [and] an adequate, built-in mechanism for rigorous self-criticism."

Such analyses have complemented, rather than contradicted, the simpler, more strongly expressed, views of Fuller and Liddell Hart of peacetime armies as hopelessly conservative. And the latter stuck to his guns. His last work, a revision of his 1943 *Why Don't We Learn from History?* (1971), still held that bureaucratic loyalty was so critical, both to promotions and to morale, that "authoritative schools of Military thought" were bound to miss "the evolution that was so *consistently revealed* [my italics] throughout the wars of the nineteenth and early twentieth centuries." As historians became less interested in policy lessons, or had exhausted the most obvious organizational, intellectual, and technological problems, they turned to other aspects of peacetime military history. This helps to explain why this introduction, the essays which it introduces, and their suggestions for further research may differ widely from field to field.

A Final Note

Regiment and regimentation are not quite the same thing. One feature of these essays was the difficulty of regimenting the authors, largely because their topics were so disparate. This author is no exception. Though he has eschewed footnotes, he has greatly exceeded his space for research suggestions, and has too few suggestions for further reading. All of the works cited are so familiar that titles and dates seemed sufficient. Washington's 1783 "Sentiments on a Peace Establishment" can be found in Russell F. Weigley, ed., *The American Military* (1969), a fine collection of *Readings in the History of the Military in American Society*. The differences between the kinds of topics it covers and these essays indicate some of the new directions of research in the history of armies in peacetime. Huntington's classic work is *The Soldier and the State* (1957); Cunliffe's, which seems more perceptive with each reading, is *Soldiers and Civilians* (1968); Andreski's is *Military Organization and Society* (1954). The quotations from Tocqueville, Spencer, and William James are in Leon Bramson and George W. Goethals, eds., *War* (1964), an excellent collection of *Studies from Psychology, Sociology, Anthropology*. For reasons already noted, many, if not most, specialized studies dealing with various aspects of the Army's contributions to American life belong on the public relations or public defamations piles. This is not true of one of the best post-Vietnam analyses, Colonel Hauser's *America's Army in Crisis* (1973).

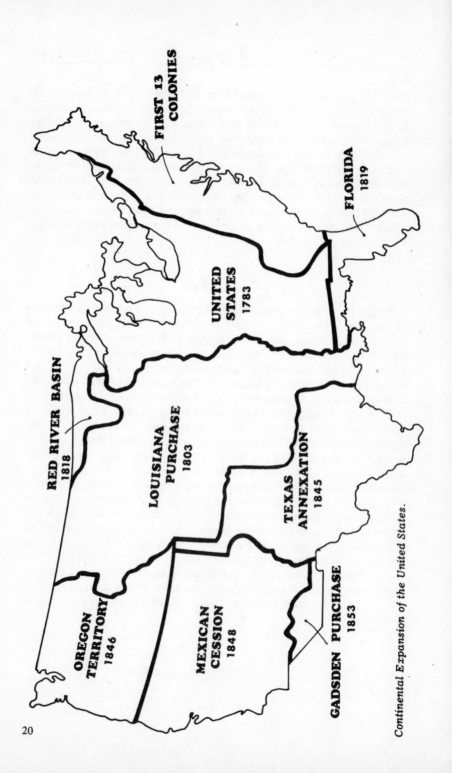

FIRST 13 COLONIES

FLORIDA 1819

UNITED STATES 1783

RED RIVER BASIN 1818

LOUISIANA PURCHASE 1803

TEXAS ANNEXATION 1845

OREGON TERRITORY 1846

MEXICAN CESSION 1848

GADSDEN PURCHASE 1853

Continental Expansion of the United States.

Chapter 2

THE ARMY AND
CONTINENTAL EXPANSION

Leo E. Oliva

As soon as it was clear that American independence was secure, following the War of 1812, the fever and fervor of continental expansion dominated American thought and action and carried the new nation from the Mississippi River to the Pacific Ocean. The movement west was a combination of good luck, diplomatic negotiations, mass migration of people, and reorientation of American thought and culture from the Atlantic community to the interior of North America. A significant contribution to continental expansion was made by the institutionalized military structure of the young and growing nation.

The peacetime Army of the United States, organized after the winning of independence, was created and existed primarily to protect and aid the westward expansion of the nation. Soldiers were in the vanguard of pioneers who occupied and developed the region between the Appalachian Mountains and the Mississippi River, settled the vast area of the Louisiana Purchase, claimed the Oregon country, and penetrated the Mexican Cession, extending the boundaries of the republic from sea to shining sea. Despite the persistent image of the individualism of pioneers who settled the West, frontiersmen did look to the national government for assistance in meeting many challenges too big for individual confrontation; and the Army often answered their demands. Throughout the era of westward expansion, the Army was the major institution of the federal government's partnership with the pioneers in the conquest of the continent.

In addition to the military duties performed in the expansion of the nation, including the Indian wars and the conflict with Mexico, the Army

21

provided numerous non-military services. Soldiers explored and mapped the West, gathering information that attracted settlers and showed them the way to lands of new opportunities. Boundaries of territorial acquisitions were surveyed by military engineers. Troops were assigned to protect routes of travel, construct and improve roads, give police protection and security to settlers, monitor the Indian trade, extend aid and comfort to victims of natural disasters, and build forts which served as bases for operations and as nuclei for settlements.

The garrisons of frontier posts provided a market for produce of early settlers, and enlisted men often planted gardens and introduced farming into a new frontier (growing such crops as corn, wheat, oats, and potatoes). Timber was cut for firewood and for logs, which were sawed in mills operated by soldiers to provide lumber for construction of forts. After building the quarters and warehouses, the soldier-laborers brought the cleared lands into production. They cut and stored hay from nearby meadows to supply winter feed for animals. In all, soldiers were pioneers who opened and helped make possible the development of the western three-fourths of the United States.

Until 1849 the Army was assigned the additional task of administering the nation's Indian policies, and military protection of Indian rights often brought public criticism. Although the military was called upon to use force in dealing with Indians when other methods failed, the Army used more than force or the threat of force to maintain peace and prevent hostilities. Officers assisted with treaty negotiations, soldiers were responsible for fulfilling federal guarantees of protection, and civilian agents and sub-agents of the war department's office of Indian affairs were assigned to distribute annuity payments, regulate liquor traffic, and see that traders were honest in their dealings with the natives. From its creation in 1796 until its termination in 1822, the factory system of government-owned and operated trading posts was administered by the office of Indian affairs and assisted by troops stationed at the posts. The Army carried out the removal of eastern tribes to new lands in the West, and western forts were built to protect those Indians from indigenous raiders and white encroachers.

The Army was assigned numerous tasks in the course of national expansion, but it always worked under serious handicaps that prevented success in some areas. Fears of a large standing army in a republic, coupled with a tight-fisted Congress, meant that manpower and financial support were inadequate. The westward marching Army never received support commensurate with its significant role in that movement. Thus, its achievements in exploration, perhaps the most notable Army contribution in continental expansion, were remarkable. The stories of reconnaissance and surveying missions compose the essence of the Army's non-military contributions to the winning of the West.

The most remarkable, although not the most fruitful, Army exploring expedition was that of Lewis and Clark from St. Louis to the Pacific and back from 1804 to 1806, following the Missouri River-Rocky Mountain-Columbia River route (a difficult path which helped put the lie to the myth of an easy Northwest Passage to the Pacific). This small military party, comprised of Captain Meriwether Lewis and Lieutenant William Clark, four non-commissioned officers, 22 privates, civilian employees, and Clark's slave, York, was sent to discover what the United States had obtained from France with the Louisiana Purchase.

They observed and recorded information about the land and Indians throughout their long trip. With unbelievable good fortune, losing only one man the entire distance (he apparently died of appendicitis), they visited numerous tribes, spent the first winter encamped near the Mandan villages in present North Dakota, crossed the Bitterroot range of the Rockies, descended the Columbia, spent the second winter at Fort Clatsop on the coast, and returned to St. Louis the next year.

They gave the United States a solid claim to the Oregon country, directed attention to the riches of the northern reaches of the Louisiana Purchase and the Pacific Northwest, saw the potential for fur trade, opened friendly contacts with most tribes (the Blackfeet being a notable exception), gathered vital data on natural phenomena, and stimulated new demands for continental expansion. The expedition marked the beginning of federal aid to the development of the trans-Mississippi West. Later expeditions could be launched with reference to the landmarks they recorded.

Attempts by civilian-led parties to explore the southern regions of the Louisiana Purchase were less fruitful; in fact, the William Dunbar-George Hunter Expedition of 1804-1805 and the Thomas Freeman exploring party of 1806 resulted in little or no new information. Two military explorations, both commanded by Lieutenant Zebulon M. Pike, were more valuable to the growing nation.

Pike's first mission was to search for the source of the Mississippi River, gather information about the country, seek friendly contacts with Indians of the region, and counteract British influence among the tribes. He did not reach the true source of the mighty river, mistaking Leech Lake as the source, and he did not counter permanently the British domination of the natives in the area; they joined Britain in the War of 1812. Although he gathered no new information, he did create new American interest in the Minnesota area and gave the United States a stronger claim there. His experiences in exploring may have been the

Escort duty for the Overland Stage Company in this case has been drawn by men of the Negro 24th or 25th Infantry at Fort Wallace, about 1867. (NARS 111-SC-87712)

most beneficial result, for he was better prepared to lead his more important investigation into the Louisiana Purchase.

In July 1806, Lieutenant Pike and 22 soldiers pushed up the Missouri River from St. Louis. They visited the Osage, Pawnee, and other tribes in the eastern plains before marching to the Rocky Mountains. There they named Pike's Peak (but failed to climb to the summit), searched for the source of the Arkansas River (but did not find it), and, supposedly seeking the headwaters of the Red River, were captured by Spanish troops on the Rio Grande. Held prisoner at Santa Fe and Chihuahua for a brief time, Pike and his men were released without the notes they had recorded and escorted across Texas to the United States in 1807. Although his field notes were confiscated, Pike prepared a detailed report on the region he had traversed.

Despite some inaccuracies in his report, Pike provided the best account of the Southwest to that time, and his observations on the potential for trade with northern Mexico helped mark the frame of reference that later created the great Santa Fe Trail and trade. He had followed a portion of that natural highway to the land of enchantment, a trail that was opened by William Becknell in 1821 to become the route of trade, penetration, conquest, occupation, and eventually Anglo settlement. His venture into Spanish lands was an advance warning of the expanding United States, and the Mexican War in the 1840s would be a direct result of the forces Pike's expedition had set in motion.

The image that would dominate American thinking about the Great Plains for at least a generation was begun by Pike. He compared the region to "sandy deserts," declaring that an agricultural-based society could not exist there and that the "wandering and uncivilized aborigines" should be left on the land. Pike saw this obstacle to the expansion of the United States as a blessing for the young nation, however, believing it would prevent the spread of the republic over a region too vast to be controlled by one government and thus assure "a continuation of the Union." Pike laid the foundation for what was called the Great American Desert by the next military exploring party to pass through the area, that led by Major Stephen Long from 1819 to 1820.

The early Army explorations of the West, during 1804 to 1807, revealed to the public the extent, general features, and some idea of the resources of the Far West. Before much could be done to exploit these new lands and opportunities, the War of 1812 interrupted to capture national attention away from the West and to bring new challenges to American authority in the region. When peace returned in 1815, national attention was again directed westward. The Army provided additional aid to expansion, especially after John C. Calhoun became Secretary of War in 1817.

The Army also had to protect the Indians, here seen receiving their rations tickets at Fort Sumner, N.M., in the latter Nineteenth Century. (NARS 111-SC-87966)

Major Stephen Long was sent out with the Yellowstone Expedition of General Henry Atkinson in 1819 to gather more details about the Louisiana Purchase; later he explored along the Red River of the North. A member of the Topographical Engineers, Long led a group of soldiers and scientists up the Platte River in 1820, southward along the face of the Rocky Mountains (where his party named Long's Peak, which they did not climb, and some of the men scaled the top of Pike's Peak) and divided his expedition. One party under Captain John R. Bell descended the Arkansas River while Long led the remainder in search of the elusive Red River (which he, as had Pike, failed to find). They mistakenly descended the Canadian. Except for Long's Peak and the Canadian River, nothing new had been discovered, but much authoritative information was collected and recorded. When the reports and maps were published in 1823, new knowledge of the geography, geology, natural history, and Indian population was made available, and the desert image of the Plains was firmly established.

The Great American Desert idea, begun by Pike and confirmed by Long, was not an altogether inaccurate depiction, for the early Nineteenth Century state of agricultural technology was not sufficient to conquer the conditions of the plains. It was not until after the Civil War that the right combination of equipment, such as windmills and barbed wire, and dryland-farming methods made possible the settlement of the "Great American Desert," and even then the harsh environment of the sod-house frontier periodically drove the farmers out before they managed to bring the region into production. Thus, the Army explorers provided some service by directing attention away from the Great Plains, a fact that surely assisted the leap-frog settlement which jumped from the Missouri Valley to Oregon and California.

Long's other expedition, in 1823, to the Red River of the North and into Canada, gathered scientific data, encountered British fur traders and settlers, and prepared a significant and informative report on the region. It should be noted that while the Army explorers were compiling statistics and producing better maps of the West, mountain men of the western fur trade were exploring much of the Far West, discovering new passages and places to which they would later guide military reconnaissance and survey parties.

By the 1840s the stage was set for the force of Manifest Destiny to push continental expansion of the United States to the Pacific as Texas, Oregon, and the Mexican Cession were added to the national domain. The tasks of Army explorers increased at the same time, expanding beyond discovery and recording of data to assistance with settlement and development. As pioneers moved westward, the Army served as a helpful partner.

In this new assignment, the Army's Corps of Topographical Engineers assumed major responsibility, becoming what the historian of the Corps, William H. Goetzmann, called "a central institution of Manifest Destiny." The Topographical Engineers surveyed boundaries, laid out wagon roads, sought routes for railroads, compiled scientific data, prepared reports and maps, and assisted with public works. In all, they aided significantly the westward movement of the American people.

John C. Frémont, whom Goetzmann called the "archetypal figure of the Topographical Engineer," was the best known of the Corps' explorers, and his expeditions in the 1840s formed an important part of national expansion. His three Army expeditions stimulated new interest in the West, brought forth comprehensive and accurate maps, assisted migration, and played a role in the conquest of California during the Mexican War. Other explorers had opened the Far West, discovered the mountain passes, and gone to California and Oregon, but Frémont became the "pathmarker" who made those avenues known and of use to the thousands of emigrants who followed.

Frémont's first assignment, in 1842, was a scientific survey of the road to Oregon as far as South Pass in present Wyoming. Guided by the famous mountain man, Kit Carson, and accompanied by the accomplished cartographer, Charles Preuss, whose maps were to prove of major value, Frémont's party marched up the Platte Valley to Fort Laramie (a detachment led by Frémont pursued the South Platte River to the Rocky Mountains and Fort St. Vrain before traveling north to Laramie where they joined the main party). Proceeding westward to South Pass, the expedition turned around and made a quick trip back to St. Louis. The detailed report of the trip was rushed into print to assist the Oregon emigrants, and newspapers spread the information to an eager public, firing imaginations with vivid descriptions of the Great Plains. Frémont's more favorable views of the region, in contrast to those of Pike and Long, helped to dispel the image of the Great American Desert. In all, the first Frémont expedition fed the growing awareness of Manifest Destiny, and widespread enthusiasm in the East brought forth new demands for continental conquest.

Frémont's second expedition was sent all the way to Oregon during 1843 to 1844, to gather additional data and complete the survey from South Pass to the Columbia River (which had been explored in 1841 by naval Captain Charles Wilkes). Guided by another mountain man, Tom Fitzpatrick, the party completed that assignment. From Oregon, Frémont led his party south into Mexican California, explored the Great Basin (which was named by Frémont), and came back through Utah, Colorado, and Kansas, completing the most spectacular official reconnaissance of the Far West since Lewis and Clark.

In 1845, the reports of both Frémont expeditions were printed by Congress, and 10,000 extra copies were bound for distribution to the public. Commercial publishers brought out other editions, and newspapers printed extracts. The descriptions of the Salt Lake Valley influenced the Mormon leaders' decision to go there the following year. The fine maps executed by Preuss were the best available, and they served as the basis for several guidebooks to California gold fields a few years later.

Frémont's narrative, including information on the land, creatures, plants, and Indian tribes, provided new knowledge and also advertised the West. The widespread dissemination of the information was a factor in persuading people in the states to migrate westward. Frémont emerged from the first two expeditions as a national hero, and his reports were read and quoted more widely than all the explorers who preceded him. A Frémont biographer, Allan Nevins, declared that the two expeditions came at a most opportune time in the westward expansion of the nation and did more to stimulate westward migration than any explorer before him.

Frémont was a rallying point of Manifest Destiny. Within a short time, national expansion exploded; Texas was annexed, the Oregon question was settled, and a war with Mexico added the Southwest to the national domain. Frémont's third expedition went to California and became involved in the Bear Flag Revolt and the Mexican War. He assisted with the conquest of that Mexican province and lost his command because of disputes with other military leaders. Frémont later led two civilian exploring parties into the West, neither of which was as important as his military expeditions. In the 1840s he was the prime example of the federal government's policy of using exploration to the advantage of the pioneer as well as the nation as a whole.

With the approaching showdown over western territories with Britain in the Pacific Northwest and with Mexico in the Southwest, the United States sent three Army reconnaissance missions westward in 1845 to gather data and assist the nation in its diplomatic relations. Each added to the knowledge of the West and gained information of value in the coming conflict with Mexico.

Colonel Stephen Watts Kearny led a dragoon battalion, accompanied by a Topographical Engineer, from Fort Leavenworth up the Oregon Trail to South Pass, providing some protection for emigrants and placing troops closer to Oregon in case of a conflict with the British there. The mounted force then traveled along the east side of the Rockies to Bent's Fort on the Arkansas River, in proximity to northern Mexico, in case of a struggle there over the annexation of Texas. The dragoons returned to Fort Leavenworth via the Santa Fe Trail, protecting travelers on that road. The experiences of maintaining a cavalry force on the Great Plains proved invaluable to Kearny the following year when he led the Army of the West to occupy New Mexico and California.

Frémont's third expedition, which went to California, constituted the second mission in 1845. The third exploring party that year was detached from Frémont's command at Bent's Fort and led by Lieutenant James W. Abert of the Topographical Engineers. Abert directed a reconnaissance along the Canadian River, expanding on the initial work done by Major Long a quarter-century earlier. Fitzpatrick was the guide, and Lieutenant William G. Peck was a very capable young Engineer with the party. They explored through Comanche and Kiowa lands, gathering important new geographical data along the way. This information would soon be of practical value in the military operations of the Mexican War.

When Kearny led the Army of the West into the Southwest to occupy the territory the United States would obtain from Mexico at the War's end, he was accompanied by Lieutenant William H. Emory, a well trained and highly intelligent Topographical Engineer who led a small party of his Corps, including Abert, Peck, and Lieutenant William H. Warner. From Bent's Fort on the Arkansas to California, Emory kept careful notes and collected information about the land and all it contained. His map was the most accurate of that region to date. Emory recognized the potential of the route followed for future development of overland transportation (perhaps even a railroad) and urged the State Department to demand a boundary settlement with Mexico at 32° north latitude to secure the potential road for the United States.

Following Kearny to California was the Mormon Battalion, led by Captain Philip St. George Cooke, which opened up Cooke's Wagon Road from the Rio Grande to California (the very avenue that Emory was promoting). This Army road, following a route similar to one opened by the Spanish in the 1770s and sometimes called the Gila Trail, was later used by the Butterfield Overland Mail, followed by the Southern Pacific Railroad, and traveled by thousands of emigrants going to California after 1848. This was an example of the kind of aid the Army provided western settlement.

Because two of the Topographical Engineers with Emory, Lieutenants Abert and Peck, had been too ill to accompany the Army of the West beyond the Rio Grande, those two remained in New Mexico and surveyed that conquered province after they recovered. The resulting reports were the first compilations of data on the area and proved valuable to later developments in New Mexico. Because of their investigations and curiosity, the Corps of Topographical Engineers had compiled much important information about the Southwest prior to the annexation of the Mexican Cession. They continued to investigate the new lands in the post-war era.

The Treaty of Guadalupe Hidalgo ended the Mexican War and defined the new boundary between the two participants. The Topographical Engineers represented the United States in the survey. That difficult task, involved as it was in international diplomacy, politics, and inaccurate information in the treaty, occupied several years and was not settled until after the Gadsden Purchase of 1853 rounded out the continental expansion of the United States. That last addition to national territory settled the dispute over the boundary and added an important section of the Southwest to the overland route of travel. Engineer Emory oversaw the survey of the boundary, during 1854 to 1855, completing a task begun in 1849. During that long era of the survey, the Corps of Topographical Engineers gathered additional data and prepared reports on the region. They thus laid good foundations for further explorations in the Southwest.

Following the Mexican War, military reconnaissance parties were sent throughout the newly acquired territories to seek out routes for travel, sites for military installations to defend the land from native soldiers, and scientific information about the lands and resources. One of those exploring parties was led by Captain Randolph B. Marcy in 1849 and followed a route from Fort Smith, Arkansas, to Santa Fe via the Canadian River. Lieutenant James H. Simpson, Topographical Engineer, accompanied the expedition. A wagon road and later a railroad followed that route to the West. From Santa Fe, Marcy moved down the Rio Grande and opened a new route eastward through Texas from just north of El Paso to Fort Washita, Indian Territory, from which there was a military road back to Fort Smith. This was a more direct route to the road to California which ran westward from the Rio Grande, and it was utilized by many gold-seekers going to the mines. The Marcy-Simpson explorations aided overland travel, resulted in maps of areas not previously recorded, and gained considerable knowledge of hitherto unknown regions.

Another example of post-Mexican War reconnaissance was that led by Captain Howard Stansbury, Topographical Engineer, who conducted a thorough survey of the Great Salt Lake Valley and opened a new road from Salt Lake City to the main Oregon Trail via Bridger Pass, more than 100 miles south of the South Pass road. The significance of this work was

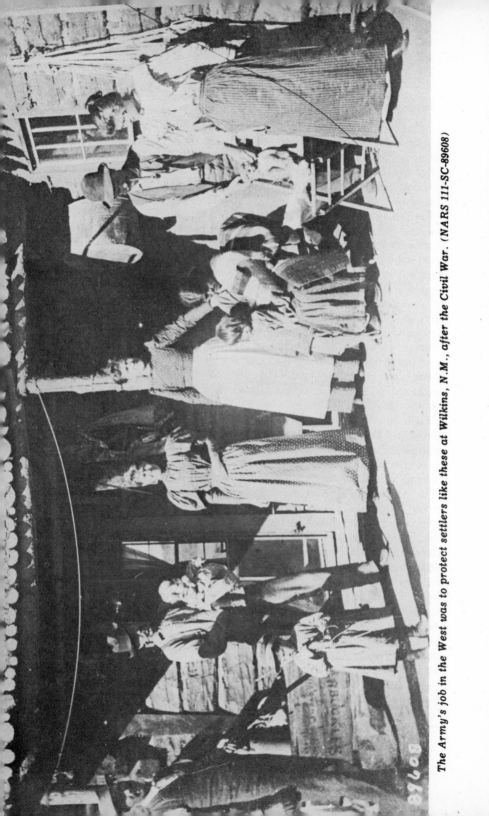

The Army's job in the West was to protect settlers like these at Wilkins, N.M., after the Civil War. (NARS 111-SC-89608)

Forts in the West were rarely the blockhouse so often pictured. Many of the famous ones like Riley, Leavenworth, Union, and Bayard, shown here in 1885, were unprotected. Although later than the period described by Oliva, this is typical of the forts in the West. (NARS 111-SC-83341)

attested by the fact that the famous Pony Express, stagecoach lines, and Union Pacific Railroad followed a portion of the Stansbury route. Other Corps of Topographical Engineers surveys were carried out in Texas, New Mexico, and California, where they opened lines of communication, built roads, assisted settlement, helped set up frontier defenses, and gathered scientific information.

After the nation's boundaries were completed and large numbers of people had moved to Oregon and California, the public demands for federal assistance to overland transportation increased. Agitation for a transcontinental railroad began in the 1840s, but conflicting interests between North and South over which section would get the line (many railroad promoters and politicians believed that only one transcontinental would be economically feasible), as well as competition among railroad interests and various states and cities, prevented Congressional action until the Civil War years. Meantime, however, the Corps of Topographical Engineers was assigned the task of surveying for possible railroad routes to the Pacific. It was the hope of many members of Congress that scientific investigation would find the best route and, thereby, remove the issue from the realm of sectional interests and politics. Those Pacific railroad surveys constituted another outstanding contribution of the Army to expansion westward, and the railroads later constructed along the routes were essential to the eventual economic growth of the West.

Congress authorized the surveys in 1853, requesting a full report on all practicable routes to the Pacific within 10 months. The time limit was impossible and precluded anything more than a general reconnaissance of four stipulated routes. Teams of engineers and scientists conducted the assignment with enthusiasm and collected an impressive amount of information, eventually published in 17 volumes, from 1855 to 1860. These reports helped create a more favorable image of the climate and resources of the West than had resulted from the earlier comparisons with deserts. But they did not resolve the conflict over the best route for a transcontinental line.

The Engineers, who had been most involved in the Southwest and almost unanimously supported the 32nd parallel for a railroad because it was the only one they knew well, now found several practicable routes, some of which possessed advantages not found along the 32nd parallel. Even so, Secretary of War Jefferson Davis slanted his recommendations, based on the surveys and his loyalty to the South, in favor of the 32nd parallel. But those who read the survey reports found good support for most of the other possible routes investigated.

This threw the decision back into the hands of the politicians and prevented any approval of federal aid to a transcontinental line until the Civil War. At that time the Union Congress subsidized the central route of the Union Pacific and Central Pacific railroads, which ironically had not been included in the Pacific railroad surveys. In the long run, the scientific results of the railroad surveys were more significant than the selection of a practicable route. Perhaps the greatest contribution of all was a new, comprehensive map of the trans-Mississippi West, prepared by Lieutenant G. K. Warren and published in 1859. The *Pacific Railroad Reports* have been called an "encyclopedia" of the West in the 1850s, and that mass of information provided a knowledge base for all future investigations. The Corps of Topographical Engineers, with the aid of civilian scientists, had done yeoman service for an expanding nation, even though the railroads were delayed for at least another decade for other reasons.

Before railroads were built, wagon roads were essential. That the Army had been involved in construction of roads since the early Nineteenth Century was well appreciated, and now that task was undertaken throughout the Far West. The Corps of Topographical Engineers contributed much to the federal road-building program in the region after the Mexican War. Before the Civil War interrupted westward expansion temporarily, the Army had assisted with the survey, location, improvement, and construction of roads in Texas, Kansas, Nebraska, Minnesota, Utah, Oregon, Washington, and New Mexico. This was justified as essential for the Quartermaster Department's task of supplying western forts, a large network of which had been erected throughout the West to provide protection from Indians who resisted the invasion of their homelands. But the roads were also invaluable to a westward-moving people. The roads brought the people and connected them with a source of supplies and with markets for their produce, both essential to economic growth. Stage lines and railroads later followed those Army roads.

By the Civil War, the Army had explored, mapped, surveyed, and opened numerous routes throughout the American West. The territory, much of it only recently acquired by the expanding nation, was secure from outside threat. Indian resistance was doomed to failure, although it was not to be crushed entirely for another generation. Wherever the Army had opened the way, commercial development and settlement followed. The stage was set for an amazing economic growth for the West and the nation, and the Army's role in the conquest of the continent was considerable.

Following the Civil War, the Army was mainly concerned with military operations against Indians, and non-military services were less in evidence. But much remained to be done. Despite all the prewar explorations and surveys, there was still need for more accurate information about the land. The Army was again assigned the responsibility for scientific investigations in the trans-Mississippi West. Three approaches to further the collection of data were developed. Engineers were assigned to each of the military departments to coordinate activities of scouting parties and lead some field expeditions. In 1867, the Army sponsored a scientific investigation, led by Clarence King, which gathered data over a wide area between the Great Plains and California in the vicinity of the 40th parallel. Finally, in 1871, Lieutenant George M. Wheeler, Corps of Engineers, inaugurated what became known as the United States Geographical Surveys Beyond the 100th Meridian. These new Army explorations yielded much valuable data for the development of the West.

Investigations carried out in the several military departments under the direction of engineers are far too numerous for consideration, but a list of major explorations reveals that much was undertaken. Among the regions explored were the Colorado River, Great Basin, Alaska, Yellowstone River, Yellowstone Park (the first national park, established in 1872), Uinta Basin, Black Hills, and others. In some cases, such as the confirmation of gold in the Black Hills by George A. Custer's 1874 expedition, settlers rushed in to exploit new-found resources. In that particular case, because Indian lands were involved, the military demands on the Army were increased. The end result in almost every case was the opening of new regions for settlement and development.

The 40th Parallel Survey by King was the most scientific investigation undertaken by the Army and lasted for several years. Concentrating on geological data, it located resources missed by earlier investigations. The reports were more than mere descriptions of what was seen, as had been the common practice before, for King theorized about how natural phenomena had developed. This Army-sponsored study brought the West, as Goetzmann declared, "into the realm of academic science."

The Wheeler Survey was an attempt to produce exact maps of the West by dividing the vast region into 94 geodetic quadrangles and conducting a systematic investigation of each. The project was not completed when Congress withdrew support in 1878, but over one-third of the area west of 100° west longitude had been surveyed. The resulting topographical maps were important contributions, but the scientific investigations of civilian explorations were far superior to what the Army could accomplish in the late Nineteenth Century. After Wheeler, further survey and reconnaissance in the West fell to other agencies. The great age of Army exploration had ended.

By that time, however, the West was won and a new age of national growth, involving industries and cities as well as agriculture and natural resources, was underway which would bring the United States into the status of a world power. Throughout the era of westward expansion and settlement, pioneers had looked to the United States Army for more than military protection from foreign and Indian threats. They expected their national government to give assistance in opening the region and in developing the resources found, and the Army was the principal institution that responded. Frontiersmen everywhere, including trappers and traders, miners, cattlemen, merchants, freighters, and farmers, had benefited from the aid provided. The Army's contribution to continental expansion is a vital chapter in national development.

Suggestions for Further Research

Some phases of the Army's contributions to continental expansion, such as military protection and exploration, have been rather carefully researched. This does not mean that studies of frontier campaigns, expeditions, and Indian wars should be stopped, for new information and interpretations are vital to the study of all history. But there are several areas of peacetime, non-military services provided by the Army which deserve considerably more investigation. The significance of the soldier as pioneer, ably demonstrated in the Old Northwest through the studies of Francis Paul Prucha, has received little attention in the frontier west of the Mississippi River. It would be valuable to know exactly how much soldiers contributed to the actual conquest and settlement of the land as well as the claiming, mapping, initial occupation, and protection of it.

The economic significance of military installations remains largely unknown. The importance of the military market for early settlers, value of payrolls for civilian employees, investments by officers in various business endeavors, and the military partnership in community development (of towns and transportation networks) remain to be determined. The total impact of military contracts, which have been shown to be so important to the economy of the urban-industrial nation in the present century, needs to be assessed in relation to continental expansion and frontier growth. The economic relationship of the Army to livestock producers (cattle, horses, and mules), grain farmers, lumber suppliers, and transportation corporations are obvious areas for further research. Such data, when compiled and evaluated, will contribute much toward a better understanding of the role of federal aid in the early development of the American West and provide additional perspective for viewing the continued importance of such aid in the modern West as well as the nation.

SOURCES

Continental expansion of the United States has been treated in general and specialized studies. Those seeking an introduction should see Albert K. Weinberg, *Manifest Destiny* (Baltimore: Johns Hopkins Press, 1935); Richard W. Van Alstyne, *The Rising American Empire* (New York: Oxford University Press, 1960); Fredrick Merk, *Manifest Destiny and Mission in American History* (New York: Alfred A. Knopf, 1963); and the more specialized study of the 1840s by David M. Pletcher, *The Diplomacy of Annexation: Texas, Oregon, and the Mexican War* (Columbia: University of Missouri Press, 1973).

The Army in westward expansion is told best in three volumes in the Macmillan series on *The Wars of the United States*: Francis Paul Prucha, *Sword of the Republic: The United States Army on the Frontier, 1783-1846* (New York: Macmillan, 1969), and two books by Robert M. Utley, *Frontiersmen in Blue: The United States Army and the Indian, 1848-1865* (New York: Macmillan, 1967), and *Frontier Regulars: The United States Army and the Indian, 1866-1891* (New York: Macmillan, 1973). Prucha devoted much attention to non-military services of the frontier army in an earlier study, *Broadax and Bayonet: The Role of the United States Army in the Development of the Northwest, 1815-1860* (Madison: The State Historical Society of Wisconsin, 1953).

Other significant books dealing with western military history include Henry P. Beers, *The Western Military Frontier* (Philadelphia: University of Pennsylvania, 1935); Averam B. Bender, *The March of Empire: Frontier Defense in the Southwest, 1848-1860* (Lawrence: University of Kansas Press, 1952); Francis Paul Prucha, ed., *Army Life on the Western Frontier* (Norman: University of Oklahoma Press, 1958); Robert Frazier, *Forts of the West* (Norman: University of Oklahoma Press, 1965); Robert G. Athearn, *Forts of the Upper Missouri* (Englewood Cliffs: Prentice-Hall, 1967); Don Rickey, Jr., *Forty Miles a Day on Beans and Hay: The Enlisted Soldier Fighting the Indian Wars* (Norman: University of Oklahoma Press, 1963); Justin H. Smith, *The War with Mexico*, 2 vols. (New York: Macmillan, 1919); and K. Jack Bauer, *The Mexican War, 1846-1848* (New York: Macmillan, 1974), one of the series *Wars of the United States*. The contributions of the military to road construction in the Far West are assessed in W. Turentine Jackson's valuable *Wagon Roads West: A Study of Federal Road Surveys and Construction in the Trans-Mississippi West, 1846-1869* (Berkeley: University of California Press, 1952).

William H. Goetzmann's *Exploration and Empire: The Explorer and the Scientist in the Winning of the American West* (New York: Alfred A. Knopf, 1966) is the best study of the subject, as is the same author's *Army Exploration in the American West, 1803-1863* (New Haven: Yale University Press, 1959), which provides a solid history of the Corps of Topographical Engineers. Richard A. Bartlett's *Great Surveys of the American West* (Norman: University of Oklahoma Press, 1962) gives another overview; Reuben Gold Thwaites, ed., *Early Western Travels*, 32 vols. (Cleveland: Arthur H. Clark Company, 1904-1907) includes many primary sources, military and non-military.

Specialized accounts of army exploring expeditions are found in Elliott Coues, ed., *History of the Expedition Under the Command of Lewis and Clark*, reprinted in paper edition, 3 vols. (New York: Dover Publications, 1965); Donald Jackson, ed., *The Journals of Zebulon Montgomery Pike with Letters and Related Documents*, 2 vols. (Norman: University of Oklahoma Press, 1966); Louis Pelzer, *Marches of the Dragoons in the Mississippi Valley* (Cedar Rapids, Iowa: Torch Press, 1917); Richard G. Wood, *Stephen Harriman Long—Army Engineer, Explorer, Inventor* (Glendale: Arthur H. Clark Company, 1966); and Allan Nevins, *Frémont: Pathmarker of the West* (New York: Longmans, Green and Co., 1955). For maps, see Carl I. Wheat, *Mapping the Trans-Mississippi West*, 5 vols. (San Franciso: Institute of Historical Cartography, 1957-1963). Finally, for anyone seeking a good general history of the Army, another volume in the series *Wars of the United States* is recommended: Russell F. Weigley, *History of the United States Army* (New York: Macmillan, 1967).

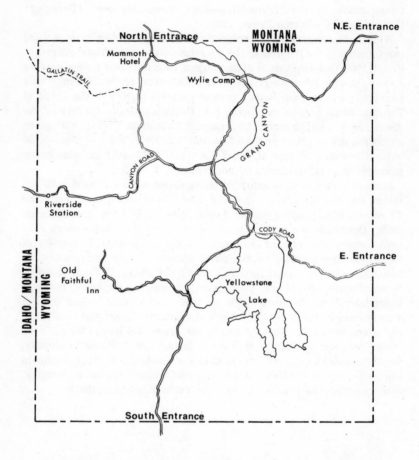

YELLOWSTONE NATIONAL PARK

Chapter 3

THE ARMY, CONSERVATION,
AND ECOLOGY: THE
NATIONAL PARK ASSIGNMENT

Richard A. Bartlett

In the mind of the layman, the Army is linked to war and destruction. With regard to the United States Army, however, such an image is not entirely correct. True, it exists to protect the nation in time of war, but in time of peace it has had many other duties. Some have not been pleasant, nor have they been of a kind to inspire affection on the part of the American people. But one assignment was popular with Army personnel, most members of Congress, presidents of the United States, and the citizenry that was touched in one way or another by the Army while it carried out its duties. This was the policing of the Yellowstone National Park and later of Sequoia, General Grant, and Yosemite National Parks in California. Because Yellowstone is the first national park, because the Army was first assigned to that park, and because policies evolved there tended to become policies followed elsewhere, an analysis of the Army's role in Yellowstone serves as an example of the military role in fostering conservation and ecology.

The Yellowstone region has a long history antedating by far its creation as a park in 1872, and the Army enters into some of this early story. Lewis and Clark, both Army regulars, may have heard tales whose foundation in fact was the thermal phenomena of the upper Yellowstone River. William Clark wrote in his Journal of 20 June 1805, from a point near the Great Falls of the Missouri, of an unexplained loud noise; and he followed his conjectures as to its origin by adding that the Ricaras [Arikarees, a tribe of Indians along the Missouri] informed the members of the expedition of "many other wonderful tales of those Rocky Mountains." On the return journey from Oregon to St. Louis, Clark's group crossed Bozeman Pass and then went down the Yellowstone; at one point they were about 60 miles north of the park boundaries. Clark, interviewed later by Nicholas Biddle, who published the Journals, told of "the Yepi pi band of Snakes of 200 men" who lived at the headquarters of the Roche Jaune (the early name for the Yellowstone). This could have been a reference to the Sheepeater Indians who resided in the headwaters area, the site of the present Park.

Even while Lewis and Clark were exploring, Brigadier General James Wilkinson of the Louisiana Territory was writing to the Secretary of War about a small expedition he was sending up the Missouri and then the Yellowstone, "which my informants tell me is filled with wonders ...." Six weeks later he sent President Jefferson a buffalo pelt upon which was a crude map showing the Missouri, Platte, and Yellowstone Rivers. "Among other things a little incredible," he said of it, "a volcano is distinctly described on the Yellow Stone River...."

Perhaps the first white man to enter the area now embraced by the park was John Colter, a private with Lewis and Clark. Near the Mandan villages (near present Bismark, North Dakota), on the return journey, the expedition members met two American trappers, Joseph Dixon and Forest Hancock, who made an offer to Colter to return west with them. Colter was permitted to go, and he spent four more years in the wild upper Missouri country before finally returning home. He witnessed some thermal phenomena: it may have been the hot springs near present Cody, Wyoming, or it could have been the hot springs of the West Thumb of Yellowstone Lake. An intriguing dotted line on the Biddle map in the first edition of the *Journals* lists Colter's Route, which seems to have taken him through the park by way of Two Ocean Pass, probably the West Thumb, down the Yellowstone River and across at a ford above the Falls, then over an Indian trail to the Lamar Valley on the east side of the park, over the mountains and back to the buffalo plains. (He could have gone the other way: there are no arrows on the map to indicate which way he went.) Whatever he did, this ex-Army man had his name given to thermal phenomena somewhere in northwest Wyoming, and the name Colter's Hell has stuck.

In 1860 a reconnaissance under the command of Captain W. F. Raynolds of the Topographical Engineers attempted to work to the source of the Wind River and from there to cross to the headwaters of the Yellowstone in the mountains to the west. From the source of the Yellowstone, Raynolds was to trace the river onto the plains where it bends east, in central Montana. If he had achieved this, he would have seen much of Yellowstone. He was very curious, for by 1860 rumors of all kinds had been heard about the mysterious region. But Captain Raynolds was unable to penetrate the snow cover separating him from the Two Ocean area to the northwest, which could have led him into Yellowstone. He had to accept a trip across Jackson's Hole, over Teton Pass to Pierre's Hole (now known as the Teton Basin) in eastern Idaho, north over a pass known as Raynolds' to this day, down the Madison River outside of the present park boundaries, and down the river to the Three Forks where the Missouri is formed. He had swung about much of the park area but had not penetrated it.

Had the War Between the States not intervened, it would probably have been Army personnel who discovered the park. But the attention demanded by a terrible civil conflict halted Army exploration in the West, and in its absence others stepped in. Miners, some known and many unknown, traversed the park area in the 1860s, as did Father Francis Xavier Kuppens, a Jesuit priest. And in 1869, three intrepid men, Charles W. Cook, David E. Folsom, and William Peterson, crossed much of the present park. In 1870, a party of Montana Territory's Very Important Persons led a widely publicized expedition into the upper Yellowstone country. Known as the Washburn-Langford-Doane expedition, it is to be noticed that one member was an Army officer. Lieutenant Gustavus C. Doane was an Army regular stationed at Fort Ellis outside of Bozeman. Doane's narration of the trip is written with unusual literary flair.

In 1871 Dr. Ferdinand Vandiveer Hayden entered the park region with his United States Geological and Geographical Survey of the Territories. He was accompanied by Colonel John W. Barlow and Captain David P. Heap, who had been sent there by General Sheridan to conduct their own reconnaissance. Sheridan was so interested in the region that his biographer incorrectly gives him the major credit for the creation of the park. Actually it was interests of the Northern Pacific Railroad, who contemplated a lucrative tourist business, who were the prime movers in the passage of the park bill.

Fourteen years after the creation of the park in 1872, the Army was given the task of securing it. The assignment was formidable. The park is about 65 miles from east to west and 55 miles from north to south. Except for a very small strip in Montana on the north and northwest and on the west of Idaho, all of it is in extreme northwestern Wyoming. Within its boundaries are over 3,000 hot springs and geysers, a grand canyon of the Yellowstone River, a huge lake, hundreds of small streams and lakes, valleys, mountains, forests, and wildlife. So remote was the park that most visitors as well as park personnel entered by one of two entrances: via Virginia City, Montana, and the Madison river on the west; and via the Northern Pacific railroad to Livingston, Montana, and up the Park Branch line to Cinnabar, thence via horse-drawn conveyance seven miles

The re-enactment at Yellowstone National Park on 25 August 1960 of General Washburn sighting Smith and Stickney arriving in the park. (NARS 79-G-26F-2)

south to Mammoth Hot Springs. (Later the railroad moved to Gardiner, the main street of which is part of the park boundary.)

The Department of the Interior had managed the park since 1872 and, when the Army took over in 1886, Interior was still trying to cope with a myriad of problems that simply would not go away. Headquarters were at Mammoth, in the extreme north of the park. There also, since 1883, was a huge, barn-like hotel. Concessionaires of questionable integrity had also been allowed to construct hotels of varying quality at principal scenic spots in the park: at Norris Geyser Basin, Lower and Upper Geyser Basins, Lake, and the Grand Canyon. Miserable roads constructed under the supervision of the second superintendent, Philetus W. Norris, led south out of Mammoth through Norris, Lower, Middle, and Upper Geyser Basins, eastward to the West Thumb of Yellowstone Lake, along its shores to a hotel, then along the west bank of Yellowstone River to the Grand Canyon. From there the visitor crossed westward to Norris Geyser Basin and then retraced his route back to Mammoth.

Visitors complained to Congress about the bad roads, poor service at the hotels, poaching, and spoliation of the hot springs formations. Lobbyists representing Cooke City, Montana, a mining camp just northeast of the park, campaigned for a railroad from Gardiner through the park to Cooke City; sometimes they advocated the severance of the northeast quarter from the park, placing it in the private domain and opening it to private entry. Much of the population in areas surrounding the park was hostile to the authorities and participated in the poaching and spoliation. Within the park the concessionaries were constantly haggling with the authorities over extensions of their rights. All in all, the possibilities for failure exceeded those for success.

Nevertheless, there were elements of the Army that had long coveted the task of administering the Yellowstone Park. As the frontier drew to a close and Indian wars became incidents of the past, it was only natural for military men to seek new peacetime tasks. From the reconnaissance of Captain W. F. Raynolds in 1860 through the explorations of Lieutenant Gustavus C. Doane, Colonel John W. Barlow, and Captain David P. Heap in 1870 and 1871; Captain William A. Jones, Captain William A. Ludlow, and Lieutenant Doane again in the mid-1870s; and the excursions into the park by Secretary of War William Belknap, Generals Sherman, Miles, and Howard, the Army had manifested an interest in Yellowstone. Much of the official exploration of the region had been Army led. Within 200 or 300 miles of the park were a number of military installations, the closest being Fort Ellis at Bozeman, less than 60 miles north of the park. In that sparsely settled country, freed from the Indian menace, it was quite natural for military personnel to think in terms of the park's security being assigned to the peacetime Army.

But the interest in Yellowstone went deeper than mere searching for a peacetime role. Although it is dangerous to generalize, it is a fact that Army officers are often adventurous, romantically inclined, sensitive to the world around them, and desirous of being of service to their nation. Some were avid sportsmen. Many military men loved Yellowstone for its primitive beauty, for its game (which many of them hunted in the 1870s), and for the proposition that had led Congress to create the park in 1872 — as a great reservation to be kept as much as possible in the primitive state, as an area of scenery and thermal phenomena, and as a game refuge for all time to come. They were appalled at the destruction they witnessed in the park — vandalism of the thermal phenomena, such as hacking away at geyser cones or soaping geysers; the frequent forest fires obviously caused by human negligence; and the poaching of hundreds of game animals, especially deer, elk, and buffalo. As military men, they reacted with the positive statement that if the Army policed the park, it would put a stop to all this.

As early as 1875 Secretary of War Belknap, who had accompanied a party of Army officers through the park, suggested in his *Annual Report of the Secretary of War* that the spoliation could be ended by stationing troops at strategic points there. Similar statements were made by Generals Sherman and Sheridan, and by officers of lesser rank such as Lieutenant Doane, who always manifested a great interest in the park.

The Army's opportunity came as a result of a congressional hassle over appropriations for the park in 1883. The measure, part of the Sundry Appropriations bill, included a clause that specified that the Secretary of War, if so requested by the Secretary of the Interior, was authorized to order troops into the park to prevent spoliation. In 1886 the fight over the park appropriations increased in intensity, the park defenders lost, and the appropriations bill was passed with no money allotted for the supervision of the park. The Secretary of the Interior had no choice but to formally request troops as specified in the 1883 law.

That is why, on 17 August 1886, Captain Moses Harris arrived at Mammoth Hot Springs in command of Troop "M," First United States Cavalry. It had been a two-day train ride from Fort Custer, Montana Territory, to the terminus of the Park Branch railroad at Cinnabar. A few more days would elapse before the horses arrived. Captain Harris may have considered this a blessing in disguise for this was a new assignment, not only for him but for the Army. His orders were to proceed to Yellowstone Park and police it — to protect it, but just exactly how the Army was to accomplish this was not specified. Wisely, he refused to accept his new responsibilities until the horses arrived and the command could be mounted; in the interval he could, and did, appraise the situation and determine how to go about his tasks.

For the next 30 years, from 1886 to 1916, the steady methodical routine that characterizes peacetime service life guided the reservation (as personnel often called the park) through the most massive changes of its official existence. Until 1886 the park had suffered from official lethargy, a lack of congressional support, and insufficient funds; moreover, the officials simply did not know how to go about running a park of vast dimensions in a remote area. No one had ever been assigned such a task before, anywhere.

Interior Department officials assigned to park affairs had done their best, committed many errors, and were subjected to political pressures. Yet that department deserves fair treatment and the indications, borne out by historical research, indicate that it was developing a workable park administration and security system when Congress denied it the necessary appropriations and thus made mandatory the calling of troops. (Interior stepped down but never out: the Army officer in command was always "Acting Superintendent," taking orders from both the Secretary of War and the Secretary of the Interior — an obvious source of frustration. After a few years, an Interior Department clerk was stationed permanently in the park.)

Whatever the situation, the Army carried out its orders. From the Acting Superintendents down through the officers, non-coms, and enlisted men, their natural *esprit*, their desire to do the best job possible "for the good of the service," demanded that the task, whether a stopgap assignment of six weeks or a lengthy tour of a generation, be well done.

The assignment was of a generation, and it was well done. The Army managed Yellowstone during a crucial period in which decisions had to be made and policy had to be evolved. Through dedication, hard work, common sense, intelligence, and determination to succeed, the Army ran Yellowstone well — so well that when the national park service took over in 1916, it merely had to carry on the policies and methods already in use, policies and methods adapted by the Army through a system of trial and error.

Captain Harris in August 1886 had two resources to fall back upon. First was the Army experience in policing military camps and bases. The neatness and cleanliness of a military encampment, especially in peacetime, was already a tradition. In a way, administering the park could be viewed as a great expansion of a task every Army man already knew. Secondly, one segment of the Army had been in Yellowstone since 1883. This was a contingent of the Army engineers under Captain Dan Kingman. He was there because the same appropriations bill that had cut off funds for the park supervision by Interior had included expenditures for road and bridge construction. From 1883 until 1918 (two years after the other Army contingents had been withdrawn) the Army engineers worked on the park roads, constructed permanent buildings, and made other improvements.

Captain Kingman is the first of two Army engineers who deserve special mention in the history of Yellowstone. To him goes the credit for laying out the basic loop road system that still exists in the park. (It is actually more of a figure eight with roads from the north, northeast, east, south, and west entrances tying into the eight.) When he arrived in Yellowstone, he found about 160 miles of road, all of it atrocious and much of the time impassable. Superintendent Norris had planned the roads on the premise that a road must be the shortest distance between two points. His roads led up the steepest hills, through bogs, and along precarious canyon walls. Stumps were left in the roadways, there were extensive washouts in wet weather, the dust was suffocating on dry days, and the steepness of grades was a horror to horses and travelers alike. On the road from Mammoth to Swan Lake Flats, in the northern part of the park, it was not at all unusual for passengers, concerned over their safety as well as the condition of the straining horses, to get out and walk.

Kingman appraised the situation, made his recommendations, and in the four summer-autumn seasons he was assigned to the park (1883-1886), he made such a good beginning that his basic road plan was accepted and completed by his successors. To him goes the credit not only for laying out the basic road system but also for designing roads that least detract from the natural beauties of Yellowstone. Rather than cut fresh timber that would leave a scar in the forest, he used wood from an 1882 burn in the park that had killed the trees without destroying much of the timber. He insisted upon well-built roads of "the solid, durable and substantial quality that usually characterizes the works constructed by the national government." He established some excellent standards for park roads, and is responsible for the present route from Gardiner to Mammoth and from Mammoth up through the Golden Gate to Swan Lake Flats. Kingman loved the wilderness and desired to keep it in nature's hands. The thing to do, he emphasized, was "simply to keep the park as nature made it .... [If it should] become the resort of fashion, if its forests are stripped to rear smooth hotels; if the race course, the drinking saloon, and the gambling-table invade it; if its valleys are scarred by railroads and its hills pierced by tunnels ... if, in short, a sort of Coney Island is established there, then it will cease to belong to the whole people and will be unworthy the care and protection of the National Government." No better statement of policy for the park has ever been enunciated.

The second Army engineer, and the better known, was Captain Hiram Martin Chittenden. He, too, fell in love with the park and worked diligently on the road system. He did, however, construct the road to the top of Mount Washburn, which may have been an engineering feat but was of questionable value and a scar on the mountainside. A good publicist and lobbyist, Chittenden's greatest contribution was his ability to wrest funds from Congress; his second was his history of Yellowstone Park.

Captain Harris probably conferred at length with Kingman. In any event, in a very short time, Army routine was taking shape; "M" Troop pitched tents south and out of sight of the Mammoth Hot Springs hotel, dubbing it Camp Sheridan. "Conformation of the ground is such," Captain Harris reported to his superiors in the Interior Department, "that the buildings are not visible from any portion of the 'hotel terrace' nor do they obstruct either the view or approaches to the Hot Springs formation." The Army, even at this early date, was not blind to aesthetics. (Five years later it moved to the east side of the terrace fronting the Hot Springs hotel and there, as Fort Yellowstone, it remained; when the Army left, the park service took over the buildings, which are still in use.)

Once his men had their horses and he had his orders (those from Interior arriving two weeks late), Captain Harris moved rapidly to secure the park. The Interior Department had provided for assistants stationed at strategic points of the park; Captain Harris considered this a viable policy and, therefore, he replaced those vacated posts with Army detachments. The need was also apparent: tourists were more prevalent than ever, drifters located their tents or lean-tos wherever their inclinations directed, and there was no satisfactory enforcement of regulations, though the last Interior Department superintendent, David W. Wear, had done his best. In short order Captain Harris had his men "roaming the back trails and canyons, flushing out hunters, woodcutters, and souvenir collectors."

By 1916 there were 15 soldier stations, sometimes called "outpost stations," the most important ones being at the park entrances. In summer, duties included sealing firearms, making sure the family dog was on a leash, and making rounds of the neighborhood. "People come here for pleasure," reads one set of Orders to Station Commanders. "It is our duty to treat them politely and give them all information possible when requested. Don't forget that the National Parks belong to the people. Never lose your temper." Within a few years there was published a small book of park regulations for use by Army personnel. Before the men were sent out, they had to study this book and pass an examination on its contents. While on summer duty, the men wore the garrison

The Army ran Yellowstone Park until 1910. Here the 25th Infantry bicycles through in 1894 on their 1,900-mile journey from Fort Missoula, Montana, to St. Louis, Missouri. (NARS 111-SC-88515)

uniforms consisting of the blue forage cap, blue blouse, blue trousers, and black shoes. At that time, 4 troops of from 45 to 62 men each were on duty policing the park; in addition there was a clerical staff, a hospital corpsman, a signal corps attachment, and the Army engineers.

Once the Army had a fixed routine for policing the park, it was a short step beyond to the evolution of policies designed to prevent forest fires, vandalism, and poaching. According to Captain George S. Anderson, the most successful of the Army superintendents (he was there six years, 1891-1897), the men on duty in summertime paid particular attention to the prevention of forest fires. "For this purpose," he said, "a mounted man leaves each station every day during the season, soon after breakfast. He rides leisurely along the road, carefully examining all recently abandoned camps. Should unextinguished fires be found, the guilty parties are arrested and brought here [to Fort Yellowstone] for trial. At a point about halfway to the next station a man from that post is met; the two eat luncheon and spend an hour or two together, and in the afternoon they retrace their steps, exercising the same vigilance as in the forenoon." To Captain F. A. Boutelle, Anderson's predecessor, goes the credit for establishing regular campgrounds, a policy still being observed. Telephone lines, strung and maintained by a contingent of the Signal Corps, connected the outpost stations with headquarters. Later fire lanes were cut at strategic places, making it easier to control fires once they had started.

Besides guarding against forest fires and policing the roads and camps of the visitors, the Army paid meticulous attention to the protection of the thermal formations. For years tourists had been hacking away at the sinter that had formed the geyser cones and constituted the edges of hot springs. In its original form, this was often lacy and exquisite, but even by the time the Army arrived, much of the beauty of the more frequented hot springs and geysers had been destroyed. Tourists had also discovered that some words scraped into the sides of a hot spring would remain for years to come. The Army took a very dim view of this vandalism. "A very picturesque figure," wrote Captain Anderson, "is a sentimental youth at twilight as he transmits his name by writing on the 'formation' — the hot springs deposits. A much more interesting figure is the same youth at sunrise the next morning when, followed by a mounted soldier, he proceeds, scrub-brush and soap in hand, to the same spot and removes the perishable evidence of his late precence."

The killing of game, whether by tourists in summer or poachers in winter, posed a serious problem for the Army because from 1886 until 1894 there existed no statutes — territorial, state, or federal — to impose penalties for the killing of game or spoliation of the thermal phenomena of the park. Stories were told of skin hunters killing as many as 300 elk in a herd and of one hunter who found a herd of deer floundering in the snow and killed 40 of them in a single stand. Tooth hunters, so called because all they wanted from the elk they killed were the molars, which commanded a stiff price from members of the Benevolent and Protective Order of Elks who made watch fobs of them, likewise poached in the park. The Yellowstone buffalo were in special danger as a head of one of these vanishing beasts was worth $500 in the 1890s.

Because of the lack of statutes imposing penalties, about all the Army could do was harass the culprits. If caught, the poacher was relieved of his gear — his horse, saddle, bridle, rifle, field glasses, pack, and cartridge belt — and was escorted out of the park — sometimes after an illegal incarceration in a jail cell at Fort Yellowstone while the slow means of communication between there and Washington eventually brought an order to release the suspect, an order the officer in charge knew all along was coming. The poachers, men of the mountains who knew their way around, tried to outsmart the Army, but often were surprised to see an armed patrol come into sight, be it in the remote southwest "Cascade Corner" of the park or the Black Tail Deer Plateau, Hell Roaring Creek, or Pelican Valley.

The Army used a secret telegraph code to prevent residents at Livingston or Gardiner, north of the park, from knowing what it was doing, and personnel could be ordered "on the quiet" to remote places "to carry out the verbal instructions received concerning poaching in the vicinity." Patrols were advised not to follow the known trails but to make their way into remote areas, off the beaten path. The poachers began to feel the pressure. Year by year the list increased of those culprits who were caught and expelled from the park.

In the winter of 1894, two officers on patrol up Pelican Valley northeast of Yellowstone Lake came upon a cache of six buffalo scalps and skulls and hides. The trail was clear and they followed it, soon coming upon a man busily skinning five more buffalo he had just shot. He was caught in a daring capture and brought to Mammoth where Captain Anderson threw him in the guardhouse. Fortunately the photographer, F. Jay Haynes, had photographed the dead buffalo, and the well known western writer, Emerson Hough, was present to write a stirring article on the incident. The publicity helped the passage through Congress of the Lacey Act which made illegal the hunting, killing, wounding, or capturing of any animal "except dangerous animals when it is necessary to prevent them from destroying human life or inflicting injury." Penalties could be levied up to a fine of $1,000, two years imprisonment, or both, plus forfeiture of guns and equipment. This was just what the Army had needed; protection of game was much more successful thereafter.

Although the buffalo were then safe from poachers, their numbers diminished in the park until there were possibly as few as 22 by 1902. It was the general feeling at the turn of the century that this useful game animal, which once numbered 32,000,000, was soon to be extinct. That the buffalo was saved is a remarkable story involving ranchers with nostalgia for the vanishing frontier, some private game keepers such as Austin Corbin in New Hampshire, a few conservationists such as Dr. William T. Hornaday of the New York Zoological Park, and government officials including Theodore Roosevelt and President Harrison's Secretary of the Interior, John W. Noble. When Noble was informed that 60 or 70 buffalo had wandered out of the park and were being slaughtered, he contacted Acting Superintendent, Captain Fraser Boutelle, to check on the rumor. He was pleased to find that the story was false.

In spite of Army interest in the buffalo, the Yellowstone herd was not thriving; there was, in fact, considerable indication that it was declining. In 1895, the Smithsonian Institution gave funds for the building of a corral in which to better protect the beasts, but only eight buffalo wandered in to make use of the forage and, because the gates were left open for others, they departed and no more came in. Then, in 1902, Congress passed a resolution calling upon the Secretaries of Interior and Agriculture to transmit facts concerning the status of buffalo in the United States and Canada and to determine "whether or not steps might be taken by the United States for the prevention of extinction of such animals."

The Acting Superintendent at the time, Major John Pitcher, cooperated by making a survey of buffalo in the areas around the park and inquiring of the owners about the possibility of purchase. He was searching for pure-blooded buffalo. This made his task more difficult because many so-called buffalo contained strains of the domestic cow. Subsequently he was given $15,000 by Congress for the purchase of additional buffalo and a further sum for the maintenance of the herd. In due time, primarily because of Major Pitcher's efforts, more buffalo were brought in, park personnel learned how to handle the shaggy beasts, and two herds in the park began to flourish.

It was during the Army period in the park that bears, which previously had not been a marked feature of Yellowstone, began to be seen more frequently. Somehow their animal minds comprehended that they were safe in the park. By 1899 a few black bears had begun frequenting the garbage dumps. At first they were there only at night, and quickly left at the appearance of man; but within a few years, they came to accept, if

Conservation continues to be an Army interest. Here, antelope are released on the range at Fort Riley, Kansas. (FR)

not welcome, his presence, and went right on scavenging as people watched.

Other park animals benefited from the Army years. Antelope, which by 1900 were in danger of extinction, in Yellowstone grew from a very small number to nearly 1,000. Mountain sheep, black tail deer, and moose flourished on the reservation, and the American elk, or wapiti, by 1916 numbered more than 32,000 and constituted a serious problem. The tendency of elk, deer, and antelope to migrate down the Yellowstone valley was partly halted by the erection of a strong fence along open portions of the northern boundary. Acting Superintendents also cooperated with the United States Fish Commissioner in stocking Yellowstone waters with several types of trout, and even planted bass in one lake.

Errors were made also: the delicate ecological balance of nature was not then understood. Predators — coyotes, wolves, mountain lions, and wildcats — were considered fair game in all seasons, so that mountain lions and wolves were completely eliminated and the number of coyotes and wildcats greatly reduced. Nature's balance being upset, the living things they preyed upon, from rodents to elk, multiplied in the absence of their natural enemies. On occasion the Army disregarded its aim of keeping the park in the natural state by planting timothy and alfalfa in park meadows for harvesting, the hay to be fed to buffalo, elk, and deer in winter. At various times, consideration was even given to introducing reindeer and other exotic animals into the park; fortunately, this never materialized.

Finally, the Army sided with such conservationists as Senator George Graham Vest of Missouri, George Bird Grinnell (the crusading editor of *Forest and Stream*), and the organization known as the Boone and Crockett Club (of which several ex-Army Acting Superintendents were members), in opposing attempts by commercial interests wanting to expand into Yellowstone at the expense of the wilderness. A concessionaire was prevented from erecting an elevator in the Grand Canyon. With the railroaders who wanted to crisscross the park, and the Cooke City miners beyond the northeast boundary who wanted a railroad through the park between Gardiner and Cooke City, there was no peace. Year after year these interests lobbied in Congress, and year after year they failed. Most, but not all, of the Acting Superintendents cooperated in every way with the conservationists in opposing this railroad legislation, and the railroads were never built.

The Army made still other innovations which were continued by the National Park Service. The facet of park service activities known as "interpretation" — the policy of giving lectures and otherwise informing tourists of the geology and natural history of the park — was inaugurated by the Army. Books and pamphlets explaining park phenomena were made available to tourists, and an arboretum and botanical garden were started. As historian H. Duane Hampton has pointed out, "Troopers detailed to patrol the natural curiosities in the Parks were instructed to give what information they could, in a courteous manner, when requested to do so."

When the Army left the park in 1916 (only to return and then leave for good in 1918), Yellowstone was more secure than it had ever been before. In the crucial generation from 1886 to 1916 the Army had given the park stability, security, and a system of management involving the handling of visitors, fire protection, and animal control. The Army had done its job well.

It had done it so well that as early as 1890, just four years after it had taken over in Yellowstone, the Secretary of the Interior, without hesitation and with the support of President Harrison, requested troops to police the newly created Yosemite, General Grant, and Sequoia National Parks in California. (Not until 1900 did Congress specifically provide for troops in the California parks.) Problems in these reservations were concentrated in fire protection and trespass, especially by cattle and sheep men and their herds. The problem was aggravated by a lack of well marked park boundaries and the existence of much private land both adjacent to and even surrounded by the new parks. Yet the Army took its charge seriously. In the absence of statutory authority, harassment of intruders and their herds worked quite well. When a sheepherder was evicted at one point and his herd at another, the trouble caused him was often sufficient to keep him from trespassing again. Soon the grass and flower cover began to return to overgrazed areas. Likewise, game began to return. When the Army left the three California parks in 1914, those reservations were secure, the surrounding populace had changed in attitude from hostility to friendship, and the management of the parks was so efficient that the changeover to civilian rangers was easily made.

So well had the Army carried out its duties that the great American parks became known worldwide, and the Acting Superintendents were consulted by authorities of such countries as Japan and Germany for advice in administering large parks and game refuges. Less than two decades later the Army would once again show its presence in the national parks, administering Civilian Conservation Corps activities. They built roads and trails, bridges, camp grounds, fireplaces, and strung telephone lines, and, in Yellowstone, they removed abandoned dwellings, cleared old hotel sites of debris, and removed long abandoned trash dumps.

The military men assigned to protect the parks from 1886 to 1916 were dedicated servants of their government. By nature they were outdoorsmen, and they enjoyed the duties. Most of them were intellectually alert and were prepared to carry out orders not only to the letter, but with imagination and enthusiasm. For the better part of three crucial decades the Army acted as conservator of Yellowstone, Sequoia, General Grant, and Yosemite. In doing so it demonstrated how well it can conserve as well as destroy; it showed that protecting a nation does not always involve defending it in time of war or from internal violence.

Suggestions For Further Research

For the historian, conservation and ecology take on the nature of a will-o'-the-wisp. One plunges into research only to find that the abundance of material anticipated fails to appear. What there is amounts to very little, and often as not, it has already been "mined" and synthesized into a scholarly study.

There are, however, some hitherto uninvestigated facets in conservation/ecology history, and one of them is the role of the Army in the movement. For example, military bases are found in almost every state. Some of them, such as Fort Sill in Oklahoma or Fort Sam Houston in Texas, have existed for decades; others date from as recently as the Second World War, but even that is now a generation into the past. All of these bases are well kept. Many cover hundreds of thousands of acres. What has the Army done to protect the flora and fauna on these enormous reservations? The answer lies in official reports and Army archives, and in investigating them the dubious researcher will be in for a pleasant surprise. The Army has done much in the areas of game control and preservation of the flower and grass cover of these vast areas. It is a generally unknown facet of peacetime Army activities which deserves scholarly study.

In addition, many Army men have become ardent conservationists on their own. Several Acting Superintendents were members of the Boone and Crockett Club. In the lonely years of Army duty on the frontier, some officers became amateur geologists, paleontologists, zoologists, botanists, and ornithologists — the latter was the particular love of Army surgeons. The accomplishments of such individuals, either singly or in the aggregate, warrants research. During the years of Franklin Roosevelt and the New Deal, the Army administered the Civilian Conservation Corps. Many of its activities were concerned with conservation.

It would be interesting to learn the Army's role in programming such projects.

In sum, the researcher will discover that the peacetime Army manifested a love of the land that is altogether praiseworthy and deserving of historical notice.

SOURCES

The following books of interest should be available at the public library of any medium-sized city: H. Duane Hampton, *How the U.S. Cavalry Saved Our National Parks* (Bloomington, Ind., 1971) (this is an excellent survey of the Army's role in the parks); Hiram Martin Chittenden, *The Yellowstone National Park*, various editions; Merrill D. Beale, *The Story of Man in Yellowstone*, rev. ed. (Yellowstone Park, Wyo., 1960); Marie M. Augspurger, *Yellowstone National Park* (Middletown, Ohio, 1948); and Richard A. Bartlett, *Nature's Yellowstone* (Albuquerque, N. Mex., 1974.)

Lewis and Clark's *Journals* may be found in various editions, and John Bakeless, *Lewis and Clark, Partners in Discovery* (New York, 1947), and Paul Russell Cutright, *Lewis and Clark, Pioneering Naturalists* (Urbana, Ill., 1969) are excellent single-volume accounts. There are two brief biographies of John Colter: Burton Harris, *John Colter: His Years in the Rockies* (New York, 1952), and Stallo Vinton, *John Colter, Discoverer of Yellowstone Park* (New York, 1926). An interesting biography of Lieutenant Gustavus C. Doane is Orrin H. and Lorraine Booney, *Battle Drums and Geysers* (Chicago, 1970). For special studies written for the layman about Yellowstone flora and fauna, consult the book list of the Yellowstone Library and Museum Association, Yellowstone Park, Wyoming.

There is no biography of Dan Kingman, but his successor has been the subject of a recent biography: Gordon B. Dodds, *Hiram Martin Chittenden: His Public Career* (Lexington, Ky., 1973). Two new books have appeared on the buffalo: Tom McHugh, *The Time of the Buffalo* (New York, 1972), and David A. Dary, *The Buffalo Book* (Chicago, 1974).

For conservation, see publications of the Boone and Crockett Club, especially James B. Trefethan, *Crusade for Wildlife: Highlights in Conservation Progress* (Harrisburg, Pa., 1961); Theodore Roosevelt and George Bird Grinnell, eds., *Hunting in Many Lands: The Book of the Boone and Crockett Club* (New York, 1895); and George Bird Grinnell, ed., *Hunting at High Altitudes: The Book of the Boone and Crockett Club* (New York, 1913).

Carl P. Russell, *One Hundred Years of Yosemite* (Berkeley, Cal., 1932); Francis P. Farquhar, *Yosemite, the Big Trees, and the High Sierra* (Berkeley, Cal., 1948); and John R. White and Samuel J. Pasateri, *Sequoia and King's Canyon National Parks* (Stanford, Cal., 1949), give some information on the California parks. John A. Salmond, *The Civilian Conservation Corps, 1933-1942: A New Deal Case Study* (Durham, N.C., 1967), is adequate.

Soldiers from Fort Riley helping protect Junction City in the 1951 flood. (USA)

Chapter 4

THE ARMY AND
FLOOD AND DISASTER RELIEF

B. Franklin Cooling

In the middle of the traumatic 1960s in this country, Defense Department officials attempted to codify the principal roles or requirements for military support to the civil powers of the United States. They saw these as the employment of military resources for civil defense, natural disaster, and civil disturbances. The nature of events in the last decade have focused more attention upon the last of these functions through urban agitation, civil rights unrest, and anti-Vietnam rallies. Receiving relatively fewer headlines, yet nonetheless important and even more controversial in some ways, are the other two sides of the civil-support triad, particularly as they have related to the functions and mission of the United States Army.

It may be true, although history leaves the picture obscure, that military aid to civil authority in disaster relief has been a traditional military function. The military might of the Roman empire included the Watch or *Vigiles* — a fire brigade for the city of Rome. Military forces have always possessed the organization, leadership, and technical skills for disaster relief, although military commanders continue even to this day to decry this mission as it lends little gloss to the ideal of beau sabreur or "defender of the faith" — in this case, national defense.

The origins of the United States Army's participation in disaster relief remain cloudy. Few notations in the record occur in this regard until after the Civil War, because the American Army was neither numerically nor technically equipped to play a major role. The demographic distribution of the populace during the early years of the republic mitigated against this function. Protection and pacification on the frontier, coastal defense, and maintenance of arsenals served as the principal missions of the Army and the disorganization of the militia rendered that institution useless as an instrument for disaster relief. Given the American spirit of self-help, the relatively few urban areas of consequence that might require aid in the wake of civil disaster, and the Army's deployment away from the populations, it may be fairly posited that the military forces of the young nation seemed destined to play only a minor role here. Local military help to civilians undoubtedly took place, but such sporadic occurences commanded few headlines and even less space in the reports of promotion-conscious officers spoiling for combat glory and accolades from absentee authorities in Washington. The Army's mission was to defend the country and uphold the laws of the land. All else was secondary — a tradition which continues to pervade military planning and operations even today.

The Army became more active in treating the effects of disasters after the Civil War. Union Army wartime experience with firefighting in Columbia, South Carolina, and Richmond, Virginia, for example; occupation responsibilities of Reconstruction; and the quality of the national military as symbolic of unity possessed of unique resources, manpower, and equipment, may have served as a spur in this direction. Then, too, the mere absence of any official national relief agency apparently contributed to the need for military involvement in relief operations during the last third of the Nineteenth Century. The American Red Cross was founded in 1881 and figured in several emergencies. Yet its national organization remained embryonic, and it lacked official standing until 1905.

Meanwhile, the military institutions often had to fill the breach. Major General Philip H. Sheridan dispatched troops to help combat the Chicago fire of 1871, and the War Department authorized issue of 200,000 rations and 10,000 tents to ease the plight of the victims. The Army contributed more than 150 tons of food and assumed the task of delivering civilian-contributed relief supplies to victims of a yellow fever epidemic along the lower Mississippi River in 1878. Army tents sheltered survivors of the Charleston earthquake of 1886; Army and Pennsylvania National Guardsmen prevented an even greater loss of life than the 2,000 dead claimed by the Johnstown flood of 1889; and fires such as those in both Seattle and Baltimore in 1904 found regulars and guardsmen called upon to maintain law and order. Similarly, the Army participated in flood relief along the Rio Grande, Mississippi, and Red Rivers in 1897, in the Galveston flood of 1900, and in several other turn-of-the century disasters in the South and Midwest. In 1902, when a volcano devastated the French island of Martinique, U.S. Army forces on Puerto Rico dispatched food to feed 50,000 people for over a month. Uniquely, the Army even helped citizens battle the effects of grasshoppers in 1874-1875. Soldiers helped to feed more than 100,000 people across four states and two territories beyond the Mississippi who faced famine caused by drought and destruction of crops by the locusts.

Despite such experiences, which might have spawned even closer ties between the nation and its military institutions, countervailing influences of this era prevented the formalization of civil-military ties in the work of disaster relief. Although the Army might readily accept responsibilities in such fields as surveying and internal improvements, Army leaders felt that disaster relief hampered the normal military mission and usually offered little opportunity to perfect those skills and techniques that could not be developed in the course of normal military activities. Similarly, the Army was uncomfortable in an assignment where it had to intrude unduly in civil affairs, and even when it approved of some relief operations, legality-conscious bureaucrats in the War Department remained sensitive to the service's lack of statutory authority for relief missions. In 1874, for instance, Sheridan simply turned a deaf ear to pleas by his local subordinates seeking relief supplies for the famine-stricken western settlers, on the grounds that any extra-legal distribution from Army storehouses would only lead the people to exploit the situation of the dole. Fortunately, wiser opinions prevailed and the citizenry avoided starvation.

But all the inhibitions did not lie solely on the military side of the equation. Prerogatives of states rights, grave suspicion of any evidence of undue influence from Washington, and the prevailing social and economic values of rugged individualism, self-reliance, and *laissez faire* were all thought to be undermined by many citizens when Federal troops entered the picture. Congress usually indicated its support of Nineteenth Century relief operations by appropriating additional funds to replace items expended by the military in such operations. Still, when approval was not unanimous, military authorities saw their doubts reinforced about the utility and legality of rescue and relief. Given this state of hesitancy, reluctance, or outright hostility, it is little wonder that complete ties were so long in coming in this sector of military support of civil authorities on a regularized basis.

War Department gratitude to Congress for finally designating the Red Cross as the nation's official relief agency in 1905 evaporated less than 18 months later when the Army found itself shouldering disaster relief burdens on a scale unmatched since the end of the Civil War. The San Francisco earthquake and fire of 1906 posed tasks so large that they could only be compared with post-combat situations where it was necessary for

a military force to occupy, govern, and sustain a conquered community. Not since the initial stages of Reconstruction during the Civil War had the Army faced such chores; but San Francisco was not enemy territory — a fact which simply complicated the problem. Barring martial law, a condition never imposed during the crisis, the Army simply could not take charge of rescue and relief operations. The Army could be faulted for being so legalistic in an hour of obvious need, but civil authority continued to operate spasmodically, the American Red Cross was also on the scene, and the lack of clear lines of authority and organization, as we know them today, must be taken into consideration. Yet, as is often the case, institutions learn best to work together in an actual crisis. So it was in San Francisco in 1906.

The earthquake and fire that swept the city in April of that year exceeded the facilities and capabilities of civil authority. Army demolition teams were quickly called into play to prevent the spread of fire, although with marginal effect and much subsequent criticism. Brigadier General Frederick Funston, in the absence of his immediate superior, Major General Adolpheus W. Greely, directed military help in manning refugee centers, restoring public order, and offering succor in the city. Actually, the War Department never sanctioned such activities until 27 April — nine days after the initial earthquake and fire. Meanwhile, quartermaster elements dispensed bedding and shelter in city parks and other open areas; signal corpsmen struggled to cope with the crippled communication system; medical teams tended to the injured; and engineers set up sanitation facilities. Most of the soldiers possessed no military specialty immediately applicable to the emergency, so they served as a valuable manpower pool for firefighting and damage control.

The post-disaster environment of looting, lawlessness, and general chaos produced a ragtag force of Marines, Navy personnel, National Guardsmen, and police and deputized civilians to aid the regulars. Only the Army had the requisite strength and organization to control all of the elements, but the sources of the aid effort were so varied that proper coordination and control proved inadequate during the early, crucial

---

When a major disaster strikes, the nearest armed forces will frequently find themselves aiding the civilian population. Though the guidelines were far from clear, the U.S. Army immediately moved into San Francisco after the earthquake of 1906 and began feeding the destitute and homeless. (NARS 92-ER-13)

Refugees leaving San Francisco after the earthquake and fire of 1906 with two of the many soldiers on duty (foreground) to keep order and prevent looting. (NARS 92-ER-26)

days after the disaster. In fact, when Greely returned to take charge, he disagreed with Funston's decisions regarding imposition of near-martial law. He properly refused to guide the Guard. Such attitudes were superimposed on confused local civilian authorities, and a plethora of official and semi-official relief missions produced great difficulty and suffering. Arbitrary enforcement of the mayor's proclamation concerning shooting of looters led to punishment of innocent and guilty alike — to the detriment of the image of the military as preservers of law and order. Some evidence exists that the uniformed ranks — including the regulars as well as the National Guard — actually participated in the looting of Southern Pacific railroad cars. Fortunately, the Army performed another mission in the wake of the crisis.

The citizenry still needed relief once the fires had been extinguished and order restored to the scene. Thousands of homeless, injured, and even the unaffected, required food and water. While relief parcels piled up in storehouses on the edge of the torn city, residents of the quake area went hungry due to lack of proper distribution facilities. Civilian agencies lacked resources and the ability to handle the chore, so the military intervened once more. The Army rapidly increased the number of food distribution points from 7 to 200, placed a doctor at nearly every place of immediate need, and improved the sanitary conditions at the refugee camps. Six-hundred soldiers fed 250,000 people for eight weeks after the earthquake had struck. The drama of firefighting or law enforcement was gone, but the Army's experience in disaster relief through this quiet, unsung fashion may well have provided its greatest contribution in the catastrophe. Although 500 people perished in the quake and fire, almost none perished during the days when the U.S. Army administered relief in the San Francisco area.

In the early years of the Twentieth Century, Army aid in disaster relief continued periodically. Soldiers helped flood victims along the Mississippi River in 1912, feeding 185,000 people, sheltering 20,000, and supplying 50,000 head of cattle with forage. Some of the same victims received similar aid when the river overflowed its banks the following year. Flooding of the Brazos River in Texas in 1913 killed 500 people and rendered thousands more homeless. Still, Army troop transports saved more than 400 people from drowning, and other soldiers fed and sheltered refugees on land. Farther north, the city of Omaha was also visited by disaster that year, as a tornado tore a 5-mile swath through the residential area, killing 250 people and leaving 3,300 more homeless. As in San Francisco, the Omaha city fathers could not cope with the impact of the disaster and they called on the local military for aid. Major Carl F. Hartmann, commandant of nearby Fort Omaha, had only a small contingent at his disposal, but he offered their services immediately, intervened personally, and brought a very delicate situation under control. Elsewhere across the United States in 1913, military authorities provided food, shelter, and medical aid to victims of a cyclone in Alabama, and soldiers fought forest fires from California to the Adirondacks.

Disaster-relief operations seemed to be almost a routine feature of military activity by the 1920s. The U.S. Army published its first regulations governing such work in 1924. AR 500-60, relatively unchanged until 1939, provided guidelines to commanders faced with disaster-relief missions. But it was even more interesting as a reflection of War Department thought on the task. Justifiably pleased with accomplishments in this vein, military authorities nonetheless remained uneasy about a continuing role in such work. Civilian suspicions about military involvement, as well as federal control of local affairs, was receding but legalistically inclined authorities in the War Department worried about statutory authority for disbursement of government property in disasters. AR 500-60 limited intervention to most desperate situations, where "overruling demands of humanity compel immediate action" or local resources were clearly inadequate to meet the need. In any event, local commanders were still forced to receive permission from the War Department before undertaking relief operations, and they had to retain control of Army property during the exercise. Another indication of the place of disaster relief in military thinking at the time may be gleaned from the General Service Schools text on military aid to the civil power. Nowhere was disaster relief even mentioned, but rather, the focus was placed on traditional contingencies of military government, martial law, and domestic disturbance.

Perhaps the largest unresolved question lay with the relations between the U.S. Army and the American Red Cross. The Red Cross was the country's primary relief agency, but it was heavily dependent on military resources in all types of disasters, and its officers felt that its primary responsibility would be usurped by a military institution which might veto relief in some of the gravest situations. Red Cross officials pressed the War Department for over a decade to modify its regulations so that the primacy of the relief agency would be recognized officially. But the military resisted such change, fearing that it would lead to Red Cross control over Army personnel and equipment. Meanwhile, circumstances forced change upon both institutions.

Numerous natural disasters in the late 1920s and 1930s honed the Army's techniques of disaster intervention. Army engineers participated in the relief effort in the wake of the great Mississippi River flood of 1927.

During a nine-month period in 1928 and 1929, the Army provided succor after hurricanes in Puerto Rico and Florida, an earthquake in Venezuela, floods in Florida and Alabama, and a tornado in Georgia. The Chemical Warfare Service aided in a Cleveland fire investigation and made recommendations for construction and fire regulations to help prevent future tragedies. Yet, in retrospect at least, the War Department seemed quite content to continue the *ad hoc* response to disaster relief — it certainly showed little inclination to change until after the major disasters of the 1937 floods.

Torrential precipitation in the winter of that year rapidly inundated the Ohio valley. Sections of Pennsylvania, Ohio, Indiana, Kentucky, and Illinois were ravaged by flood waters. Red Cross officials found themselves caring for 600,000 homeless people after but a single week of crisis. The Public Health Service and the Narcotics Bureau provided medical aid, the Works Projects Administration and the Civilian Conservation Corps placed laborers at strengthening the dikes and levees, and even the Coast Guard employed small boats to rescue flood victims. But the U.S. Army once more received the largest assignment as flood waters reached the Mississippi system.

Army engineers directed a 150,000-man effort to avert disaster from Cairo, Illinois, to the Gulf of Mexico. The War Department announced plans to evacuate the entire Mississippi flood plain if necessary. Fortunately, a much greater catastrophe was averted and only 250 people died during the floods. Dozens of disparate organizations coordinated their efforts and operated under the general direction of the Red Cross — perhaps it was the spirit already engendered by hard times of the Depression and the cooperative uplift of the New Deal. For the military, at least, this cooperation was somewhat spontaneous and quite dependent on the good relations between commanders and Red Cross officials at the local level. Yet, it seemed a somewhat weak reed upon which to continue to base relations in the future. Traditional interservice cooperation in the military had been learned the hard way over the years, and, after the disaster of 1937, the War Department became less reluctant to come to a positive understanding on disaster relief with the Red Cross.

The War Department and the Red Cross reached a modicum of agreement in 1938, and the following year the Army revised its regulations to reflect the first formal understanding of the difference of approach to disaster relief. The Red Cross received recognition from the War Department as the nation's official relief agency. It would command a position of primacy in future disaster operations. Requests for military aid from individuals or other agencies would be referred normally to the Red Cross for approval. Only Washington might still give authority for military intervention in a disaster, but local commanders were supposed to consult with Red Cross officials before reporting a disaster situation to the War Department. The Army retained final authority on the use of its personnel and materials. Requests for aid, even though cleared by the Red Cross, might still be vetoed at the Washington level. Still, both sides felt that the agreement provided a sound basis for future cooperation.

The great crusade in World War II solidified the bonds of cooperation, organizational ties, and unity of effort between the civilian and military sectors of American society in ways still dimly perceived by historians. The program that was labeled civil defense was in effect disaster oriented, with a focus on man-made rather than natural catastrophe — but it employed many of the same tools and agencies to a similar end. Thus, the framework and functions of the Office of Civil Defense from 1941 to 1948 cannot be discounted nor disconnected from the overall pattern of relationships between the Army and civilian disaster relief organizations. While the Army throughout the wartime period rightfully claimed a primary focus on combat activities — and even the 1946 report of a civil defense board chaired by Major General Harold R. Bull decided that civil defense problems lay outside the scope of military responsibility because they were civilian in nature — proliferation of institutional arrangements, liaison activities, and grassroots organization in the civil defense program pointed the direction for postwar conditions. But "proliferation" not "cohesion" seemed to be the norm as the Army and the nation emerged from a second world conflict into a period of uneasy peace.

The unstable nature of the world environment, plus untoward developments in international armaments, produced a postwar atmosphere in which relief from both man-made and natural disasters assumed new dimensions. Despite the American proclivity for compartmentalization in management, the twin issues of civil defense in nuclear holocaust and disaster relief in natural catastrophes were handmaidens in disguise. Neither federal officials — military or civilian — nor the nation as a whole recognized the connection. Just as it required 15 years for the War Department and the Red Cross to adjust their institutional arrangements to insure cohesion in natural disaster relief before the war, it would take nearly two decades for the military establishment and the rest of the federal, state, and local bureaucracies to weld together the various facets of post-attack and post-disaster relief after World War II. Meanwhile, threat of nuclear attack and actual natural disasters produced uncoordinated legislation designed to cope with the twin problems of the homefront which seemed so dissimilar to that generation of officials. The results included the federal disaster relief legislation of 1947 and 1950 as well as the Civil Defense Act of 1950. Elaborate institutional arrangements were spawned, and they remain essential to understanding postwar disaster relief and the Army. But, in each case, the military was a distinctly minor and recalcitrant partner.

Prompted mainly by the reported need for national aid in the hurricane-affected Gulf Coast area, the flooded regions along the Mississippi and Missouri Rivers in 1947, and the Texas City explosion in April of that year, Congress broke with its traditional pattern of piecemeal authorization to organizations such as the Red Cross, Corps of Engineers, and Commissioner of Public Roads to provide material assistance. Public Law 233 of the 80th Congress authorized the War Assets Administrator to transfer certain surplus property to the Federal Works Administrator who in turn could aid state and local governments in alleviating the damage, hardship, and suffering caused by disasters. The Federal Works Administrator could authorize and act through any other national agency or any state or local government, and other federal agencies were supposed to cooperate to the fullest possible extent. Three years later, the first of the so-called "Disaster Relief Acts" was passed to enable state governors to seek assistance from the President following a major calamity. Later that year, under the impetus provided by the Korean conflict and escalating threats to national security, President Harry Truman established the Federal Civil Defense Administration. All of this legislation prescribed the role of military involvement, at least on paper. However, the long sensitive years of implementation that followed showed the need for Army interest and participation in both facets of disaster relief. Practice proved as necessary as theory.

The U.S. Army responded quickly to the Texas City explosion on 16 April 1947. Army officials at Fort Crockett sent uniformed personnel to work with civilian officials on police patrol, food distribution, and medical and shelter aid. The commanding general of the Fourth Army, Jonathan Wainwright, surveyed the problem personally and placed the entire resources of his command at the disposal of the relief effort — much in the tradition of Funston at San Francisco some 40 years before. Army withdrawal from an active role in the emergency occured only when Red Cross and civil officials seemed to have stabilized the situation. Similarly, in the 1953 Waco tornado disaster, the First Armored Division used its heavy equipment to rescue people trapped beneath collapsed buildings, to clear rubble, and to demolish hazardous structures. Military engineers participated in Operation Noah in 1955, a long-range relief effort designed to mitigate the effects of Hurricanes Connie and Diane along the east coast. Even Army aviators played a role in disaster relief

When a tornado struck the city of Topeka, Kansas, in 1966, the National Guard was ordered out to protect property, here outside the State Printer's Office. (Kansas State Historical Society)

as in 1956 when they made a perilous descent into Grand Canyon in an effort to rescue survivors from the collision of two airliners. The year before, Army pilots had undertaken vital transport and damage-survey missions after a volcano eruption in Hawaii, and two years later they again participated in such activities.

Postwar responsibilities abroad also involved Army units in disaster relief. A severe storm pounded the Netherlands in 1953 and produced the worst flooding in that country since the Fifteenth Century. The resources of that nation were inadequate to cope with the disaster, and the U.S. Army in Europe was among those American military commands that intervened in Operation Tulip with food, gasoline, labor, rescue services, and equipment for containing the flood waters. The Army sent medical teams to Pakistan in 1955 to prevent epidemics arising from a flood and soon extended their services to cope with other medical problems in that country. Similarly, Operation Amigos in 1960 had an Army field hospital dispatched to Chile as part of one of the largest emergency relief operations ever undertaken in peacetime.

Thus, by the 1960s, U.S. Army participation in disaster relief at home and abroad had become so commonplace that few seasons passed without some involvement in flood, hurricane, tornado, blizzard, or other form of help for civilians in emergencies. The National Guard was particularly outstanding in this regard, faced with such bizarre catastrophes as the chlorine-gas emergency at Natchez, Mississippi, in 1961-62, and "operation Water Wagon" in 1964 when the Vermont National Guard trucked 25,000,000 gallons of water to keep 18,000 cows alive on 200 farms during a drought-ridden winter. The proficiency of the Guard led many military spokesmen to advocate disaster relief and civil-defense missions as the only viable functions for the Army's reserve components in a world of nuclear deterrence.

Whether it was a tornado in the Texas panhandle, floods along the Ohio River, or blizzards in northern California, Army forces always seemed to be ready to render aid. One of the most publicized instances came in 1964 when the Alaskan earthquake affected not only civilian communities but also part of the nation's first line of defense in that area. The earthquake, whick struck shortly after 5:30 p.m. on Friday, 27 March, spread devastation throughout a large portion of south-central Alaska, which contained about half of the state's population. Military installations were also affected, although the damage was less severe, and the Army was able to rapidly turn its attention to aiding the stricken civilian community. Fortunately, the positioning of Army installations at Forts Richardson, near Anchorage, and Wainwright, outside the region, permitted a logical division of labor and relief. Actually, the conditions in outlying areas such as Seward and Valdez were more difficult due to breakdown of communication links with Anchorage. Army aviation proved especially effective as helicopters and aircraft were able to provide the first reliable information about the plight of those communities. The Army even found itself running a dog shelter in Valdez rather than killing off the roaming animals.

Although the earthquake produced destruction and damage of large proportions, the death toll was limited to 115, due mainly to widely scattered population, absence of serious fire in Anchorage, calmness of the citizenry, and the coordination and cooperation of various agencies charged with coping with disasters. Substantial experience with disasters over the years had finally yielded good results in Alaska, as such diverse agencies as the military (active and reserve), civil authorities, civil defense organizations, and the Red Cross had learned to work together with minimum friction and duplication of effort.

Throughout the history of disaster relief runs the thread of local cooperation and unity of effort, while at higher echelons may be found confusion of organization, responsibilities, and lines of communication. The postwar years particularly surfaced a confusing matrix of people and agencies all charged with varying responsibilities in several areas roughly grouped as "disaster relief." For example, presidential delegation of authority to administer the Federal Disaster Act of 1950 followed a tortuous path. By 1953, authority had passed from the Administrator of the Housing and Home Finance Agency to the Federal Civil Defense administrator, with all Federal agencies responsible for varieties of support. President John F. Kennedy sought to bring some order out of the years of chaos when in 1962 he signed an executive order detailing the responsibilities of the Director of the Office of Emergency Planning (later the Office of Emergency Preparedness) in the Executive Office of the President. Within the Department of Defense, responsibility for disaster-relief activities passed originally through the Office of the Assistant Secretary of Defense for Civil Defense (which would act as liaison with the OEP, Red Cross, and other government agencies), before finding a final home with the Secretary of the Army on 31 March 1964, when the Director of Civil Defense was settled within that level of the bureaucracy. Although mirroring the declining importance of civil defense in the minds of military and civilian leaders in this country over the years, the transition finally collated properly those allied functions of civil defense and disaster relief in an environment more promising for correct implementation of the mission in the future. Ironically, it had taken nearly 20 years, and internal streamlining would continue into the

1970s. But, the Secretary of the Army has remained the DOD Executive Agent for providing military assistance to civil government in times of civil disaster.

The series of disasters that struck with lightning fury in various sections of the nation after March 1964 further emphasized the importance of the entire program of federal participation in disaster relief. In addition to the Alaskan earthquake, the Pacific Northwest floods of December and January 1964, the Upper Plains flooding, and the tornadoes in Indiana, Michigan, Illinois, and Ohio in late April 1965, gave impetus to a new Disaster Relief law, originally passed in 1966, which with its 1970 revision attempted to improve the control mechanisms for alleviating distress that accompanied disasters. Nevertheless, problems were to remain, as noted in a study by the Disaster Research Center at the Ohio State University in 1968. These analysts isolated certain factors that were responsible for problems in military-civilian relations during natural disasters. Among these were (1) the failure of civilian officials to understand and to appreciate military structures and operations, and similarly (2) the less frequent failure of military authorities to comprehend and to accept the manner in which civilian organizations are structured and how they operate. Then, too, the Ohio State group saw "the absence in many cases of any viable civilian means for coordinating and integrating the activities of the numerous groups and organizations — both civilian and military— that assume emergency tasks." Clearly then, some basic questions remained to be asked, some answers sought, and implementation effected. With each successive disaster — Dell City, Texas, flood of 1968; Hurricane Camille in 1969; Operation Haylift during the mid-winter blizzards of 1971; floods in California in 1971 and in South Dakota in 1972; and Hurricane Agnes in 1972 — slow, but steady progress came through the stern lessons of experience. Yet, disaster relief continued to be plagued by inadequate planning and coordination, lack of ample communications, presence of curious official visitors who clogged actual operations, and the never-changing complexities of operations in the wake of a major catastrophe.

In each case, the Army and other disaster-relief organizations responded quickly and affirmatively, saving lives and easing misery. But, the determination to help has always characterized the Army's traditional participation in disaster relief. The long-term trend has been one of improvement because of growing technical competence, and the substitution of planning, experience, and a degree of managerial skill for the earlier impromptu, spectacular, and sometimes marginally successful efforts. All echelons of the Army have disaster-relief and civil-

Cattle may not be citizens, but they are the property of Americans, and so when a blizzard strikes, the Iowa National Guard, in this case in January 1975, operates a hay lift. (Iowa NG)

defense plans by regulation. Yet, the Department of the Army maintains its uneasy feelings towards over-involvement in this sort of noncombat activity. Admittedly, the Army has come a long way since its earlier aversion to anything that did not contribute directly to combat efficiency. Secretary of the Army Robert Froehlke's approval of equivalent training credit for flood-relief duty by the Pennsylvania National Guard after Hurricane Agnes, in lieu of federal annual training, attests to that fact. Still, the army regulations blithely pronounce that: "Utilization of US Army Reserve units or individuals during inactive duty training in the event of disaster is not authorized. US Army Reserve units or individuals may assist in disaster relief operations only on a volunteer basis as private citizens ...." Lieutenant Governor Ernest P. Kline of Pennsylvania took a decidedly more positive stance on this issue when he cited flood duty as providing opportunities for exercise of command and control, small unit leadership, staff procedures, communication, unit movements under duress, logistical missions, field administration, medical support, and other aspects of training.

The basic role of the U.S. Army continues to be provision for the defense of the nation. In wartime, then, combat will take precedence over civil defense and post-attack recovery in the eyes of most military professionals. But, the peacetime situation can be viewed somewhat differently. The unpleasant memories of Vietnam, antimilitary rallies, and the ending of the draft in the late 1960s and 1970s support the view that the Army must act in a positive manner to convince the American public that it is and will remain an extension of civilian society. Perhaps this has always been more apparent on the local level where men in uniform have traditionally worked side by side with harried civil officials in floods, earthquakes, and famine. Perhaps, it is only the officialdom of the central government, disassociated from the actual disaster scene, which fails to perceive the note of thanks in the eyes of the citizen as he receives medical aid, a food package, or other form of help from an Army regular or National Guardsman on the scene of calamity. By insuring that the public image of the military is enhanced through domestic action activities such as disaster relief and civil defense, inroads can be made to assure that a viable military force can be manned and made available for the primary mission of national defense. The good will, exposure, and utilitarian results produced by years of U.S. Army work in disaster relief remains both incalculable and indelible. The dilemmas, the problems, and the tradition will remain. Armies in disaster-relief operations, whether American or foreign, whether the catastrophe be man-made or natural, may be expected in the future. Neither antimilitarism,

Children assist men of the 62nd Engineer Battalion as they fill sandbags for reinforcing dikes along the Atchafalaya River, Morgan City, Louisiana, in April 1973. (USA)

aversion to noncombat missions, nor the changing human environment in the world has altered that fact in over 1,000 years.

Suggestions For Further Research

Accounts of specific disasters document U.S. Army experience in modern relief activities fairly well. However, we know all too little about pre-Twentieth Century experiences in this vein, either by pattern or by individual case. We even fail to understand how the American experience relates to the historical ramifications of the issue on the international scene. Although some studies have been done by U.S. Army professional officers at the Command and General Staff College and at the War College, neither the military nor the civilian communities truly appreciate the historical dimension of military institutions and disaster-relief responsibilities. We need to know more about the managerial relationships, the individual experiences and impressions of participants in the disasters, and their view of military involvement. Is disaster relief an aberration, merely to be tolerated as an inevitable part of the human response to his environment, or does it have wider and more relevant meaning than either the military or the civilian communities would like to assign to it? Have all the widespread organizational arrangements and position papers produced at various echelons of government since World War II inhibited or expedited the actual practices of military-civilian interlock in disaster relief activities? Are disaster-relief operations really any less productive for combat readiness and efficiency than sterile maneuvers and sandbox training exercises, as military professionals have claimed for so long? Are civil defense and disaster relief really twin facets of the same non-combat defense effort, or should some paramilitary organization be charged with their implementation, leaving the U.S. Army and its reserve components free for the primary mission of active defense? Historically, these questions pervade the issue of disaster/civil defense operations and the military institutions. Still, the nation has forgotten little and learned little on the question of the Army in disaster relief — simply because all the dimensions of the past have not been explored fully so that the United States may plan for the future.

SOURCES

Sources are rich and varied concerning disasters and disaster relief, although one may search in vain for a single account concerning military activity in such work. Official reports of the War Department (and

Department of Defense), the Militia Bureau, and the National Guard and Reserve components, as well as journals such as the *National Guardsman* must be diligently researched for the isolated cases in which the military has aided civil authorities. Even then, the primary focus will be on post-World War II activities with earlier treatment limited to such case studies as Gilbert C. Fite, "The United States Army and Relief to Pioneer Settlers, 1874-1875," *Journal of the West*, 6, January 1967, 99-107; Carroll A. Devol, "The Army in the San Francisco Disaster," *Journal of the United States Infantry Association*, IV, July 1907, 59-87; U.S. Army, Pacific Division, *Earthquake in California, April 18, 1906; Special Report of Major General Adolpheus W. Greely* ... (Washington: Government Printing Office, 1906); and Gordon Thomas and Max Morgan Witts' revisionistic *The San Francisco Earthquake (New York:* Stein and Day, 1971). Also useful on the U.S. Army's philosophy toward aid to civil authorities is the U.S. Army General Service Schools', *Military Aid to Civil Power* (Fort Leavenworth: General Service Schools Press, 1925) as well as Army Regulation 500-60, *Emergency Employment of Army Resources, Disaster Relief*, 1924- .

Analyses of post-World War II disaster relief might profitably begin with Edward A. McDermott, "Emergency Planning," *Military Review*, XLIV, February 1964, 19-28; U.S. Cong., 81st, 2nd Sess., Senate, *Report 2571, Authorizing Federal Assistance to State and Local Governments in Major Disasters*, 14 September 1950 (Washington: Government Printing Office, 1950); U.S. Commission on Intergovernmental Relations, Subcommittee on Natural Disaster Relief, *Report* (Washington: Government Printing Office, June 1955); U.S. Cong., 88th, 1st Sess., Senate Committee on Government Operations, *Federal Disaster Relief Manual*, rev. ed. (Washington: Government Printing Office, 1963); U.S. Cong., 89th, 2nd Sess., *House Report, 2141, Disaster Relief Act of 1966* (Washington: Government Printing Office, 1966); and William A. Anderson, *Military-Civilian Relations in Disaster Operations* [Disaster Research Center Report Series 5] (Columbus: Disaster Research Center of the Ohio State University, 1968).

Reports on specific disasters in this period include: U.S. Army Europe, Historical Division, *U.S. Military Flood Relief Operations in the Netherlands* (Heidelberg: HQ, USAEUR Historical Division, 1953); Douglas Courtney, et. al., *Operation Tulip; A Study of Military Assistance in the Netherlands Flood Disaster* (Washington: National Academy of Sciences, 1954); U.S. Army Engineer Division, New England, *Operation Noah, May 1958* (Boston: Office of the Chief of Engineers, 1958); Mattie E. Treadwell, *Hurricane Carla, September 3-14, 1961* (Denton, Texas; U.S. Department of Defense, Office of Civil

Defense,1961); U.S. Department of Defense, Office of Civil Defense, *Hurricane Dora, 1964* (Washington: Government Printing Office, 1964); Howard Kunreuther and Elissandra S. Fiore, *The Alaskan Earthquake; A Case Study in the Economics of Disaster* (Arlington, Va.: Institute for Defense Analyses, February 1966); and John J. Koehler, "Dell City, Texas, Flood Disaster," unpublished student essay (U.S. Army War College, Carlisle, Pa.: Army War College, 1968).

Useful U.S. Army disaster-relief operations plans and manuals include: U.S. Army Corps of Engineers, *Disaster Operations* EM 500-101, 3 June 1957; U.S. Army Materiel Command, *Disaster Control Plan* (Washington, HQ USAMC, 1972); and U.S. Army, Fourth Army, *Joint Operations Plan For Disaster Relief, Central Area* (Fort Sam Houston, Tex., HQ Fourth Army, 1971). The interface with civil defense can be traced in Dino A. Alberti, "Civil Defense," *Military Review*, XLV, December 1965, 34-38; as well as in Donald W. Mitchell, *Civil Defense: Planning for Survival and Recovery* (Washington: Industrial College of the Armed Forces, 1966).

Several treatments of the role of the National Guard include: Bernard B. Abrams, "The National Guard in Civil Disasters," *The Military Surgeon*, 114, February 1954, 100-103; R. Ernest Dupuy, *The National Guard; A Compact History* (New York: Hawthorne, 1971); "Disaster! The Guard Against the Elements," *The National Guardsman*, May 1964, 12-14; Roger M. Griffith, "Guard's 'Operation Water Wagon' Saves Cows — and Vermont Farmers," *The National Guardsman*, April 1964, 28-29; W. D. McGlasson, "Gas!", The National Guardsman, December 1962, 2-6, 29-30; and Larry Zoeller, "The Big Shake," *The National Guardsman*, May 1964, 8-11, 37.

Particularly important are unpublished student theses in the library of the U.S. Army War College, Carlisle Barracks, Pennsylvania, including: Archie E. Carpenter," Military Aid to Civil Authorities," 1967; Early J. Rush, "Disaster Relief: Domestic Action in the Spotlight," 1973; and Joe H. Sheard, "Control or Confusion During Natural Disasters," 1970. Equally important is Benjamin F. Sharp, "The Role of the Army in Disaster Relief," unpublished professional study (Montgomery, Ala.: U.S. Air War College,1973).

U.S. Sanitary Commission Hospital at Brandy Station, Virginia, 1863. This Matthew Brady photograph depicts one of the earliest developments of Army medical activities. (NARS 111-B-445)

Chapter 5

THE ARMY AND PUBLIC HEALTH

James O. Breeden

The debt of modern medical science to the military surgeon and to the battle casualty is beyond calculation.
— General Edward Croft, 1935

The story of man, a leading historian of military medical history has stated, is largely the story of his wars. True though this statement may be, war has precious little to recommend it. Its legacy has been death, destruction, and pestilence — horrors that cannot be too indelibly etched on man's memory. Yet, for all its carnage, war has another side. Armed conflict is the supreme test for a society and commands its mightiest effort. The fruits of such a challenge, especially the solutions to its special and pressing problems, have frequently produced profound and lasting changes, benefiting not only the people tested but all mankind. Nowhere has this mitigating side of war been more noticeable than in the field of medicine. Rare indeed has been the wartime medical advancement that has had no peacetime application.

The catalytic effect of war on medicine is the product of many factors. These range from an unparalleled opportunity for experiment to the military's centralized organization and supervision of the medical effort, resources, and patients. But the single most important factor is the urgency of the problems confronting military medicine. Thus, solutions and breakthroughs which might have required years in peacetime have often been reached in a fraction of the time during war.

The pages of medical history are studded with the brilliant accomplishments of military medicine. The resulting incalculable enrichment of medical knowledge has greatly increased the ability of the physician, military and civilian alike, to save lives and preserve health. For example, such taken-for-granted, but essential, features of the modern health care system as the hospital and the professional nurse are the products of war. The former was developed by the practical-minded Romans to restore soldiers to fighting fitness as expeditiously as possible, and the latter grew out of the carnage of the Crimean War. Further examples can be found in American history. A random sampling of the Army's important contributions to medical progress on the eve of its bicentennial anniversary might include: America's first medical book; the first American pharmacopoeia; America's first vital statistics; the founding of American meteorology; the creation of the world's largest medical library; the first studies in the physiology of digestion; the pioneer work in photomicrography; the founding of America's largest medical museum (which has given rise to the world's foremost diagnostic and consultative institution for tissue pathology); America's first bacteriologist and first book on bacteriology; America's oldest school of preventive medicine, one of whose original faculty members verified the vector role of the mosquito in the transmission of yellow fever; the world's leading center for the treatment of burns; and successful campaigns against a host of health hazards.

This list of contributions dates back to the American Revolution. Founded in July 1775, almost a year before the signing of the Declaration of Independence, the Medical Department of the Army (now the Army Medical Department) played an indispensable role in the contributions of America's first war to medicine and public health. Especially noteworthy is the crucial part the Medical Department played in the marked increase in the dissemination of medical knowledge among physicians. The lack of contact between the approximately 3,500 members of the medical profession in pre-revolutionary America had produced an inhibiting parochialism in both medical thought and practice. The war, by bringing at least one-third of these physicians together on the battlefield and in the military hospitals, helped break down the barriers of isolation. As a result, medical provincialism began to give way to constructive dialogue and progressive thought.

A number of useful medical publications, growing out of wartime needs and personal experiences, further promoted the sharing of medical knowledge by the new nation's physicians. The earliest of these appeared in 1775, shortly after the beginning of the hostilities. John Jones, the professor of surgery at King's College (now Columbia University) and subsequently a surgeon in the Continental Army, compiled a surgical volume entitled *Plain Concise Practical Remarks on the Treatment of*

Wounds and Fractures. Although not original, it was the first medical book published in America. Three years later, William Brown, Physician General of the Middle Department of the Continental Army, brought out his *Pharmacopoeia for Use of Army Hospitals.* It, too, was the first book of its kind in America and was widely consulted by both military and civilian pharmacists. The end of the war did not halt such publications. Benjamin Rush's subsequent writings on military diseases, alcoholism, smallpox, and tetanus, for example, drew heavily on his Army experiences. But the best known of these post-war works is James Tilton's *Economical Observations on Military Hospitals and the Prevention of Diseases Incident to an Army.* This volume contains a wealth of practical information, not only on military medicine but also on hospital architecture and medical administration. In fact, along with John Jones, Tilton pioneered in civilian hospital planning and construction in America.

Of more immediate benefit to society was the considerable progress the Revolution stimulated in surgery and preventive medicine. America could claim but a handful of first-rate surgeons at the onset of the hostilities, but the exigencies of the battlefield and the ample opportunities for experimentation, including dissection, soon began to rectify this situation. By the war's end many military surgeons had become highly skilled. In preventive medicine there developed a greater awareness of the important connection between such things as physical condition, exercise, personal cleanliness, clothing, shelter, food and drink, and an individual's state of health. The most noteworthy single advancement in preventive medicine probably was the Army's demonstration of the efficacy of compulsory inoculation in the prevention of smallpox.

But military medicine's most important contribution to public health during the American Revolution was more long-range than immediate. This war gave a powerful impetus to professional medical education and the licensing of physicians — two of the cornerstones of modern medicine. Wartime experiences showed that the few college-educated physicians were much better qualified than those who were self-taught or preceptor trained. This realization placed a premium on a formal medical education, and with the cessation of hostilities, the enrollment of America's few existing medical schools increased and a number of new ones were started. The end of the war was also accompanied by a movement aimed at establishing procedures for examining and licensing of physicians, a development attributable in large measure to the practice instituted by the Continental Congress during the Revolution of

The Civil War spawned an active interest in hospital design and ambulance trains. This Brady photograph shows the airy interior of Carver Hospital in Washington in September 1864. (NARS 111-B-358)

setting up special committees to test applicants for military medical posts. It seemed only natural to a growing number of farsighted state medical leaders that if it were necessary to license military physicians, then it was equally essential that civilians be accorded the same protection.

The end of the Revolution was accompanied by the rapid demobilization of America's armed forces and the nearly complete disbandment of the Medical Department of the Army. All that remained was a handful of regimental surgeons serving at scattered isolated posts. Thus, when a second war with Great Britain broke out in 1812, a medical organization had to be devised under wartime conditions — a lesson that was painfully repeated with each new war down to World War I. Aptly called an exercise in inefficient mediocrity, the War of 1812 is not one of the brighter chapters in American military history. Such was indeed the case on the medical front where little of value accrued to either the soldier or society. The most significant developments were the Army's substitution of vaccination for inoculation in the prevention of smallpox and James Tilton's pioneer work in systematic meteorological observations in America. Vaccination had been introduced into the United States as early as 1800 by Benjamin Waterhouse, who served as a surgeon in the War of 1812, but its adoption by the Army during this conflict greatly accelerated its general acceptance. A veteran of the Revolution, Tilton served as Physician General of the Army from 1813 to 1815. It was in this capacity that he directed hospital surgeons in 1814 to record the weather, noting specifically its influence on disease.

One man, Joseph Lovell, dominated American military medicine between the War of 1812 and the Civil War. In fact, it has been stated, the story of Army medicine during much of this period is in large measure the story of his efforts. Lovell was named the first Surgeon General of the Army when the post was created by Congress in 1818, a position he held for nearly two decades. A man of marked ability and foresight, Lovell was an ideal choice as his accomplishments — a boon to the health of the civilian as well as that of the soldier — well illustrate. Chief among them were his meteorological registers, vital statistics of the Army, and Library of the Surgeon General's Office.

Shortly after his appointment, Lovell extended and enlarged the meteorological investigations initiated by Tilton. This careful recording of meteorological data, published periodically in register form, culminated in the establishment of the U.S. Weather Bureau in 1890, a development largely attributable to Army medicine. In 1819 Lovell initiated a system of detailed reporting of the Army's vital statistics. These reports, America's first vital statistics, helped lay the groundwork for the epidemiological basis of preventive medicine. In 1836 Lovell founded the Library of the Surgeon General's Office which, after several name changes, became the National Library of Medicine in 1956. Today this outstanding facility, often called America's greatest gift to medicine, is the world's largest and most complete medical library and is open to the physicians of the world.

Lovell is to be further commended for the encouragement and support he offered William Beaumont in his experiments on the physiology of digestion. Beaumont, one of the Army's best known medical officers, while stationed in the Michigan backcountry, in 1822, attended a half-breed who accidentally had been shot in the stomach. The victim survived but his wound failed to heal, providing Beaumont the opportunity to observe the process of digestion through the resulting fistula in his stomach. His findings, *Experiments and Observations on the Gastric Juice and the Physiology of Digestion*, were published in 1833 and became a pillar in the evolution of gastroenterology.

Although the most celebrated, Beaumont was not the Army's only noteworthy antebellum experimental scientist. William A. Hammond, who joined the Army Medical Service shortly after the Mexican War, is another. Although largely remembered for his Civil War career, Hammond was a pioneer in the therapeutic use of animal extracts during the 1850s. His *Experimental Research Relative to the Nutritive Value and Physiological Effects of Albumin, Starch, and Gum, When Singly and Exclusively Used as a Food*, which appeared in 1857, was honored by the American Medical Association and served as a model for subsequent nutritional and metabolic studies.

The Civil War was the bloodiest and most costly war in American history. Despite its captivation of the public mind, it was not a glory road, as some would have us believe, but a horrible fratricidal struggle which left a heart-rending trail of unmitigated suffering and misery in its wake. Nowhere is the validity of this assertion more demonstrable than in the field of medicine. Medical education actually deteriorated as a result of this war, a promising public health movement that had been gathering momentum in the late 1850s was set back at least a decade, and a benumbing blight paralyzed Southern medicine for a generation.

Yet some good resulted — even for the South. The Civil War was said to have been fought at the very end of the medical middle ages, immediately before bacteriology and aseptic surgery. The experiences of the war's military physicians helped bring about a more advanced medical practice and a greater receptiveness to the bacteriological revolution when it spread to America from Europe in the 1870s. Surgery, owing to the frightful slaughter of this war, received noticeable impetus. Promising lessons were learned in preventive medicine. America's first formal medical group, aimed at preserving the health of the soldier through the cooperation of the Army and civilian volunteer workers, appeared in the war's early days. This agency, the United States Sanitary Commission, was modeled after the British Sanitary Commission of the Crimean War and resembled the present-day Red Cross. Military and civilian cooperation also accounts for the dating of professional nursing in America from this war, as both sides came to depend heavily upon women to care for the sick and wounded in their large hospitals.

The Civil War was the catalyst for major advances in the evacuation and care of the sick and wounded. In the former, an area in which the

Army has always shown the way, the most notable accomplishment was Jonathan Letterman's founding of America's first ambulance corps. As for the latter, a constant concern of the Army, important progress was made in hospital design. The war's unparalleled casualties stimulated action on both sides. As a result, improved hospitals were constructed which served as models after the cessation of hostilities. The principal developments were the one-story pavilion-type hospital and the designation of separate wards (and sometimes entire hospitals) for certain diseases.

Although not remembered for its research, some highly significant investigations were conducted during the Civil War. Surgeon General William A. Hammond, one of the war's truly farseeing medical figures, helped set an encouraging tone. In 1862 he founded the Army Medical Museum, the mission of which was the preservation of specimens illustrating the major causes of disease and death in the Army in the hope that this would stimulate their investigation and lead to a reduction of mortality. From this modest beginning there has emerged the Armed Forces Institute of Pathology, the world's foremost diagnostic and consultative institution for tissue pathology. Pathologists from all over the world, both military and civilian, train here. Hammond also sponsored *The Medical and Surgical History of the War of the Rebellion*. Designed to preserve every bit of known experience for the use of future Army physicians, this monumental undertaking set a precedent for the careful recording of the medical history of America's wars, which has been faithfully followed down to the present. Medicine and public health have greatly benefited from these histories. A final contribution of Hammond's was his *Treatise on Hygiene*. This was America's first comprehensive textbook on public health and military hygiene published in the English language, and it set the stage for a lengthy series of similar treatises.

The response to Hammond's stimulus and example, while not extensive, was rewarding. In 1864, for example, S. Weir Mitchell, George R. Morehouse, and William W. Keen published their findings on injuries of the nerves. Regarded as a classic in neuropsychiatry, this volume contains the earliest recognizable descriptions of ascending neuritis and the psychology of the amputee. In addition, although not bearing fruit until after the war, Joseph J. Woodward, assistant to the curator of the Army Medical Museum, began his pioneer work in photomicrography. Long interested in microscopy and photography, Woodward was the first to apply them to the study of pathology — research that earned him international acclaim.

The third of a century between the end of the Civil War and the outbreak of war with Spain in 1898 has been called the day of small things in the Army. Reduced to a series of posts on the Western plains, its only action was a number of bloody skirmishes with hostile Indians. For the Army Medical Service, it was a time of routine duties. Yet, for all its stagnation, this era produced one of the giants of American military medicine — George M. Sternberg. Sternberg was both a brilliant military physician and one of America's foremost scientists. A self-taught bacteriologist, he was the pioneer in this field in America, having commenced his studies in 1870 when bacteriology was still in its infancy. His chief interest was the discovery of ways to prevent and control infectious diseases. In the course of his investigations he discovered the pneumococcus in 1881, photographed the tubercle bacillus for the first time in 1882, and 10 years later published America's first textbook on bacteriology.

In 1893 Sternberg began a decade of service as Surgeon General. He was without doubt one of the ablest men ever to hold this post, as his impressive record shows. Within a month of his appointment he established the Army Medical School (now the Walter Reed Army Institute of Research), America's oldest, and perhaps most successful, school of preventive medicine. Sternberg is also responsible for the creation of the Army Nursing Corps and the Dental Corps. In addition, his foresight prompted him, as we shall see, to tackle the Army's most pressing health problems through a number of highly effective special scientific investigatory boards and commissions.

The Spanish-American War ushered in one of the most fruitful eras in the Army's long history of contributions to public health. Gains were made on a wide front and at the expense of many of man's most feared biological enemies. These advances were the result of an especially fruitful cooperation between military and civilian scientists, the extraordinary talents and indefatigable zeal of a group of young military physicians who eagerly responded to the challenge of the times, and the successful application of a number of promising new research tools, especially in epidemiology.

The celebrated contributions of Walter Reed to the conquest of typhoid and yellow fever are the best known of these breakthroughs. The alarming incidence of typhoid in American Army camps moved Surgeon General Sternberg to secure the appointment of a board of medical officers in August 1898 to investigate and report on its origin and spread. Composed of Walter Reed, Victor C. Vaughan, and Edward O. Shakespeare, this board examined more than 20,000 typhoid cases in the course of its clinical, epidemiological, and etiological investigations.

Their famous findings showed that the disease was not caused by contaminated drinking water, as most people thought, but by direct contact.

In 1900, before the Typhoid Board had finished its report, Reed was called upon to head the Yellow Fever Board in Cuba. Labeled the most famous scientific group in Army medical history, this commission, consisting of Reed, Aristides Agramonte, James Carroll, and Jesse Lazear, performed a veritable scientific miracle within the span of a single year. In exhaustive research that saw Carroll survive an experimentally induced attack of yellow fever and Lazear succumb to an accidental infection, the Reed Commission proved that yellow fever was caused by a filterable virus and confirmed the hypothesis of Carlos Finlay that the disease was transmitted by the mosquito. As a result of this board's work, immunization for the whole category of insect-borne diseases was made possible — an invaluable service to mankind.

The first fruits from the Reed Commission's findings were dramatically obtained by William C. Gorgas as Chief Sanitary Officer first of Havana, in 1901, and later, beginning in 1904, of the Panama Canal Zone. In the former capacity he effected the first control of an insect-borne disease by attack on the vector; in the latter, he made possible the building of the Panama Canal, constructed between 1904 and 1914, a project which disease had forced the French to abandon a quarter of a century earlier.

But as commendable as the accomplishments of Reed and Gorgas were, they represented but the tip of the iceberg. Less celebrated Army scientists were also at work. Advancements in the control of tropical diseases, necessitated by America's newly won insular empire, were especially numerous. If indeed, as some maintain, the first two decades of the Twentieth Century constituted a golden age of tropical medicine in the United States, then Army scientists played a paramount role in making them that. Examples abound: between 1900 and 1933 three Army medical boards investigated the principal diseases of the Philippines; military researchers like Richard P. Strong, Joseph F. Siler, and E.B. Vedder confirmed that dengue fever was transmitted by mosquitoes, uncovered a new species of malaria, discovered the cause and treatment of beriberi, and initiated the treatment of amoebic dysentery with emetine; and Bailey K. Ashford, studying what appeared to be an epidemic of pernicious anemia in Puerto Rico, learned that the disease was actually hookworm. Ashford's discovery was especially beneficial to public health in the United States in that the success of his recommendations for a campaign to eradicate hookworm led to the worldwide crusade of the Rockefeller Foundation for its control — a godsend for the American South.

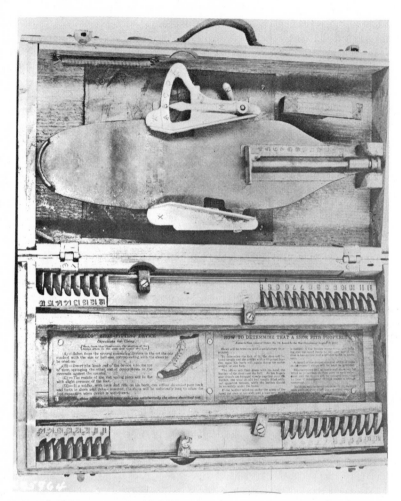

Accurate measurement of soldiers' feet was a matter of concern because ill-fitting shoes could incapacitate, so the Army developed the "Resco" shoe-fitting device. (NARS 111-SC-37388 and 95964)

Contributions to other areas of medicine by Army scientists kept pace with those in tropical medicine. The Roentgen ray (x-ray), which had been first used for medical purposes in the United States by the Army Medical School, was extensively tested in the Spanish-American War.

With the enthusiastic endorsement of Surgeon General Sternberg, it was widely used to locate bullets and shrapnel. Tragically, owing to an ignorance of the dangers of radiation and the absence of protection for the operators of early x-ray machines, a number of unsuspecting Army physicians became martyrs to science. In 1907, periodic physical examinations, so essential to public health, were introduced by the Army. Fear of a resurgence of typhoid fever spurred Frederick F. Russell to investigate ways to prevent it. In 1909, after detailed observations abroad, he introduced antityphoid vaccination in the United States Army. Two years later it was made compulsory, setting an example for the American people. In 1910, Carl R. Darnall originated the use of liquid chlorine to purify water. Three years later, William J.L. Lyster invented the "Lyster bag" to sterilize drinking water in the field. These developments have proved of inestimable value in the reduction of typhoid fever and other water-borne diseases worldwide. In 1911, Ernest R. Gentry and Thomas L. Ferenbaugh showed that Malta fever, a form of brucellosis first described by an Army physician a decade earlier, was endemic in the American Southwest. Finally, the Army, which had pioneered in separate left and right shoes during the Civil War, pointed the way to correctly fitted shoes in 1912 when it adopted the "Munson last," upon the recommendation of Edward L. Munson, President of the Army Shoe Board.

World War I was a gigantic laboratory for medicine. Thousands of physicians, mobilized to meet the medical challenge of total war, were confronted with diseases, injuries, and health problems seldom seen in peacetime. The outcome for medicine and public health was decidedly advantageous. Not only were many important advancements made, but existing practices were thoroughly inspected and improved.

Wound treatment and research, necessitated by the great number of wounds produced by a large variety of explosive devices ranging from shells to bombs, was perhaps the area of greatest medical activity. As a result, several important advances were made in the successful management of wounds. Chief among these were the development of new surgical antiseptics such as Dakin's solution, acriflavine, and dichloramine; the perfection of delayed primary closure for gunshot wounds, which minimized infection while preserving primary healing; and the perfection of debridement for traumatic and gunshot wounds, which sharply reduced the necessity for amputation.

But World War I's most promising contributions to public health were in preventive medicine. A truly brilliant record, the result of the direct application of the science of infectious diseases to military sanitation, was compiled here. Army medical officers in the field, encouraged by

Using the Resco machine a supply lieutenant measures World War I doughboys for their boots, an application of physiological science to the mass needs of a large Army. (NARS 111-SC-37386)

special preventive medicine agencies set up by the Medical Department, conclusively demonstrated that the infected or exposed individual is a far greater threat to the health of an army or society than the disease itself and stressed the importance of hygienic organization and an educated sanitary force in the battle against infectious diseases. Impressive wartime gains in preventive medicine were scored in immunization against infectious diseases, typhus control, and venereal prophylaxis. Great success was realized in the eradication of smallpox, typhoid, traumatic tetanus, and diphtheria through preventive vaccination. Typhus, the louse-borne scourge of many a European army in the past, was controlled by an elaborate delousing procedure. Venereal disease, a persistent problem for the Army throughout its existence, was attacked with commendable success. Owing to such things as public information programs and the establishment of special venereal disease hospitals and centers, the rate of infection among the American Expeditionary Force in France fell below that of the peacetime Army. The dissemination of the war's lessons in preventive medicine to the general public was expedited by returning veterans of the Sanitary Corps. Established in 1917, this organization was largely composed of non-medical personnel from civilian life with special skills in sanitation, sanitary engineering, bacteriology, and related fields. It not only promoted cooperation between military and civilian scientists, but also played a major role in protecting the health of the American soldier.

The gains made in medicine during World War I were by no means limited to wound management and preventive medicine. On the contrary, there was considerable activity and progress in almost every field. In internal medicine much valuable information was learned about the nature and treatment of a wide variety of disorders. New techniques were perfected in the treatment of shock and burns. Blood transfusion was simplified, greatly extending its applicability as shown in the Army's pioneering of its use in the control of shock. Skin grafting and plastic surgery advanced tremendously. Giant strides were made in surgery of the chest, especially in radical thoraco-plastic surgery. Orthopedic surgery was essentially a product of this war. Psychiatrists were provided with their first real opportunity to study large numbers of men under stress. They were also confronted by a host of neuropsychiatric conditions lumped together under the misnomer "shell shock." Both physical therapy and occupational therapy were given serious consideration for the first time. Improved artificial limbs were designed. Radiology was used on an unprecedented scale. Notable improvement was made in the standardization of drugs and other medical stores. Finally, the Army produced the first specialist in aviation medicine during this conflict.

Demobilization, inactivity, and economy sharply reduced the Army's contributions to the nation's health during the two decades separating the

First and Second World Wars. But military medical research continued and progress was made. Epidemiology, an area of preventive medicine given strong impetus by World War I, was the scene of a good deal of activity. Medical scientists, military and civilian, came to realize that as a result of the advent of bacteriology, so much emphasis had been placed on the search for the infectious agents of communicable diseases that noncommunicable disorders and the factors of host, environment, and cultural and social conditions as determinants of health and disease had been increasingly neglected. Thus, there was begun a return to a holistic interpretation of both individual sickness and community disease. The outcome was a marked strengthening and enriching of epidemiology. This development sparked several noteworthy books on preventive medicine. One of the best was George C. Dunham's *Military Preventive Medicine*, which first appeared in 1930. Widely consulted by both military and civilian physicians, it was in its third edition in less than a decade.

These years saw similar contributions made by Army scientists in other fields of medicine: Calvin H. Goddard conducted extensive studies on the identification of projectiles, and his technique for determining the exact manner in which gunshot victims were killed was of great benefit to forensic medicine; Hiram W. Orr, drawing on his experiences in World War I, proposed the closed plaster technique for treating compound fractures (the value of which was demonstrated in the Spanish Civil War); Fernando G. Rodriquez pioneered in the study of the bacteriology of dental caries in America; and finally, medical officers in Panama field-tested atabrine which had been introduced in 1932 as a substitute for quinine in the control of malaria.

The most important test for military medicine between the world wars, and one of tremendous significance for public health, began in the early days of the New Deal when the Army Medical Service was asked to provide medical care for the newly created Civilian Conservation Corps. Subsequently, between 1933 and 1942, the health of hundreds of thousands of young Americans was guarded. The record compiled was outstanding without doubt. Its high point was the conclusive verification of the value of protective immunization in the prevention of communicable diseases. In fact, this was probably the first time in history, it has been stated, that so large a body of young men had been brought together in camps and barracks without a serious epidemic.

As impressive as the military medical record of World War I had been, that of World War II eclipsed it. The medical advancements growing out of this challenge of global warfare indeed make up one of the brilliant chapters in the history of medicine. The unparalleled success of military medicine, which yielded immeasurable good for public health, was the result of the total and effective mobilization of America's medical talent, both clinical and research and civilian as well as military. Service ranged from active duty in the field to participation in one of a great variety of advisory and research organizations.

Preventive medicine again received a great impetus and responded with fresh victories. The fact that for the first time in American military history battle casualties exceeded deaths caused by communicable diseases and non-battle injuries attests to its success. Much of this success is attributable to the rendering of the major infectious diseases innocuous by immunization. But the greatest victory, and one of the landmarks in the history of preventive medicine, occurred in 1942 when Army scientists discovered the effectiveness of penicillin in the treatment of gonorrhea and syphilis.

World War II was a boon to pharmacology. Many new drugs were developed and the knowledge of old ones advanced. In the fight against malaria, for example, atabrine (and later chloroquine and primoquine) was substituted for the hard to get quinine. But the most dramatic breakthroughs in this field centered around penicillin, the most celebrated of the antibiotic agents, and DDT, a wartime savior of man now in disfavor. Penicillin, discovered as early as 1929, required the stimulus of war to make it an indispensable ally of the modern physician. It proved phenomenally successful in combating a surprising array of infections. Although synthesized as early as 1870 by a Swiss chemist, DDT was ignored until World War II when it emerged as a substitute for arsenic in the war against the insect carriers of disease. Like penicillin, DDT proved amazingly effective.

Surgery benefited greatly from global warfare. Surgeons learned that debridement should be kept to a minimum; that viable nerve, muscle, tendon, and bone should be preserved; that in most instances wounds should not be closed by first intention; that shock was best managed through the use of whole blood or plasma; and that tantalum plates were effective replacements for damaged or destroyed cranial bone. Chief among the new surgical techniques developed were peripheral nerve surgery and the use of bone transplants, bone screws, and metal plates. The Army Medical Service also demonstrated the effectiveness of the intramedullary pin. Its adoption permitted patients with leg fractures to walk weeks sooner than with previous methods.

World War II marked an epoch in the understanding of the human mind. Building upon the foundation laid in World War I, military psychiatrists tremendously expanded medicine's knowledge of human behavior and relationships. Especially noteworthy were the successes they achieved in dealing with combat fatigue, a neuropsychiatric disorder erroneously explained as "shell shock" in World War I. Treatment varied, ranging from occupational therapy, rest, and hypnosis to psychotherapy and electric shock. Some treatment with drugs, such as intravenous injections of sodium pentathol which allowed the patient to relive his trauma, proved highly successful. Psychiatrists also tried to anticipate this condition's early signs in soldiers sent from the front for rest and recreation. Likely victims were afforded preventive therapy with encouraging results.

World War II also produced important advancements in the use of whole blood and plasma, the treatment of burns and skin grafting, radiology, and the evacuation of the sick and wounded. The use of whole blood and plasma came of age in World War II with the development of preservative solutions that made blood transfusions feasible worldwide; and the use of blood plasma eliminated the need for matching blood. Consequently, beginning in 1942, the Army developed blood banking on a large scale. Valuable experience also was gained in the treatment of burns and skin grafting. In fact, it has been suggested that no other aspect of medical treatment received as much attention during World War II as did burns. As a result, old methods of treatment were improved and new ones were developed. Disfigurement cases were sent to special plastic surgery centers where spectacular results were achieved. The specialty of radiology, which had been greatly advanced by the Spanish-American War and World War I, came into its own in World War II. In addition, this conflict was the stimulus for the perfection of the evacuation of the sick and wounded by air. There had been a few isolated attempts at long distance air evacuation of casualties in World War I, but in World War II, this practice became common.

Unlike previous American wars, World War II was not followed by an immediate and drastic reduction of the Army's contributions to public health. This sharp break with the past, and one that has produced much good for mankind, is the product of a potentially cataclysmic "cold war" which engulfed the world after 1945, dividing it into two armed camps. As a result, military preparedness became equated with survival. The Army Medical Department has not only demonstrated its ability to perform its mission, as its record in Korea and Vietnam shows, but in maintaining its readiness, it has greatly advanced world health. In 1956, for example, the Walter Reed Army Institute of Research developed a vaccine against Asian influenza in time to halt its march across Europe and the United States. This was the first time in the history of medicine that an epidemic was fought with a vaccine specially prepared to combat it. But such feats, it should be noted, could not have occurred without the close cooperation between military and civilian scientists. Indeed, modern America's unprecedented success in research and development, so noticeable since World War II, is attributable to the stimulation and pooling of the talents and energies of the nation's entire scientific community. At present, all research having military medical pertinence is coordinated and supervised by the Army Medical Research and Development Command.

The periods of greatest military medical activity since World War II occurred, of course, during the Korean conflict, at the beginning of the 1950s, and during the recent war in Vietnam. Public health gained from the fighting in Korea as the result of several important developments: the Army proved the effectiveness of the helicopter for the speedy evacuation of the sick and wounded; further advances were made in preventive medicine as shown by this war's lower disease rate than the previous low set in World War II; the Army Burn Treatment Center, the uncontested world leader in the treatment and pathophysiology of burns, was established at Fort Sam Houston, Texas; Army scientists perfected a technique for the repair of arterial injuries to preserve extremities; the principles of the neurosurgery of trauma developed in World War II were refined; and, finally, the Army began to develop the concept of disseminated intravascular coagulation, a new concept of disease production which has shown great promise in the treatment of a surprising number of clinical syndromes.

It is too early to attempt a definitive assessment of the effect of the Vietnam War on public health, but the early results look promising. Especially significant are two potentially invaluable advancements in the basic concepts of health care delivery. The first, total area medical care, was under development before America's involvement in Southeast Asia. The heavy medical burden resulting from the hostilities there gave it added impetus. This concept, designed to provide total care to everyone on an equal basis at a minimum cost in both personnel and money, involves a number of outlying self-contained medical and dental clinics supported by a central hospital for specialized services. A principal feature of this plan, and one that civilian medicine has found increasingly appealing, is the widespread use of medical assistants — highly trained technicians who perform a variety of functions usually performed by physicians or other professional medical personnel in civilian practice. The second, definitive emergency care for the injured in a minimum of time, is a product of the Vietnam War. Its basic features are helicopter evacuation and around-the-clock hospitals staffed with personnel highly trained in emergency treatment and equipped with sophisticated laboratory and treatment facilities and advanced monitoring devices. This development is the result of one of Vietnam's major medical lessons — the advantage of the prompt delivery of skilled attention to the

wounded. Convinced of its value to continued progress in total health care, the Army has encouraged and assisted civilian communities in the adoption of aeromedical evacuation.

Among the other medical benefits accruing to society from the Vietnam War, those most promising are: the development of new drugs to combat malaria strains found to be resistant to previously used compounds; improved treatment of shock; the development of vaccines for meningococcus meningitis and measles; the launching of the first trauma research unit; the development of new techniques to halt otherwise fatal hemorrhaging from internal injuries; and improved artificial limbs. A final contribution, and perhaps the most celebrated one, is drug control. In early 1971 the Army discovered that it was in the midst of a serious heroin epidemic. Following President Nixon's initiative, Army scientists immediately formulated a drug-screening program that produced dramatic results. This vigorous, well directed campaign consisted of identification, detoxification, treatment, rehabilitation, and prevention through education. It achieved a degree of success unmatched in the free world, setting a superior example for civilian society as it tries to cope with its mounting drug problem.

As the foregoing attempts to show, the Army Medical Service has performed its mission well. It has forged a towering tradition of service to mankind which has bridged the years and the ebb and flow of history. This lofty position is firmly grounded in numerous contributions of inestimable value to medical science and public health. Indeed, it should be readily apparent that medical knowledge growing out of the carnage of the battlefield has remained to benefit both the victor and the vanquished long after the guns have fallen silent. Tragic as war is, then, some solace can be found in the belief that its contributions to medicine will save lives in the succeeding years of peace. And, hopefully, at some point in time, the knowledge thus gained will spare more lives than were lost on the field of battle.

Suggestions for Further Research

Military medicine's contributions to public health, which this author sees as essentially the story of military medicine, is an inviting area of scholarship. A great deal has already been written, to be sure, but much

The boredom of garrison life had to be whiled away in some fashion. Here medical corpsmen at Fort Riley in the post-Civil War years relax with boxing gloves and skeletal friends. (FR)

101

of it is now either outdated or spotty in coverage. In addition, the quality of many of these works is questionable as a result of the professional historian having largely abandoned this field to the amateur. There is, then, ample room for research in every major area of military medical history.

Examples abound: there is no comprehensive up-to-date history of either the Army Medical Department or its contributions to medicine and public health; there are no medical histories for the majority of America's wars; there is no single account of medicine in the Civil War covering both sides; the monumental official medical histories of the Civil War, World War I, and World War II need synthesizing into manageable accounts; although, its luminaries have received much attention from biographers, military medicine's many unsung heroes, who have contributed mightily to the advancement of medicine and public health, have been largely ignored; military medicine's conquest of particular diseases and health problems merits investigation; the major military health and research groups, which have played paramount roles in military medicine's gains, are worthy of examination; and, finally, the cooperation between military and civilian scientists for the advancement of medical knowledge is a very promising topic.

In general, there are abundant sources, ranging from firsthand accounts to official reports, for the study of military medicine. Equally important, the bulk of them are readily available, for the student of military medical history is blessed with the existence of several enviable repositories: the Army Historical Unit, Ft. Detrick, Maryland; the National Archives, Washington, D.C.; the National Library of Medicine, Bethesda, Maryland; and the Army Historical Collection, Carlisle Barracks, Pennsylvania.

SOURCES

Sources for the study of the Army's contributions to public health, as we have seen, are of varying quality. Those singled out here were principally used in the preparation of this essay and hopefully represent a sampling of the most significant sources. Although in need of updating, the best overall account of the Army Medical Department is Percy M. Ashburn's *History of the Medical Department of the United States Army* (Boston, 1929). Invaluable assistance was also rendered by two specialized studies: Edgar E. Hume, *Victories of Army Medicine* (Philadelphia, 1943), also in need of updating; and Stanhope Bayne-Jones' narrower in focus *Evolution of Preventive Medicine in the United States Army, 1607-1939* (Washington, 1968).

A large body of important periodical literature complemented these monographs. Most of it is to be found in the specialty journal, *Military Medicine*. The leading articles consulted were: Edgar E. Hume, "Medicine and War," 1948, 103, 169-93; Leonard D. Heaton, "The Army Role in Medical Progress," 1961, 126, 14-17; William S. Middleton, "Military Medicine: Its Role in World Health," 1968,133, 257-64; Hal B. Jennings, "Army Medical Department," 1972, 137, 344-49, and 1973, 138, 554-58; Robert M. Hardaway, III, "Contributions of Army Medicine to Civilian Medicine," 1973, 138, 409-12; and Richard R. Taylor, "Army Medical Department," 1974, 139, 792-94. Useful studies from other journals included: "Military Medicine" and "War & Health," *MD*, 1968, 12, 125-34, 187-91; "U.S. Army Medical Service Contributions to Civilian Health and Medicine," *Ohio State Medical Journal*, 1959, 55, 178-79, 332-34, 492-94; and Gustave J. Dammin, "Military Medicine and its Influence on Medicine," *Bulletin of the New York Academy of Medicine*, 1971, 47, 1455-72.

Numerous period studies were consulted, only the most essential of which can be noted here. The best account of medicine in the Revolution is Howard L. Applegate's "The Revolutionary Hospital Department," *Military Medicine*, 1961, 126, 296-306, 379-82, 450-53, 616-18. There are admirable medical histories of the Civil War for each side: George W. Adams, *Doctors in Blue; the Medical History of the Union Army in the Civil War* (New York, 1952), and Horace H. Cunningham, *Doctors in Gray; the Confederate Medical Service* (Baton Rouge, 1958). Mention should also be made of the official *Medical and Surgical History of the War of the Rebellion* (Washington, 1870-88), 3 vols. in 6. Nicholas Senn's *Medico-Surgical Aspects of the Spanish American War* (Chicago, 1900) is this conflict's most authoritative study. The definitive source for World War I is its multivolume official medical history, *The Medical Department of the United States Army in the World War* (Washington, 1921-29), 15 vols. in 17. The global warfare of World War II has given rise to a truly monumental medical history — *Medical Department of the United States Army in World War II* (Washington, 1952-). At last count, 43 of a projected 50 volumes had appeared. Although covering only a portion of the period, the best study for post-World War II military medical history is Rose C. Engleman, ed., *A Decade of Progress: The United States Army Medical Department, 1959-69* (Washington, 1971).

Only a handful of the leaders in military medicine have been the subjects of biographies. Among these, those worthy of mention are: Jesse S. Myer, *New Print of the Life and Letters of Dr. William Beaumont* (St.

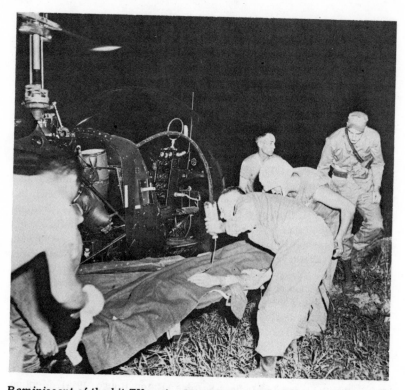

Reminiscent of the hit TV series M*A*S*H* is this scene of corpsmen in Korea lifting a wounded soldier off a helicopter while administering blood plasma. The air evacuation of wounded has now been translated to civilian activities with the MAST program of air evacuation of accident victims, thus saving precious minutes and lives. (Bell Helicopter photo)

Louis, 1939); John M. Gibson, *Soldier in White; the Life of General George Miller Sternberg* (Durham, 1958), and *Physician to the World; the Life of General William C. Gorgas* (Durham, 1950); and Laura N. Wood, *Walter Reed, Doctor in Uniform* (New York, 1943).

There are many other works of value in the study of the Army's contributions to public health. Excellent guides to them are: *Bibliography of the History of Medicine* (Bethesda, 1965-); Genevieve Miller, ed., *Bibliography of the History of Medicine of the United States and Canada,*

1939-1960 (Baltimore, 1964); and *Index-Catalogue of the Library of the Surgeon-General's Office, United States Army,* 1st-5th ser. (Washington, 1880-1961).

The 10th Cavalry's troopers at a bivouac somewhere in the Southwest, probably in the 1880s. (NARS 111-SC-83343)

Chapter 6

THE ARMY AND MINORITY GROUPS

Marvin E. Fletcher

The United States Army has generally been a significant influence in the lives of the minority groups of this country. For white male immigrants in the Nineteenth Century it served as an avenue for educational and social mobility. More recently, for blacks and women it has provided opportunities for travel, career development, and education. Within the last decade the Army has set an example for the civilian population in how to deal with the problems of minority groups.

For the purposes of this discussion, the word minority will be defined as anyone who is a member of a group whose ethnic, racial, and sexual characteristics differ from the majority of the Army. In this brief overview, the position of several minority groups in the military will be considered in terms of the treatment given them by the Army, the reasons why a minority group member might join the Army, and the elements that fostered a change in the intraservice position of the minority groups.

First are the immigrants. The period of foreign immigration began in the 1840s and lasted until 1914. The immigrants perceived service in the Army as a means by which they could improve their lot. In the period immediately after the War of 1812, about 20 percent of the enlistees declared themselves as being born overseas. By 1850 the foreign-born percentage of the Army had risen to 60 percent. From the end of the Civil War to 1914, about 40 to 45 percent of the enlistees were foreign born. Toward the end of this period the Irish and the Germans, who had been the predominant immigrant groups in the service, were replaced by eastern and southern Europeans.

An analysis of enlistment rosters during the mid-1870s tells us much about the foreign-born enlistees. In 1874, 50 percent were born outside of the United States. Of these foreign born, 45 percent came from Ireland, 25 percent from Germany, and 14 percent from Great Britain. Very few came from eastern or southern Europe. The foreign-born soldier was slightly older than his native-born counterpart, probably indicative of the fact that he already had served at least one tour of duty. Foreign-born soldiers had a lower desertion rate than native-born. These figures suggest that the immigrants viewed service in the Army as beneficial to them.

The Army was attractive to immigrants; it offered a wide variety of opportunities. For example, Private William Hustede, First Cavalry, fresh from Germany, joined the Army with the intention of learning English. He attended the post school at Fort Assiniboine, Montana, and acquired a rudimentary knowledge of the language. Many posts had libraries stocked with magazines and books; a few stations offered opportunities for advanced instruction. Soldiering also provided the enlistees with a vocational education. Carpentry, baking, and brickmaking were among the many skills that could be learned by the individual soldier. Many units provided the labor forces to build and repair the forts, lay telegraph lines, and build roads. All of these jobs meant that the foreign-born soldier gained a broad traditional and vocational education which could be useful in the civilian labor market.

The Army also aided in the process of Americanization. The foreign-born soldier was able to get a better perspective of the customs and the country as he traveled to his post, which was often far from his point of enlistment.

Although people on the frontier were not enthusiastic about foreigners in general, as seen in the attacks on European bankers in the Populist writings of the 1880s and 1890s, these foreign-born soldiers were treated differently. They were representatives of the government, opening up the West, controlling the Indians, and civilizing the frontier. As such, they were as well thought of by the settlers as any soldier who could trace his lineage back to the *Mayflower*. This attitude also existed within the Army ranks. Living together, under threat of danger in isolated posts, broke down many of the language and cultural barriers. It is apparent from the high reenlistment figures that the foreign-born soldiers found the Army a congenial place to work.

For the foreign-born members of the military in the Nineteenth Century, the Army offered opportunities for advancement. However, as they became Americanized, the attractions of the Army diminished. Other, more profitable, outlets for their talents appeared. Consequently the Irish and German immigrants began to be replaced by those from eastern and southern Europe. Then, by the 1920s these too began to diminish in number. First-generation Americans were not as enthusiastic as their parents about the Army. They no longer needed it as a vehicle for social mobility.

Another minority group which served in the Army in the post-Civil War period were the native Americans, the Indians. They served as scouts for most of the Indian War period. For example, General George Crook employed 500 Apache scouts in his 1871-1872 campaigns against the Apaches in Arizona. This did not mean that they were really part of the regular Army; instead they operated on their own. In 1891 Secretary of War Redfield Proctor authorized the enlistment of one company of Indians for each of the 26 regiments of white cavalry and infantry west of the Mississippi. By the end of that year, seven companies had been fully recruited and seven more were partially manned. Within a few years, the experiment of integrating the Indians into the regular Army had collapsed and the last company was disbanded. These few years in the Army had no noticeable impact on the native Americans. Their service was too short and too isolated for the contact to really mean anything.

The other primary minority group in the Army in the Nineteenth Century was the black American. The general attitude of the Army at that time towards blacks was resigned acceptance. In the first years of the Twentieth Century the attitude became one of hostility. Only in the last 25 years has the black minority become an accepted and integral part of the Army.

In the years before the Civil War the Army occasionally used black manpower, but mainly as servants or laborers. During the Civil War, over 180,000 blacks served in the Union Army in a variety of capacities including infantry and cavalry. After the end of the war, Congress created four all-black regiments as part of the expansion of the regular Army. These four regiments, the Ninth and Tenth Cavalry and the Twenty-fourth and Twenty-fifth Infantry, were the only ones in which blacks could serve in the peacetime army until after World War II. These black soldiers were governed by several unwritten rules. One was that they were to be segregated. Another was the belief on the part of most white officers that blacks were inferior and would make good soldiers only if commanded by whites. The Army also accepted many of the commonly held stereotypes about blacks: they were lazy, prone to stealing, told lies frequently, often sang and played musical instruments, and were close to animals in their behavior.

But despite the discriminatory treatment, the Army in the period from 1865 to 1898 was a very attractive place for a black. For most of the late Nineteenth Century, blacks in civilian society faced discrimination, disfranchisement, and lynchings. Few blacks owned the land they worked on, and most had a very small income. Public education was

Quartermaster black troops meet Arabs near bivouac area in Casablanca, North Africa, in February 1943. (USA)

minimal or non-existent. Most blacks were confined to the rural South by the debts which were a normal part of the share-cropping system. In this environment the Army was the better alternative. Blacks could earn a steady salary and build up credits toward retirement. And the Army provided an education. In addition, service in the military afforded an opportunity to travel to the West and to participate in the opening of the frontier. Blacks could take part in a variety of recreational activities, many of which were unavailable to them in civilian life. Finally, they could fulfill one of the duties of citizenship.

The black enlistees of 1874 differed from their white counterparts: they were older, and they had a higher reenlistment rate and a lower desertion rate.

Although life in the Army was very attractive for blacks, it was not perfect. Many Army officers did not want to serve with a black command. Frontier communities did not welcome black soldiers. A number of racial clashes occurred and the Army did little or nothing to protect the black soldiers. An incident in Suggs, Wyoming, in 1892, is indicative of this. A group of men from the Ninth Cavalry went to visit a white prostitute, a woman whom they had known at their previous station at Fort Robinson, Nebraska. In Suggs, however, the white clients protested the presence of the black men. Later the blacks went to a bar and were refused service there also. They drew their pistols, as did the whites, but the bartender managed to calm things down before shooting began. The next evening a number of black troopers rode through Suggs shooting their pistols. On the way back to camp, a hidden gunman killed one of the black soldiers. The Army's reaction was to confine the blacks to camp, and to do nothing to track down the killer or to pressure the civilian authorities to get involved in the case.

As the status of blacks in civilian society deteriorated after 1898, it also began to change in the Army. Certain aspects of military life, however, continued to be attractive to black civilians. The educational programs continued and even expanded. These programs were open to blacks, though at times segregation was involved. The Army required that two people at a time take the course for bakers. Only when two blacks were assigned to the course could they both begin instruction. Athletics continued to involve inter-regimental competition, and the Twenty-fifth Infantry had an outstanding baseball team which regularly beat white teams. Also, the opportunities for travel were broadened. Blacks were stationed throughout the United States and the American possessions overseas. They were among the first American troops returned home from the Philippines via the Suez Canal. However, other aspects of life in the Army became less favorable. Black efforts to expand their presence in the service were met with great resistance by Congress and the War Department. Blacks were denied entry into the artillery because it was believed that they did not possess the necessary technical ability. When the Army expanded the number of infantry and cavalry regiments, no new black regiments were added. When black soldiers met discrimination in civilian society, the Army made no effort to correct the situation or protect the soldiers. Civilians shot at the black soldiers, segregated them, and made it perfectly clear that they did not want them around.

As a result of these changes within the Army, military service became less attractive. Although the units were kept up to strength, the reenlistment rate declined and the desertion rate climbed.

In the 1920s and 1930s the situation remained the same. The Army really did not want black soldiers but felt that it was easier to retain the small number than to get rid of them. The black units became essentially service detachments. The cavalry regiments acted as stablemen at West Point and Fort Leavenworth, Kansas. The only black officer during most of this period, Benjamin O. Davis, Sr., received assignments that kept him out of the mainstream of Army life. Yet despite this situation, the black units were always filled. Economically blacks in civilian society were not well off in the 1920s and even worse off during the Depression. Many blacks left the South in search of economic and political improvement in the North. They usually did not find it. In comparision to conditions in civilian society, the black soldiers' life was rather good. Even for black officers, the situation was good when compared to civilian life. An excellent example of this is the decision of Benjamin O. Davis, Jr., to enter the military academy and pursue a career in the service. When he made the decision in 1932 he knew the discrimination and isolated assignments that his father had received. He understood the general hostility of Army officers toward black officers. Despite this he went ahead, for it was his belief that service in the military offered good career possibilities.

As World War II approached, the Army came under increasing pressure to lower the barriers to black enlistments. The leadership reacted with a quota system related to the percentage of blacks in the total population. When the draft went into effect in 1940, blacks were accepted up to a limit of 10 percent of the total Army. Most job classifications in the service were closed to them, though the Army piously claimed that this was not the case. As a result, black leaders, such as A. Philip Randolph, head of the Brotherhood of Sleeping Car Porters, protested vehemently against expanding the segregated Army. As the war drew near, America was preparing to fight a fascist enemy with a racist Army.

The end of World War II saw that racist Army still in existence but there were many forces in operation that soon led to a change. An experiment in integration had occurred in the last months of the war, at the urging of General Benjamin O. Davis, Sr. It had proved to be successful. The new president, Harry S. Truman, was sincerely interested in civil rights and opposed to discrimination in the armed forces. Black leaders, such as Randolph and Lester Granger, of the Urban League, were emphatic in their demands for an end to discrimination and segregation in the Army. In 1948 President Truman issued Executive Order # 9981, which prohibited discrimination in the armed forces. Under pressure from Truman and his advisors, the Army, after two years of stalling, in March 1950 ended segregation and the quota system. The Korean War, which began the following month, accelerated the process of change. By 1954 the system of segregation which had existed since 1866 had disappeared. The Army had taken the leadership, albeit unwillingly, in social change. It was one of the first major institutions of American society to become desegregated. The Army again was a very attractive place for blacks. Once more the number of blacks in the Army increased. However, although the system of segregation had disappeared, discrimination within the service became more obvious and annoying.

In the last ten years this remaining discrimination has come under attack and changes have begun. One of the factors that caused the upheaval was the large number of blacks drafted as a result of the Vietnam build up and the inequitable way in which the draft operated. The blacks that were inducted brought with them a heightened black consciousness. They had distinctive hairstyles and customs, many of which clashed with the Army's way of doing things. As a result there were many incidents of racial friction in the states and in Vietnam in the late 1960s and early 1970s. The black reenlistment rate dropped from 66 percent in 1966 to 31 percent in 1967 and to 13 percent in 1970. In the United States and in Europe blacks found that they were denied housing on the basis of their race and their children had to suffer through segregated education. When black soldiers protested the inequities, the white commanders usually paid little attention or punished them in a variety of ways. Blacks suffered more courts-martial than did whites and received harsher penalties for the same offenses. A disproportionate number of blacks ended up in the stockades. Administrative discharges were often used by commanders to get rid of blacks whom they considered undesirable, and though the blacks thought this was a quick way of getting out of the service, the stigma followed them into civilian life and made jobs hard to find. The fact that there were few black officers also intensified the grievances.

Meanwhile, in civilian society, the black power movement was growing in strength. There was more emphasis on the black heritage. Afro hair styles and the dashiki were accepted parts of the black lifestyle; they were frowned upon in the service. When blacks tried to get soul food or music, things which they felt were important to their new black way of life, they found the Army was unwilling to cooperate. Militant black groups opposed the war in Vietnam and counseled that blacks should not go when drafted. Other such organizations suggested black soldiers should learn the techniques of guerrilla warfare and then teach their brothers when they returned home. Still other black groups protested blacks fighting orientals for the benefit of whites. In this situation, it was hard for a black man to think about making the Army a career or for staying in any longer than his required two years.

113

The old frontier Army was quite well known to those living in the West, especially the girls at Kansas State College of Agriculture and Applied Science, now Kansas State University, where an enterprising colonel in 1890 sponsored this Girls Military and Physical Education Drill team. (KSU)

When the novelty of integration had worn off and black protests and demands increased, things began to change. There were a variety of forces which were responsible for these changes. One was that racial problems were counter-productive for the military. Too much time and effort had to be spent in dealing with them. Another factor was the pressure from Congress and the black community for equal treatment. Finally, as an all-volunteer Army became more likely, the Army could not afford to lose any source of manpower. The black population had always been a good source of soldiers and the decline in the reenlistment rate therefore was disturbing.

These pressures brought about a number of changes, most of which occurred in the 1970s. In November 1969, on orders from the chief of staff, Army posts began a series of human relations seminars. Black periodicals and books were provided on the posts. Afro hair styles were accepted and the service barbers and beauticians were instructed in the techniques of cutting and styling the black person's hair. In addition, efforts were made to monitor the disciplinary actions of individual unit commanders. And the Army required off-base housing owners to sign a no-discrimination pledge before the housing would be listed as available to service personnel. Because only this housing could be used by Army personnel, this was a powerful economic weapon. The Army required that all of its officers and enlisted personnel take classes in race relations. They admitted that racial discrimination "past and present, real and perceived, is the root cause of the problem."

The pinnacle of the new system is the Defense Race Relations Institute (DRRI) at Patrick Air Force Base in Florida. There the instructors teach enlisted men and officers about the causes of racial problems and how to deal with them. These officers and enlisted men then go back to their own units as instructors. The first commander of the project, Colonel Claude M. Dixon, believed that ignorance of the background and history of minority groups lay behind the problems of the services. He believed that the DRRI would begin to deal with the situation through education. At the beginning of each DRRI program every student is given a multiple choice examination which involves various words with meanings particular to a racial group, perceptions of racial stereotypes and ideas, and the history of the different minority groups. The students' performance makes them aware of their own cultural bias. The students also spend their time in a small black community near the base, which allows them to familiarize themselves with previously unknown aspects of black culture and how this relates to military customs. For example, when the parent of a soldier dies, emergency leave is usually granted. This regulation does not take into account the fact that many blacks have been raised by a grandmother or an aunt, which means that the soldier might have to go AWOL in order to attend the funeral. Other phases of the course of instruction acquaint the students with the culture and needs of the Chicano, Puerto Rican, and native American minority groups.

As the result of these programs, life in the Army for the black soldier has evidentally been improving. The reenlistment rate has gone back up and the percentage of blacks in the military is on the rise. By mid-1974 it had risen to about 20 percent of the enlisted force and about 4 percent of the officer corps. These figures indicate that the Army has not had much difficulty in obtaining more black enlisted men, but blacks who could become officers have been harder to get. Civilian opportunities for advancement, monetary rewards, and educational benefits have been showered on those blacks who are prime officer material. As a result, the percentage of black officers has only slowly risen from the level it was at in the early 1970s. And racial problems and incidents have not totally ceased in this improved Army life. Recently, Secretary of Defense Schlesinger noted that "Race relations in the services remain a problem as racial incidents continue to occur." Blacks have continued to perceive inequities in the application of discipline and punishment. "These perceptions contribute to polarization which in turn leads to confrontations." The military is still in the forefront of the effort to deal with the problem of racial discrimination. Yet, despite its flaws, it has again become an attractive place for the black soldier. The job opportunities, the educational programs, the travel experiences, and the pay are better than that available to many blacks in civilian America. For this minority group, the peacetime Army is a very attractive segment of American society.

The other primary minority group in the military today is women. Though they constitute a majority in American society, in the military they are a small, but growing, minority. Like blacks, they were accepted reluctantly, were treated differently, and found life difficult. Yet for them, also, the situation has improved in the last few years.

Women have been associated with the American military from the Revolutionary era onward. However, they were always in an auxiliary capacity. In the Revolutionary War some women served as nurses, others as aides. During peacetime, many Army posts had women laundresses or servants. In World War I women were used extensively in the war effort, but only as civilians. When General John J. Pershing asked for 100 phone operators, his request was met by 100 civilian women who were sent under contract with the War Department. None of the women workers ever became part of the regular Army establishment. In the inter-war years Ms. Anita Phillips, working with the General Staff, tried to convince the Army to plan for the utilization of women in a future war. No plans were made, and in 1931 Chief of Staff Douglas MacArthur eliminated Ms. Phillips' position. No further planning was done on the utilization of women until 1939. In that year, as the probability of war increased, planning began again, with women relegated to the traditional military roles. Nothing was done with these plans until 1942.

This view of the woman's role in wartime found little opposition in civilian society. Most men and women accepted the idea that women should stay at home during war while men fought on the front lines. It was with great reluctance that women were allowed into factories in World War I. Yet this change began to open up new horizons for some women. During the 1920s and 1930s there was a steady undercurrent of protest against the inferior role given women. The passage of the Nineteenth Amendment in 1920, the entry of women into politics, and the shifting sexual mores of the 1920s were all in part responsible for this change. Army plans continued to keep women in an auxiliary capacity because there was little pressure for any change in the roles given women in wartime. In addition, they saw no need to utilize female personnel. They believed that the draft would provide more than enough manpower to fight any enemy.

The entry of the United States into World War II led to a change. Eleanor Roosevelt and Congresswoman Edith Nourse Rogers pushed the concept of a separate women's Army corps. The Army, "to avert the pressure to admit women to actual membership in the army," was willing to go part way. The compromise was the Women's Army Auxiliary Force (WAAF), which was as its title implied, not really part of the regular Army. When it came into existence in May 1942, the problems it had were tremendous. There was no compensation for service-connected disabilities, the pay was lower than that for the regular Army, the officer ranks were not equivalent, and there was no real respect for the WAAF from male Army officers. In 1943 some of these problems were resolved with the creation of the Women's Army Corps (WAC). Chief of Staff George C. Marshall was of great assistance in lobbying with Congress for the legislation. The head of the WAAF, Oveta Culp Hobby, had a great deal of influence with Congress and this also helped overcome the resistance of many Congressmen. As a result of the legislation, the WAC became a real part of the wartime Army. The director was to be at the temporary rank of colonel. No woman was to command a man, except by special permission. During the war the members of the WAC helped meet the unexpected personnel shortage by performing clerical, administrative, and technical tasks in the United States, Europe, and the Pacific. Although the initial projection was that four women would be

At Casablanca in 1943 WACS line up for chow in summer work uniforms and fatigues. (USA)

needed to replace three men, it soon became evident that three women would replace four men, because they were far more qualified than the males they were replacing. At its wartime height, the WAC had about 100,000 members.

With the end of the war, the future of the Women's Army Corps was uncertain. As a result of the original legislation, the corps began to be demobilized in 1946. However, groups within and without the Army pushed for the WAC to become a permanent part of the regular establishment. The American Association of University Women came out in support of the concept, as did Eleanor Roosevelt. Even the War Department got behind the idea. Chief of Staff Dwight D. Eisenhower stated that although he originally thought the idea of women in the Army was strange, his experiences in World War II had convinced him that they should continue to serve. "For the particular tasks for which women are qualified, they are far better than men." The War Department proposed a plan to Congress which called for a permanent WAC to be no larger than 2 percent of the regular Army's size, an officer corps of up to 1,000 women, and a director with the rank of colonel. This version easily passed the Senate in 1947, but not the House. There the opposition to the idea of women in the service came to the surface and the bill was blocked. However, the following year things were more favorable. The bill got out of the House Armed Services committee after an intense debate. Congressman Lyndon B. Johnson led the drive to expand the proposal to 4 percent of the regular Army, but that lost on a tie vote. The Army's proposal finally passed in its initial form and the WAC became part of the permanent peacetime establishment.

The Women's Army Corps faced a number of problems, some of which had appeared earlier in World War II. Most arose from the fact that the members of the WAC were treated differently than the male members of the regular Army. All of these problems were to hinder recruiting in the future, but while the WAC remained in the 7,500- to 10,000-force level, as it did until the mid-1960s, enough women volunteered to fill the ranks. The problems then were not serious enough to overcome the advantages which service in the Army provided for women. Travel, good pay, eligible bachelors, and retirement benefits were attractive to women. These advantages were closed to them in many other job categories in American society at that time. Yet the problems would not disappear. In 1952 Ms. L.B. Thompson, a major in the WAC reserve, was discharged because she had a baby. Ms. Thompson protested that she should not be discharged "solely because she performed the function for which our Creator intended her." Her protests were unavailing, and the problem of pregnancy discharges was to continue for another 20 years. More easily resolved were the protests over uniforms. Initially, the Army gave the WACs the same uniforms as the male soldiers got. Slowly they began to realize that women required special uniforms. In the beginning the Army tried to make the WACs use cotton stockings, but in 1953 they gave in and allowed nylons to be standard issue.

By the early 1950s the WAC had grown to 10,000 women and was an accepted part of the Army. As General Matthew Ridgeway said on the occasion of the ninth anniversary of the corps, "For you are soldiers, performing soldiers' duties, subject to soldiers' discipline, and proudly ready ... to share whatever the country's service may demand." By that time about one-third of the corps was stationed overseas, in the Far East, and Europe. Recognition of their status came in 1955 when permanent headquarters were established at Fort McClellan, Arkansas.

By the 1960s, as women began to question their roles in society and object to discriminatory treatment, as indicated by the creation of the National Organization for Women and the efforts toward the passage of the Equal Rights Amendment, the different rules which governed the WAC came under scrutiny. Among the major inequities were the ceilings on a WAC officer's rank and on the size of the WAC. In 1967 the Defense Department urged that these restrictions be removed. Women officers often did not have the rank comensurate with their responsibilities. Males with the same jobs had a higher rank. As a result of these arguments, and the rising pressure from women's groups, Congress removed the promotional and size limits on the WAC. Within a year six women had been promoted to the rank of colonel, and the director of the WAC had been promoted to the rank of brigadier general. The overall size of the WAC grew slowly.

The last few years, especially under the leadership of WAC Director Brigadier General Mildred C. Bailey, has seen tremendous changes in the status, role, and size of the WAC. Congress passed a law equalizing the age and parental consent requirements for male and female volunteers. It is now considering repealing the provision for a separate WAC promotion list. The number of occupational specialities closed to women is very small. In December 1974, 422 were open and only 36 combat-related specialities were closed. Women were admitted into the junior and senior ROTC programs, though not into West Point. Women are enlisted/ appointed into the Army, not the WAC, and are treated like their male counterparts. And WAC officers can attend the senior service schools. In 1974 Lieutenant Colonel Connie Slewitzke, one of five women in a class of 1,000 at the Command and General Staff School, was chosen president of her class. In July 1974, the Reverend Alice M. Henderson, a black woman, became the first female chaplain. Women were made fully participating members of promotion and school selection boards. The WAC was expanded from 12,400 in 1972 to 25,000 in 1974, and a goal of 50,000 was set for 1979. One major change came as the result of a Supreme Court decision in 1973. As a consequence of the decision in *Frontiero v. Richardson*, female members of the armed services can collect the same dependency allowances, subject to the same criteria, as can males. In fact, most WACs are assigned to individual branches, so that although the WAC remains on paper, its members are integrated throughout the Army. The Director of WAC is an advisor to the Secretary of War and the Chief of Staff on women's affairs.

The changes in the Army closely coincided with changes in society. The women's rights movement grew increasingly strong. Congress passed and over 30 states ratified the Equal Rights Amendment. Women became more politically active. Widespread efforts were made to equalize pay. It was much more acceptable for women to take a wide variety of jobs or for males to be supervised by females. And, as the woman's role in American society changed and as equality of treatment became accepted, the Army had to change also, if it was to attract women members. As the all-volunteer Army concept went into operation, the Army could not ignore this additional, largely untapped, source of personnel. An examination of the WAC in 1974 indicates that they have been successful in their efforts towards change. It is a young organization. Over 90 percent of its enlisted personnel are under the age of 25. The median age for officers is 31. Many of the women have gone to college and almost three-quarters of the officers have bachelors degrees. Since 1966 no one has been commissioned with less than two years of college. About 80 percent are single. In 1974 more than half the enlisted personnel and almost 45 percent of the officers reenlisted.

Despite all of these changes a number of the old problems still remain, and new problems have developed. One of them is command. For example, Sergeant Paul Hammond had command of a unit of WACs, but needed an escort before he could enter the barracks. And pregnancy in the service still causes problems for the WAC. Although the traditional policy had been to discharge the pregnant WAC, this has come under review in the last few years. Even more perplexing is what to do about volunteers who are either unmarried mothers or married with dependents. Traditionally they have been rejected, but this policy also has come under fire as being discriminatory. Beginning in 1971, waivers have been granted on an individual basis to women in these categories. Yet conflicts have arisen between family responsibilities and duty assignments. The WAC has insisted that "the needs of the Army will be given priority," and it also has tried not to penalize single women or those

In World War II women served not only as nurses, but as WACS, and went overseas as well. Here WACS await the order to leave their train at Algiers, North Africa, 3 September 1943. (USA)

without dependents. It is not easy to be equitable to all interests. Demands to allow women into the combat arms also have not been resolved. For example, Privates Rita Johnson and Joyce Kutsch underwent parachute instruction at Fort Benning, Georgia, in 1973, yet are prohibited by law from using that skill in combat. Private Penny Hartley graduated from the air assault course in 1974 with a skill which she could not use and had to go back to driving a truck for a supply and service battalion. Another problem is how far to carry the process of integration. At Fort Dix, New Jersey, male and female MPs are housed in the same barracks. The males have the second floor, the females the third, and they share the recreation room on the first floor.

In the WAC over the last decade, we have seen the operation of many of the same factors that led to the improvement of the position of blacks in the service. Demands by Army personnel for rectification of inequities, a heightened consciousness on the part of the minority group, and the necessities of an all-volunteer service have moved the Army to improve the position of women as they did for blacks. The consequences are shown in the willingness of women to join the WAC, the success of the program of integration, and the acceptance of the new roles by most males.

During most of the history of the United States Army, minority groups have seen it as a means of Americanization and upward mobility. It proved attractive for European immigrants, for blacks, and for women. For most of the time the Army conformed to the rest of society in its treatment of these minority groups. This is evidenced by the ways in which blacks were discriminated against and subjected to segregation, the attitude towards the utilization of women, and the reluctance to change any of this. Yet despite this climate, the Army was an attractive career. It offered the minority groups a variety of benefits that were not available in civilian life — education, travel, retirement security, and the feeling that these individuals were becoming citizens by serving in the military. This attitude toward the Army's social role is well summed up by an old Army saying: "The military's job is to fight and not to lead social revolutions." In the past decade, however, the Army has been in the forefront of social change. Willingly or not, forced by outside pressures from civilian society, the need for recruits, or the feeling that it should correct existing inequities, in the last decade the Army has worked hard to eliminate many of the manifestations of racial prejudice and sexual stigmas. Yet in so doing the Army has found that these are very complex problems. Racial prejudice is embedded deep within the core of white America and to change it will mean more than pious statements and courses at DRRI. Similarly, the end to sexual barriers and the integration of women has raised a whole series of questions as to what role women should play in the military. Instead of mirroring American society's racial and sexual ideas, the Army, along with the other armed services, has acted as a leader. The traditional Army role of providing opportunities for minority groups still remains, but more importantly, the Army has adopted a new role — the testing ground for the true meaning of equality. It is a significant and important addition.

Suggestions for Further Research

The subject of the interrelationship of the Army and minority groups really has not been studied by historians. Traditional military history has concentrated on battles, military biography, and weaponry. Only in the last few years has there been any study of the military as a social institution, and much still remains to be done.

North African Spahis, one of the most famous fighting troops in the world, line up on their white Arab steeds to watch the first overseas unit of the Women's Army Auxiliary Corps parading in the courtyard of the Palais d'Ete, headquarters of the Allied French Forces in Africa, 1945. (USA)

The role of the Army in the Americanization of immigrant groups in the Nineteenth Century surely deserves more study than it has received. It has only been briefly mentioned in the many accounts of the Indian Wars. The utilization of quantification and statistical techniques as applied to Army enlistment records can give us some insight into the numbers, origins, and skills of the immigrants. In this way we will begin to understand the impact the Army had on the immigrants. A study of the published and manuscript memoirs of soldiers and officers, especially those in the Military History Research Collection at Carlisle Barracks, Pennsylvania, would be another fruitful source for insight in this area.

The impact of the Army on the black population has been the subject of a number of studies in recent years, but there are still some gaps in our knowledge of this relationship. The period between World War I and World War II has not been researched, except in relation to the Army's handling of blacks in the Civilian Conservation Corps (CCC). The ongoing problems of the Army in the last decade in the area of race relations have just begun to be studied. Such topics as the image of the Army in the black community, the relation of the black power movement to the Army, military justice as it applies to blacks, and the efforts to deal with racial prejudice are fascinating topics for research.

Women in the Army have received almost no attention from scholars. Other than the study of the WAC in the *History of the Army in World War II*, there is really no scholarly article or book on the WAC. Among the topics that should be investigated are: the legislative history of the acts of 1948 and 1967 which shaped the present WAC; a profile of the members of the WAC and their backgrounds, interests, motivations, and roles; the interaction between the WAC and the women's rights movement; and comparisons between the WAC and foreign women soldiers, such as those in the Israeli Army. At this point in time almost any research in this field would be a contribution.

SOURCES

Only a few books deal with recruits, minority groups, and Indians in the Army. Among those used in this chapter were: Marcus Cunliffe, *Soldiers and Civilians: The Martial Spirit in America, 1775-1865* (Free Press, 1968); Don Rickey, Jr., *Forty Miles A Day on Beans and Hay* (University of Oklahoma Press, 1963); and Jack D. Foner, *The United States Soldier Between Two Wars* (Humanities Press, 1970). The demographic data for 1874 enlistees is based on Army enlistment registers.

There are a number of good books on black soldiers in the peacetime Army. The best comprehensive survey is Jack D. Foner, *Blacks and the*

Heroic charge of the United States black regulars near Santiago, Cuba, in the Sapnish-American War (Ninth and Tenth Cavalry; Twenty-fourth and Twenty-fifth Infantry. (Courtesy B. Franklin Cooling)

Military in American History (Praeger, 1974). The book contains an excellent annotated bibliography; it was the source of much of the material on blacks in this chapter. This author has studied race relations around the turn of the century in *The Black Soldier and Officer in the United States Army, 1891-1917* (University of Missouri Press, 1974). Richard Dalfiume, *Desegregation of the U.S. Armed Forces: Fighting on Two Fronts, 1939-1953* (University of Missouri Press, 1969), is a good study of the process of desegregation and the forces that led to it. Current Army policy is spelled out in Department of the Army Pamphlet 600-16, *Improving Race Relations in the Army, Handbook for Leaders,* and in articles in *The New York Times, Washington Post,* and *Armed Forces Journal.*

The basic source for the formation and early years of the WAC is Mattie E. Treadwell, *The Women's Army Corps* (Government Printing Office, 1954), a part of the *History of the U.S. Army in World War II.* The Congressional Record and the Senate and House of Representatives document set provided information for the legislative background of the WAC. In recent years *The New York Times, Washington Post,* and *Army Times* have had a number of good articles on the WAC. Typical is "Military Ideas on Equality: Some Women Wonder If It's A Forward March," which appeared in *The New York Times* on 18 April 1973. General Mildred Bailey has written a good overview of the past changes in "Army Women and a Decade of Progress," *Army* (October 1974), pp. 85-91. The author has also relied on information supplied by Colonel Maida E. Lambeth, Deputy Director, WAC.

George C. Scott as General George S. Patton in the movie "Patton." Immensely popular with audiences of both veterans and young non-veterans, the movie typified the best that the Army has stood for with its portrayal of one of the great heroic leaders of the Second World War. (Courtesy of 20th Century-Fox Ltd.)

Chapter 7

THE ARMY AND POPULAR CULTURE

Donald J. Mrozek

In popular culture, the United States Army has been actor, object, and image. The service has altered specific cultural habits and affected the legal sanctions within which those habits may be exercised. Similarly, major media and specific artists have used the Army as an important vehicle through which to express their own social and political opinions, thus also changing the culture as a whole. The Army also has been an object for imitation, by civilian sub-groups who have appropriated elements of Army style. The impact of the Army on American popular culture and the service's complementary receptivity to pressure from the culture are thus a combination of intention and accident.

For American society, which moved from a turn-of-the-century "cult of toughness" toward a later exploitation of leisure, the Army's impact on sport for the masses has had perhaps the broadest and most lasting effect on the activity of the average citizen. In all instances, however, the intent of the service was internal edification — to use sport to meet the institutional demands that officers perceived, not to alter the way civilians lived as an end in itself. Although many prominent civilians such as Theodore Roosevelt and William James credited sport with powers to produce a moral transformation in the lives of youth, the decision to make team and individual sport a part of the Army's training program emerged from within the service, often against a broader current of popular opposition or disinterest. The cases of boxing and skiing are among the most instructive, typifying the Army's role in the growth of both spectator and participant sport.

Before World War I, for example, boxing was illegal in most states and disreputable in all. Only five states allowed bouts by 1906. Yet the Army, and the Navy as well, regarded boxing as perfect for the training and conditioning of recruits, as well as for recreation. Army trainers believed that fighters developed more than agility and strength. They learned confidence and discipline that would carry them obediently into battle, and hopefully out of it alive. War was still a close, even hand-to-hand experience; and the immediacy of boxing and its dependence on the force and character of the strong lone man seemed to make it an obvious preparation for combat. Logically, then, every inductee took up boxing during training, and many later participated in service boxing teams. According to World War I author Edward F. Allen, the inter-unit bouts in a sport banned in much of the civilian world became major attractions.

Athletic competition, moreover, was an alternative to vice. Secretary of War Newton D. Baker had been embarrassed during the 1916 confrontation with Mexico by reports of prostitution, drinking, and gambling near Army camps. As a means of meeting the manners of the day and guarding against charges that military service corrupted the nation's youth, Raymond B. Fosdick, head of the Commission on Training Camp Activities for the Army (and head of a comparable Navy agency), consciously set out to change the leisure-time activities of the recruits and inductees of 1916 and the war years. Under athletic director Joseph Raycroft, the Army camps sponsored large football and baseball programs and heightened the awareness of servicemen to their availability. At the end of the war, the Army's General Staff authorized the American Expeditionary Force to conduct athletic competitions as a means of regulating the troops and consuming much of their ample free time.

It is noteworthy that the Army's athletic programs extended to black enlisted men as well as whites. Ocasionally, white officers objected to interracial competition, but such cases appear to have been exceptions. More frequently, officers of both races found in sport a solution to the training and disciplinary problems that were "color-blind," by excluding men from participating in athletics as a form of punishment. Evidence suggests that the black regimental teams made some impression on civilian white teams as well. Competition between black Army squads and college teams, usually white, was commonplace in baseball and not infrequent in football, basketball, and track. The success of blacks as Army athletes caused some to question the wisdom of barring them from professional competition on an equal basis with whites. In a 1909 divisional track meet, for example, one George Washington, stationed in the Philippines, placed first in the 100-yard dash and in the 200- and 880-yard races. Afterwards, challenged by a soldier from the British legation in Hong Kong, Washington performed so well that he was acclaimed champion runner of the Far East. As historian Marvin E. Fletcher has implied, white Americans had a choice of prejudices. They had only to ask whether they wished to feel superior to the blacks or to the British, their competitors in world affairs. The greater opportunity for personal development that the Army afforded blacks during the early part of the Twentieth Century helped to alter the image of the American black in the popular mind, and their increasing success helped to emphasize that a Jack Johnson — a superior black — was a champion but not an anomaly.

On a broader level, what occurred through the years of World War I and shortly before was a shift in the values of literally millions of men who had been drafted or who had volunteered. These men in turn affected other millions when they returned home. Immediately after its founding in 1919, the American Legion opened a campaign for the legalization of boxing. In January of that year, the Army, Navy, and Civilian Board of Boxing began its promotion of the values of the sport and its pressure for the removal of all legal sanctions. By the mid-1920s, such groups had gone far toward reestablishing American prize-fighting. The very fact of participation in the sport by Army trainees had helped to create a post-war market for professional boxing; and the association of a then popular service with a sport of dubious pedigree had broken the taboo about boxing instead of the credibility of the Army.

The Army's training activities supplied consumers for what was a kind of service-industry. For its own reasons, which had nothing to do with the purposes of private civilian fight-promoters, the Army created the demand that called forth the postwar supply of boxing and agitated for its legalization. The success of the boxing movement provided the foundation for the rise of other spectator sports such as hockey, wrestling, and basketball. For although the great indoor arenas were designed with boxing in mind, common sense and personal greed both dictated that the Madison Square Gardens of the nation be filled with paying customers for other sports as often as possible. The Army thus helped to spark a movement that took on its own force and swiftly went its own way, giving the public new pastimes in the process.

The theory that mass spectator sport is merely a function of leisure time and available money has fallen into disrepute, because it does not tell us why a nation chose the specific forms through which to spend that time and money. During the interwar period, the Army followed the lead of many prominent physical educators and placed great emphasis on sport as well as calisthenics. In programs such as the Citizens' Military Training Camps, a businesslike and sometimes severe discipline tended

Boxing became one of the first inter-racial sports and thus a means of breaking down the barriers. Henry Armstrong and Major Mark Conn, former Lightweight Champion, spar before an interested crowd in 1945. (USA)

to make what sport there was an instrument to bring order and subordination. Yet the use of boxing and other sports before the 1920s had shared this purpose to some extent as well. The change was partly one in emphasis, then, together with a new desire to find general ways in which sport might mold character.

Adopting a nearly ascetic self-image (which also prejudiced its leaders against the more flamboyant members of the Air Corps), the Army was ill at ease with the glamor of the new spectator sports. More important, it experienced a decline of interest, or faith, in its ability to affect the moral character of the recruits. Army training officials expected to use drill and organized exercise to make the soldier physically rather than morally fit. Significantly, once again the service had no desire to alter the pattern of civilian culture. Some saw advantages in using team sport, especially football, to break a supposed insubordination among the youth of the 1930s, yet such calls often came from figures on the periphery of policy — such as Navy physical training adviser Gene Tunney — and many were associated with the Navy rather than the ground forces, including James Forrestal, who served as Under Secretary and Secretary and later became Secretary of Defense. Nonetheless the supporters of the Army continued to boost the team sports — both for spectators and participants — including football, baseball, and track and field. The American Legion advocated their importance through the two decades, and numerous National Guard units followed their lead and even formed a Military Athletic League. In a broader sense, however, the war itself had generated interest in sport and triggered a transformation in physical education programs by exposing the medical deficiency of one-third of those who had been called up for service. The temper of the time, though, was such that leaders sought less to mold the spirit than to firm the body.

The Army's own concern for practical, functional applications of sport (and of anything else that might insure military victory) led to erratic experiments culminating in the formation of the Tenth Mountain Division of World War II. In 1940, skiing in the United States was distinctly a fringe sport. It was new. Its equipment was primitive. Its better-known devotees included the glamorous and the outrageous and comparatively few in between. The "Sun Valley set" gave the sport a somewhat frivolous image that made it seem singularly unsuitable for taming by the Army. Yet the service's involvement in this sport did much to build the base for skiing's rapid growth after World War II.

In 1940, after the German invasion of Norway, a young American insurance agent named Minot Dole contacted the U.S. Army to urge the formation of military ski units. As head of the National Ski Patrol System and a devoted skier, Dole was hardly a dispassionate adviser. And the

Boxing was also an international matter when the U.S. Army had occupation duty abroad. Here the U.S.A. fights the French Army in the Nouveau Cirque de Paris, 14 March 1919. (NARS 111-SC-153601)

German advances seemed to make for a wider variety in the threats that Americans might need to face. The Army adopted Dole's idea and assigned soldiers to learn to ski at Mount Rainier, Washington, and later at Camp Hale in the high Rockies of Colorado. Ill-chosen, the designated skiers included many southerners (including some who had never even seen snow) and even a company of Chicano desert soldiers. Although many men who had been mismatched to the task soon departed from the train-stop at Pando, Colorado, the idea of the ski troops endured, and its proponents fought to keep it a going enterprise.

Dole played an important part in assuring the unit's success by insisting on the enlistment of competent skiers, located by the headquarters of the National Ski Patrol, to serve in the Tenth and often in the role of instructors. This in itself constituted a major breakthrough. Until the 1940s, instructional techniques in skiing were rudimentary, and for the most part they did not accommodate groups successfully. Under the pressure of the Army's demand for ski troops, Dole's instructors and the Tenth Mountain Division's leaders inaugurated the first systematic program of skiing instruction. This significant technical achievement was ultimately to reduce the cost of learning to ski for the postwar vacationer and thus establish the sport on a more reasonable financial base.

The specific needs of the Tenth Mountain Division also affected technological development in skiing. The service underwrote the improvement of ski construction by ordering large numbers of laminated skis — indeed, as many as the major companies were able to supply. These purchases embodied a commitment to the most advanced ski technology of the day. Using the basic principle of plywood, lamination allowed the manufacture of equipment that retained the same basic shape yet had a wide range of dynamic properties. This was achieved by using different kinds of wood in varying thicknesses in the layers of the laminate "sandwich." The inventor of laminated skis, Björn Ullevold-saeter, at first concentrated on cross-country equipment. In 1938, he sold the license to produce so-called *splitkein* boards to Peter Östby who in turn licensed Denverite Thor Grosvald, Christian Lund of the Northland Company in Minnesota, and S.L. Allen of Philadelphia. Grosvald, Northland, and Allen's firm Splitkein could hardly keep up with the Army's orders, partly because the troops shattered the light skis at an inordinate rate and also because Dole's instructors had not yet made their impression on the Tenth. The service's needs forced strengthening of the skis, experimentation with sidecut, and a variety of improvements that established the standards for postwar recreational skis.

135

Cross-country ski patrol returning from a three-day maneuver in Alaska in 1948. (USA)

In addition to technical changes in the infant ski industry, the Tenth Mountain Division brought skiing to a significant number of young men who would not likely have discovered it under the social and economic limits of the 1930s. Approximately 20,000 young men learned to ski for the Army, and many of them built careers in skiing after the war. These included Aspen founders Friedl Pfeifer and Darcy Brown and Vail founder Peter Seibert. In this indirect way, then, the Tenth Mountain Division contributed much to provide the prerequisites for making skiing a business, for normalizing it by the introduction of an extensive middle-class with customary work habits, and for making it accessible to a vastly enlarged consumer market by reducing the cost and improving the efficiency of instruction. Moreover, although the postwar recreational ski boom did not transform Camp Hale into a destination resort, certain of the Army's facilities, such as Cooper Hill, later served area civilian skiers and substantially broadened interest in the sport by changing the public's pattern of recreation. If this was a consequence of Army actions, it was also the result of efforts by individuals. And so it was fitting that, when the major resort at Vail, Colorado, underwent expansion of its trail system in the late 1960s, its managers dedicated the trail "Minnie's Mile" to the Tenth Mountain Division and Minot Dole, the man who had done so much to make it possible.

Throughout most of the Twentieth Century, the Army also provided the most continuous institutional support for equestrian events. The Fort Riley, Kansas, Equestrian School carried on the post's cavalry traditions and also produced the great bulk of amateur riders for international competitions such as the Olympics. Although Congressional appropriations for equestrian training (as well as for overseas competition for amateur riflemen) often lagged, Secretaries of War persisted in their support of participation in international events. In other branches of sport as well, the Army functioned as a reservoir of amateur talent — preserved from professionalism by their military commitment and often encouraged to develop their athletic abilities as another part of their training as soldiers and for the projection of the Army's image as a builder of men. Thus it often happened that Army men and women appeared regularly on Olympic rosters in riding, shooting, track, swimming, and other sports.

The impact of the Army on the performing arts and the visual arts has been more ambiguous than its role in the transformation of sport and similar recreational leisure activities. The visual and performing arts, to the extent that they are a part of "high culture," have never been especially pertinent to the mission of the Army. In pursuing its own needs, nonetheless, the service actively affected them. As a bureaucracy, the Army assumed a conventional posture of self-glorification, or at least of recording its own development, through most of the Twentieth Century. To this end, the promotion of documentary photography, painting, and drawing met institutional demands. In World War I, the Army Signal Corps undertook an extensive program in still and motion photography to keep a visual record of the activities of the American Expeditionary Force in Europe. This occurred at a time when the nature and uses of documentary photography were in flux, and the reliance on this medium permitted rapid exploration of its limits. At the same time, the service encouraged paintings and drawings of combat and camp life. Again the function of these works was to provide a visual history and a celebration of the endurance of the American soldier in the grimness of trench warfare.

Because the access of the press to scenes of combat was often restricted on grounds of security, Army artists sometimes supplied the only images of war available to the civilians at home. They helped to shape an understanding not only of the material cost of World War I but of its human costs. In brief, because their work tended to express the emotional and psychological impact of war rather than its purely material toll, they shared a deeper kinship with the creators of "high art" than did many civilian photographers and war artists.

This accidental ascendancy of artistic result over a merely bureaucratic and self-laudatory purpose recurred during World War II and after. Army artists captured moments that were important to the lower ranks. In the global war of the 1940s, vast movements and symbolic

Baseball was a highly popular service pastime. Engineers at Fort Leavenworth practice outside their barracks. (LVN)

figures such as Churchill, Roosevelt, and Stalin usually overshadowed the concerns of the enlisted man. Although war correspondent Ernie Pyle became popular for his dedicated reporting of the common soldier's experiences, it is good to remember that his popularity owed much to the fact that he was an exception — the common soldier's combat correspondent. Those individuals in the war effort who became known were taken largely as personifications of types — an Audie Murphy as the symbol of the bravery of the common soldier, an Eisenhower as the image of humane management of the ground war, and a Roosevelt as the guiding father through times of trial. The Army's artists cared little for Audie Murphy and less for General Eisenhower. They showed simple men in the streets of French and German towns and, without intent, built a backlog for the exploration of World War II and its aftermath from the bottom up. Artists such as Bill Mauldin used humorous sketches in *Yank* and elsewhere to show the real problems of simple men at war.

The available art record of World War II is extensive, but it has not received much attention. What Army artists provided later viewers was a special lens — a medium of selection which gave later years a link to their military past. The Army at war thus appeared through the naturally selected images of the kind of people who did the fighting. Their choices tell later viewers what the men at the grass roots level — the combat level — thought most meaningful and most memorable. They provide a corrective against the insolence of experts — the viewer sees what the enlisted man saw rather than what the commander imagined.

Although the Army's artists, then, have done their most important work during wartime, the impact of their works has been most significant in peacetime. The paintings and drawings capture a war that already has been won, but they did not shape the popular mind of their own time. Their most critical impact is residual. A later age sees them for what they were instead of for what the artists thought them to be. At the same time, some of the most significant links between experience in the Army and artistic accomplishments have come in highly individualistic forms that have normally escaped study either in social history or in art criticism. For example, from his service as a painter in a Camouflage Engineer Battalion during World War II, the important American artist Ellsworth Kelly learned lessons in basic form and in the relationships of colors to which he returned in a series of prize-winning exhibitions in the 1960s and 1970s. Although unintentional, the impact of Army experience was real — the imagination of one exceptional talent had somehow gained a stimulation in techniques even in the midst of rather repetitious and uninspired work.

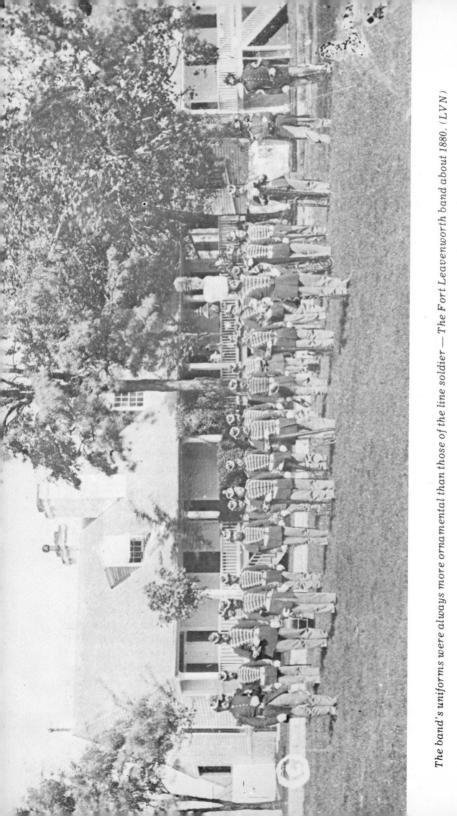

The band's uniforms were always more ornamental than those of the line soldier — The Fort Leavenworth band about 1880. (LVN)

American music has also been influenced by the Army and this in turn has affected popular culture. Thus, when Americans think of martial music, they think of John Philip Sousa and usually associate him with the Army because of his prolific authorship of marches. Yet Sousa emerged as an important figure in American music as a band director for the Marines. The very fact that Sousa was popular at all stemmed from what may be regarded as a demilitarization of martial music. The early roles of music for an Army were to keep the Army organized and orderly (by providing a clear cadence for the march), to muster its morale, and to provide audible signals through which to relay orders in the field. As the technology of communications advanced, the practical functions of the military bands became fewer and usually ceremonial. At the same time, the civilian uses for march music became, if anything, more numerous, in sports spectacles and patriotic observances (which enjoyed a great resurgence in the early and middle Twentieth Century). Consequently, the musical scores that had erroneously become associated with the Army, and others that actually had been tailored to its order, were adopted by civilian organizations comparatively soon after they were published. Sousa himself encouraged this process of dissemination by participating in the founding of ASCAP (the American Society of Composers, Authors, and Publishers). This contributed largely to the greater exploitation of the Army as a cultural object, though it did not help the Army mold popular culture through its own conscious works.

The Army also became a creator of national styles not in itself but through actions of its individuals. In clothing, for example, the personal magnetism and powerful image of Dwight Eisenhower helped to make the Army's "Eisenhower jacket" a stylish rather than a merely utilitarian form. The adaptation of this Army style by the civilian clothing industry showed the broad acceptability of the service in the public mind, at least in the post-1945 era. What has been overlooked is that the use of fatigues and field gear by many younger people in the late 1960s and the 1970s similarly symbolized the permanence of the Army as an influence in American popular culture. This was represented in the choice of costumes even among dissenting members of that society, both because they were cheap at surplus stores and because of a psychological need to belong to a dominating cult.

The Army's impact in areas such as clothing, music, and the visual arts has thus been largely associative or derivative. Many groups within the society have taken some specific part of the service's own private material culture and transformed it into a general or national property. This process of selective exploitation and popularization undertaken among civilian groups, taken in its cumulative force, helps to explain the growing popularity of the war film and the increasingly favorable presentation of the Army in the 1940s and 1950s. A significant fact that has been ignored all too frequently is that the war film was largely a phenomenon of the 1940s and after — not a constant element of film history. The Army had been characterized in film at least as early as *Birth of a Nation* (1915), but it was the preparedness movement of the very late 1930s which began to bring military problems to a wider public, even if only in a comparatively tentative and cautionary way.

It was only World War II itself that brought this particular film genre into complete vitality. Works such as *Guadalcanal Diary* and *Gung Ho* did more than praise men's courage in battle. They revealed the growing acceptability of the idea that the Army deserved standing public interest, an interest that created the chance for a large peacetime standing army for the first time in the nation's history. The reason was simple. The films developed in a sequence that finally accepted the concept of eternal vigilance. When film-makers sought to stir enthusiasm for the war in the early years of the American involvement, they exploited the notion that there was a specific, limited job to be done. As the war went on, many directors and writers began to conceive of military preparedness as a lasting obligation.

Some commentators have mistaken the import of films exploring the readjustment problems of the wounded of World War II, such as *Pride of the Marines* (1943) and *The Best Years of Our Lives* (1946), reading into them an antiwar and anti-military sentiment that was alien to their creation. These films finally praised the work of Army and other armed forces institutions and identified war, not the armed forces, as the trigger of personal calamity. Indeed, they even raised doubts about the validity of the civilians' perceptions. In *The Best Years*, for example, Fredric March remarks that what he fears most about returning to the civilian world is that "everybody's going to want to rehabilitate me." Such films forced attention to a new question. Ought not the military be given a chance to function on its own terms? Did it not have a way of its own that civilians ought to respect? Other films such as *The Men* (1950) and *Bright Victory* (1951) carried these themes into the era of the Korean War.

On a deeper level, these films argued that personal selfishness — not military institutions — were the real cause of individual distress if not of personal injury. They assaulted the myth of the loner, of the rugged individual, and they brought him into an organized society seeking an ill-defined "national security." Even more important, however, were films such as *The Long Gray Line*, featuring major box office attractions such as Tyrone Power. This film, for example, specifically praised West

Point; it honored the Army as an institution. The fact that such films extolled not the heroics of individual men but the system that trained and regulated them underscored the adjustment of popular tolerances in the culture that was making possible a gradual transformation of the Army and its place in American society. In this way, film became a reflection of the prevailing attitudes toward the Army rather than a sign of its own efforts to maintain popularity and the public favor that assured appropriations in the postwar years.

This remained true even through the 1960s despite serious public manifestations of a more shallow challenge to the political and international policies of the United States. A host of "protest films" appeared, including several that challenged the integrity of the Army's past performance. Two notable examples differing greatly in style were *M*A*S*H* (1970) and *Soldier Blue* (1970). *M*A*S*H* merely attacked the inanity of bureaucracy, albeit in a war situation. *Soldier Blue*, though it criticized the Army's treatment of Indians in the Nineteenth Century, still saw the service as an instrument of general national policy and not as an exceptional institution. At the same time, moreover, films appeared that reiterated the decades-old formula of adulation of the ground forces, such as John Wayne's *The Green Berets* (1968). Still others, such as the box-office winner *Patton* (1970), appealed simultaneously to the nostalgia of veterans and to the curiosity of the young. *Patton*, interestingly enough, was popular with large numbers on both sides of the debate over the Vietnam War, suggesting that the human values portrayed in the film were widely accepted in part for the candor of their presentation.

The Army's debut in the new medium of television grew largely from public information programs. Film footage of World War II and the Korean War series *The Big Picture* became standard fare on American networks, and their uses as tools to circulate information gradually yielded to their value as entertainment. Meanwhile, because television in its infancy produced fewer shows that stations needed to fill long air time, local distributors relied heavily on motion pictures, including a large proportion of the World War II vintage films of the Army in combat. Increasingly, the requirements that the Federal Communications Commission imposed on stations to devote time to public service and noncommercial spot announcements left the medium relying on promotional materials from the Army and the other services. In these broad ways, the new medium served to enhance the Army's visibility.

Another pattern of growing popular acceptance, marking a shift in public values and the concerns of popular culture, extended through comic books and cartoon strips. The war comic enjoyed some substantial currency in World War II, and the comic book itself had only been invented in the 1930s. The glorification of American experience in World War II, however, was tentative at best in the late 1940s and became strong only after the beginning of the Korean War. Only when the realities of the postwar world had made clear that the use of force was still very much an instrument of national policy did the war comic achieve real popularity. The praise of individual valor was fused with the portrayal of the inevitability of conflict. Even one of the most aggressive of Cold War heroes, Sergeant Rock, basically hated war and acknowledged it only as an unpleasant if necessary chore. In cartoon strips such as *Beetle Bailey*, spoofing military bureaucrats and bosses, it is bureaucracy and privilege that are basic targets of humor. Beetle Bailey's problems with General Halftrack enjoy a close kinship to Dagwood Bumstead's chaotic dealings with his boss, Mr. Dithers, in the totally civilian strip *Blondie*. Thus the cartoon, or unsophisticated cultural form, helped create national acceptance of the idea of a permanent military obligation with the Army fulfilling that obligation. The tacit acceptance did not have to be conscious to be present and crucial, and it is unlikely that the reader of a war comic thought of himself as a supporter of the Army any more than the buyer of war toys. Yet the presence and popularity of the comics and toys marked the broadened limits of popular tolerance for the Army. With the adjustment of custom that permitted boys the use of dolls as toys, "G.I. Joe" — the image of a living, current, active hero — replaced mere model soldiers that only had hinted at acceptability. Objects from the past yielded to heroic images of the Army in the present.

The impact of the Army upon American popular culture, then, has been of several kinds. The easiest to trace in a conventional historical fashion is direct impact, even when it has not been specifically intended. In these cases, one can observe the causal relationship of Army action upon civilian phenomena, as in the expansion of sport in the Twentieth Century. The development of sport in America might have occurred at other times and for other reasons, but it is a fact that it occurred as it did because of Army involvement and thus the service contributed to the real evolution of a major element of popular culture.

More difficult to assess is the Army's secondary impact on the society through the unintended efforts of its veterans, shaped by their military experience, in years long after their service. In many of these cases, the Army has become an object — a target for change proposed by those who had themselves been changed by their participation in the armed forces. Military history in the United States has always paralleled social and intellectual development. For the Army to have significant effects upon people who will be able to alter the laws of the society, then, presupposes a general predisposition in the nation for the kind of changes proposed. In such cases, the Army has served as one of several possible catalysts for the formation of opinion among those who were to return to civilian society.

Comparatively easy to record is the series of manifestations of Army subjects in American life. As a symbol, the Army has long been viable. It is a kind of promotional property available to virtually all prospective salesmen of ideas quite irrelevant to the Army. The fact that such promoters could use the Army in this way revealed the underlying respectability of the service in the post-World War II world.

In all of these modes, however, the Army's impact was essentially unintended. Officers sought to build a more efficient service, and they collaborated to present their works before the public in the most favorable light. Thus, for example, they cooperated completely in the production of motion pictures that presupposed that the Army was a basically benevolent force in the society. And even those directors and writers who harbored personal dislikes for the military usually betrayed assumptions that the Army was, in the end, a necessity and an inevitability. In this way, the portrayal of the Army by civilians reflected back upon the service, endowing it with a greater institutional security than it had ever known before in peacetime. The final effect, then, of the Army upon popular culture was that it influenced culture most at the times of its own most popular acceptance, in World Wars I and II and their aftermaths, both immediately and when the veterans reached their nostalgic forties and beyond.

For Further Research

The best work on the Army's impact on American popular culture has been done by historians of sport, who have appropriately given more attention to sport than to the armed forces. The greater bulk of material available at present deals with the first three or four decades of the Twentieth Century. What has yet to be documented satisfactorily are the origins of sport in the Army during the Nineteenth Century, the creation of institutional channels for promoting sport under government auspices, and the development of sport in the Army after World War II.

Art critics and historians have left the greatest part of the Army's role in the visual arts untouched. In general, art specialists can find little to praise in the genres popular in the paintings and drawings produced through the services, and this judgment about the quality of the works has evidently yielded a lack of interest in studying their historical development. In recent years, social and even political historians have begun to pay attention to the place of art in politics. One must hope that social, art, and military historians will follow their lead.

Students of popular culture have started to explore the function and growth of comics, cartoon strips, and similar popular print media. Although there have been works dealing with military comics, these have usually been only impressionistic. Too often the important causal relationships have eluded the observers, and it is these that current historians need to detect. In what way did "comic culture" actually affect the Army, and in what ways did the Army intentionally or accidentally shape the popular periodicals?

The ultimately most important work on the Army and popular culture has yet to be written. After specific studies of small angles of the Army's impact appear, it will remain necessary to synthesize. What should appear is a general study of war culture and the Army's role as actor and object in its development.

SOURCES

Few historians have provided more than cursory or tangential comments on the Army's impact on popular culture, usually in the setting of broader social and cultural histories. A useful general survey dealing with the early part of the Twentieth Century is Preston W. Slosson, *The Great Crusade and After, 1914-1928* (Chicago, 1971), originally published in 1930. Also see Robert H. Boyle, *Sport — Mirror of American Life* (Boston, 1963).

Some of the most useful works, however, are contemporary accounts. For example, Edward F. Allen, *Keeping Our Fighters Fit: For War and After* (New York, 1918), argues a case for permanent physical education programs on a patriotic basis. In World War II, similarly, the education faculty of Stanford University collaborated to produce *Education in Wartime and After* (New York, 1943) which provided lengthy explanations of the military value of physical education and sport in the schools and in government camps.

There are numerous books on the history of film and many on the depiction of the Army in particular. Yet most of these are superficial, and relatively few even select satisfactory stills from the motion pictures. Most important, few aspire to explain the direct efforts of government agencies to sponsor films as propaganda or to record the Army's cooperation in the production of films. A brief but useful example of what can be done appears in Richard Shickel, *The Disney Version*, in which the author comments on Disney's promotion of the Army Air Forces in World War II through the creation of an animated version of Alexander deSeversky's *Victory Through Air Power* (New York, 1942). Also see the brief but useful comments on film-making in J. W. Fulbright, *The Pentagon Propaganda Machine* (New York, 1970).

Frequently, the reader may glean useful information on the Army's impact on the culture by consulting works designed either to describe the civilian society during a war or to criticize the Army for unwarranted encroachments in time of peace. Richard Polenberg, *War and Society: The United States, 1941-1945* (Philadelphia, 1972), contains a worthwhile commentary on the social impact of the war. The more highly critical Fred J. Cook, *The Warfare State* (New York, 1962), also provides tangential information on the impact of the Army. Such works, however, must be read critically. Also see the tentative and inconclusive comments on the depiction of the Army in film and on the social uses of film for the service in David Manning White and Richard Averson, *The Celluloid Weapon: Social Comment in the American Film.*

The important research that remains to be done will depend on a substantial exploration of primary documents which are now largely available. Some of the best repositories are the National Archives in Washington and the Franklin D. Roosevelt and Harry S. Truman presidential libraries. Only through a study of agency documents and personal correspondence will the full rationale behind the Army's movement into American popular culture emerge.

The 800,000-pound testing machine at Watertown Arsenal had also the capacity to measure the strength of a single horsehair; this shows the control console. (NARS 156-WA-72A)

Chapter 8

THE ARMY AND THE

DEVELOPMENT OF TECHNOLOGY

James J. Stokesberry

Technology is "know-how": knowledge expressed in machines and applied to raw materials to achieve a finished product or desired result. The term technology should not be confined to the processes and applications alone, but must include the knowledge — how it is acquired, how it is applied, and how it is transferred, developed, and changed.

The United States Army has been a constant participant in the development of American technology. The Army's interest springs from the very requirements to support military force — the providing of arms, equipment, food, clothing, transportation, and communications. In satisfying these needs, the Army has consciously advanced American technology, but also at times has unexpectedly and unconsciously contributed significantly to non-military technology.

The Army's historical contribution to education, especially engineering education, in the United States is of great importance. During the early part of the Nineteenth Century, American engineers either came from Europe, were self-taught or the products of on-the-job training, or were graduates of the United States Military Academy at West Point.

The U.S. Military Academy began in 1802 when Congress authorized the Corps of Engineers to train a number of cadets at the Engineer depot at West Point, New York. By 1815, the then full-fledged Military Academy had engineering courses in its curriculum. In the years that followed, the Military Academy became the agency of the transfer of the best engineering knowledge then available, from France to the United States. French engineers were hired for the faculty, and native-born faculty members were sent to France to study French civil as well as military projects.

Although the United States had two rather embryonic schools of civil engineering (Rensselaer Polytechnic Institute at Troy, New York, and Norwich University in Vermont), the U.S. Military Academy was for a generation the only major educational institution offering academic training in the field. Many of its graduates left the Army for civilian service soon after graduation. Some went on to distinguished careers in engineering (surveying for and supervising the construction of the nation's railroads, for example), while others became professors in America's then emerging schools of engineering.

On 13 July 1866, the Military Academy changed its curriculum to one of general education, but in the same year, Engineer officers established the Essayons Club at Willets Point, New York, for the continued development and application of engineering principles. This effort produced the first practical electrically controlled system of submarine mines and was succeeded by the Engineer School of Application, which was officially recognized by the War Department in 1885 and moved to Washington, D.C., in 1901. Its students were West Point graduates who received instruction in military, civil, electrical, and mechanical engineering, field astronomy, and geodetic surveying. It was renamed the Engineer school in 1904 and relocated to its present location (Fort Belvoir) in Virginia. Although it became exclusively dedicated to military engineering in the period between the beginning of World War I and the close of World War II, after 1945 the curriculum was expanded to include instruction in river and harbor and flood control engineering.

But before 1800, the United States Army had been involved in technology. The U.S. government began a major effort in 1794 to encourage and foster domestic sources of armaments. In the development of this capability, so important to the national well being, certain innovations, when coupled with later developments, brought about the evolution of mass production techniques. Mass production, which came into fruition in the Twentieth Century and helped make the United States the most powerful nation in the world, grew from seeds planted in the Nineteenth Century. Some of those seeds are to be found in the history of the national armories.

The U.S. Army consisted of about 800 officers and men in 1789. Because an armed force of this size (and distribution — it was scattered along the Ohio river in various forts at that time) did not require an extensive support organization, the Board of Treasury had responsibility for procuring and purchasing military stores, and the Secretary of War was responsible for transporting, safekeeping, and distributing them. In 1794, Congress established the Office of Purveyor of Public Supplies in the

Treasury. This office operated the contract system which favored the low bidder.

Arms procurement, however, was in contrast to the contract purchase system. In 1793 Secretary of War Henry Knox recommended to the Congress that "the means upon which our safety may ultimately depend" be extended and perfected — reiterating Alexander Hamilton's conviction that the development of a domestic arms industry was essential to national independence. Congress responded by increasing the number of U.S. arsenals and magazines for the stockpiling of armaments and establishing the first national armory at Springfield, Massachusetts, and a second at Harper's Ferry (then in Virginia) later in that same year.

The mission of the armory in America was cooperative with private industry, rather than competitive, an imitative adoption of the English system of assembling arms in arsenals. Within the American armory, new weapons were invented and developed, and production methods (engineering) evolved. The armory maintained production skills and knowledge through programs of limited (but expandable) production, and became a source of technical advice and assistance to commercial manufacturers.

In 1798, when the United States began building up its armed forces for protection against hostile Indians and warring European powers, Connecticut inventor Eli Whitney contracted to produce 10,000 new muskets for the Army. Two years later, because he had produced only 500 muskets, Whitney was summoned to Washington to explain to a board of experts. There he unpacked various musket parts, placed them in sorted piles, and suggested that one of the board select one piece from each pile. Whitney then assembled the pieces into a finished musket. The principle underlying Whitney's dramatic demonstration in 1800 was manufacture with interchangeable parts. Whitney's accomplishment was also based in the water-powered machine tools he had developed to fashion the musket barrels and stocks. (Before this time, gunsmiths had built guns part by part, one at a time, no two guns exactly alike.)

Recent historical scholarship strongly suggests that Captain John H. Hall anticipated Whitney's system in the machines and methods he used at the Harper's Ferry armory. The idea of interchangeable parts was known in Eighteenth Century Europe, but Hall made it possible by providing the needed technical bases the technique required — power machinery especially designed for the work and the use of gauges to ensure measured uniformity of the pieces. The spread of the use of the technique probably owes much to Whitney, however, for the early essential elements of what became known as the "American system" of manufacture appeared and developed in the Connecticut Valley small arms industry.

The problem that the system of manufacture by interchangeable parts sought to meet was the lack of skilled labor. As Whitney's experience at the turn of the century showed, a great deal of effort had to go into the production of machine tools to make the idea work. Thus the milling machine, a distinctly American development in the field of machine tools, was developed and quickly put to work in the manufacture of small arms. Another tool, the grinding machine, previously used only in polishing and sharpening, proved useful in shaping metal parts. In 1821 Thomas Blanchard invented a machine that automatically carved out wooden gunstocks at Springfield Armory, and his duplicating principle was later applied to the manufacture of some of the metal components. Work at the armories also continued during the first half of the Nineteenth Century in the development and use of precision gauges — one gauge for each individual part, and sometimes a gauge for each step in shaping complex parts.

After 1830, the "American system" of manufacturing — complex mechanical devices produced in a series of sequential machine operations — flourished in industries beyond the arms-makers. The first industry to apply the idea was clock making. Eli Terry and Chauncey Jerome began making clocks, and later watches, with the system, which subsequently spread beyond Connecticut's boundaries. The concept was accepted by the laboring man as well as the manager, an important factor in the widening use of the system.

Manufacture by assembled interchangeable parts began an evolution towards mass production, but other elements were needed to fulfill the promise the system offered. In the 1870s, Chicago meat packers had introduced overhead conveyers that carried carcasses along a "disassembly line," and in the 1890s freight-car trucks were pulled along a track while workmen an scaffolds alongside completed the superstructures, each man carrying out an individually assigned task. The assembly line idea, based on the principle of division of labor, was brought to a conceptual efficiency through the efforts of Frederick Taylor, called the Father of Scientific Management. Taylor had earlier proved himself useful in the whole evolution of mass production by developing a high-speed tool steel. His work in the last decade of the Nineteenth Century — time and motion studies using stop watches and photography — and his planning and routing work in factory planning led to setting production standards.

It remained for someone to put all the elements together, and the newly forming automobile industry, unenslaved by tradition, offered the opportunity. Henry Ford founded the Ford Motor Company in 1903 using the techniques that we know now as mass production. Ford was imitated widely throughout the world, but mass production techniques, coupled with the United States' vast resources and energetic industries, proved the wonder of the world.

The Army's interest in effective techniques for producing small arms was paralleled by the desire for better materials for heavy artillery. This was expressed not only in efforts to better understand and control then existing types of metals and alloys, but also in the desire to develop entirely new materials, and it led, through a series of historical events, to a consciously conceived, long-term scientific program with purely civilian as well as military goals. The Army would contribute, in a quiet and unheralded way, to the everyday safety and well being of all Americans.

Repeated failures of iron led to mid-Nineteenth Century testing Programs. Wrought-iron T-rails, rarely lasting more than three months on busy routes, signalled their failure by causing painful and costly railroad wrecks. Bridges and cannon also proved unreliable. In 1844, a large wrought-iron gun disastrously exploded on board the Navy's U.S.S. *Princeton*, killing two Cabinet members who were on board at the time. The Army's Ordnance Department soon thereafter began a program of experiments to compare the available materials, reduce the variations in "standard" materials, and gather numerical data on which to base designs. During those same two decades preceding the Civil War, a solitary Ordnance officer, Thomas Jefferson Rodman, developed a method of hollow casting for large cannon which involved cooling the interior first to strengthen the mass through concentric tension produced by the different cooling rates. Rodman patented his process to American founders who produced the 10- and 15-inch columbiads — extremely reliable cannon. In his developmental work, Rodman also devised methods and devices to test the properties of his cast iron; these later provided the beginnings of the Watertown Arsenal's testing laboratory.

After 1870, steel began to emerge as a serious competitor to cast iron for cannon fabrication. The mild steel produced by Pittsburgh iron manufacturers using the Bessemer-Kelly process seemed extremely promising for rails and structural beams, but the exact strengths and weaknesses of the new material were not known.

In 1872, the American Society of Civil Engineers formed a special committee to convince Congress of the importance of a complete and thorough series of tests of American iron and steel. The necessity for determining the strengths and characteristics in the various forms employed in construction increased geometrically with greater production and proliferation of uses. The testing program envisioned by the American Society of Civil Engineers far outstripped the resources — both financial and of scientific talent — of "any private individual or corporation."

Congress's first response, although far short of what the civil engineers felt was adequate, did provide some hope. The Army appropriations bill for 1873 provided $25,000 for "improved machinery and instruments for testing." The civil engineers continued to press for a comprehensive program. Then in 1875, Congress voted to establish the "United States Board on the Testing of Iron, Steel, and Other Metals," and appropriated $50,000 for the Board's work. The engineers appointed to the Board were prominent men, both military and civilian.

But the Congressional enthusiasm turned out to be short-lived. In the very next year, Congress voted $19,396.98 "to complete the work of the Board." Although the number and usefulness of the tests actually conducted by the Board were severely foreshortened, the Board had ordered an elaborate testing machine to be built on contract by Alfred H. Emery. Emery's machine was not finished when the Board ran out of money and time, but it became the legacy that ultimately fulfilled the Board's purposes.

The sudden demise of the Board posed a dilemma as to the fate of the yet unfinished machine. The Army members of the Board felt that the machine should be completed, for it would be extremely useful in ordnance work. The civil engineers pointed out that the machine had been ordered under the auspices of the Board and should also be available to them as well as the Army. In 1878, Congress authorized the machine to be set up at Watertown Arsenal and "applied to the testing of iron and steel for all persons who may desire to use it upon the payment of a suitable fee."

In 1879 the machine was completed and ready for its acceptance test. Emery had produced something quite beyond the expectations of the men who had ordered it. The huge machine, its one end held stationary in a firm foundation, could hydraulically exert up to 800,000 pounds of force with its movable portion, which ran on railroad tracks.

The acceptance test began. A hard iron link was stretched to its breaking point — the machine's scale read 722,000 pounds of pull. Then a single horse hair was placed in the machine's holders. It snapped at a registered pull of only one pound (this was precisely confirmed in a check test with weights). The United States had a machine of great power, accuracy, and delicacy. Emery had overbuilt and overspent in his effort, and so he subsequently petitioned Congress for additional payment beyond the contractual price. Happily, upon receiving proof of Emery's expenses, Congress agreed to award the additional compensation.

The Congressional solution of civilian access to the machine, now styled the "United States Testing Machine," provided only "meagre results" in regard to the testing of structural materials, or so the civil engineers claimed. In 1883, the Army appropriations act officially recognized the American Society of Civil Engineers and provided that any program of tests submitted by that society should be carried out by the Ordnance Department.

The United States Testing Machine made some 114,158 separate tests in the years between 1882 and 1917. Of this number, 27,096 were performed for (and paid for by) individuals or individual enterprises (e.g., railroad companies). The tests made for the program of the American Society of Civil Engineers provided data from which engineers and professors of engineering deduced formulae. Emery, in testifying before the U.S. Senate's Select Committee on Ordnance and Warships on 8 August 1884, stated that certain iron columns, almost 30 feet long, were crushed longitudinally in the machine with a force between one-fifth and one-third of the equivalent strength credited to them in standard engineering texts. The earlier computations had been based upon tests of small sections of like columns made in small testing machines.

The results of the tests made between 1882 and 1917 were published annually as *Tests of Metals*. Many of the tests, both military and civilian, were concerned with the basic steel-making and forming processes themselves and were also of critical importance in comparing newly created alloys. For example, one military series concerned the physical properties and microstructure of steel castings — green (untreated), annealed, and heat treated.

American railroads found the machine useful in testing rails. After the Civil War, of the 12 early steel-making ventures begun before 1881, all used the Bessemer-Kelly-Mushet process, and 10 of the 12 concentrated their output in steel rails. Railroad men were involved in bringing the first Bessemer plant to Pennsylvania, for they had been long troubled by the cost of maintaining iron rails, were impressed by the promise of steel (longer lasting and greater load-bearing capacity than iron), and irritated by the price of English steel rails.

The demand for domestic rails spurted early, from 1867 to 1873, then subsided for five years, and then resumed a ten-year upward trend after 1878. The Pennsylvania steel makers, constantly improving their production techniques, met, and then surpassed the demand for rails. But the steel rail makers had chosen the protection of the tariff, foregoing the scientific effort necessary to improve the quality of their steel — the American steel rail remained decidedly inferior to the British rail.

The Bessemer process was not well suited to America's highly phosphorous ores. The Siemens-Martin process, also known as the open-hearth process, had been developed in Europe, and was adopted by competing American steel makers after 1878. When tested on the United States Testing Machine, the open-hearth rails proved to be of consistently higher quality. In 1893, the production of steel by open hearth surpassed that of the Bessemer-using group.

Architects and engineers discovered the relative strengths of various types of joints, and the properties of wood, concrete, marble, and even the adhesion of nails in various materials. The machine tested cables, tires, etc. Notably, it tested concrete for the construction of the Washington Monument in the nation's capitol and parts from the Brooklyn Bridge.

The United States Testing Machine continued in use from its original installation in 1879 to about 1963. It contributed to basic scientific knowledge about steel and other materials by full-scale measurement of construction members, and thus provided a way of checking and controlling the basic processes for creating and shaping the materials. The U.S. Testing Machine was eventually eclipsed as new machines were developed, and the organizational function of such testing changed with the establishment of the U.S. Bureau of Standards in Washington near the beginning of the Twentieth Century. As the Bureau of Standards widened its activities and increased its physical plant, it took over a large portion of the civilian tests.

This transfer of service functions, primarily civilian in character, to newly created arms of the federal government, was not confined to the testing of materials. The Army Signal Corps had operated the first national weather service until near the end of the Nineteenth Century, when the service was first transferred to the Department of Agriculture. It was subsequently made the primary mission of an entirely new arm of the government, the United States Weather Bureau. Removal of these functions useful to the non-military culture signalled a fundamental change in the character of the United States military establishment and the expectation of more specialized military research and development.

The U.S. Army's interest in food technology (the processing, preservation, and packaging of raw foods) has grown with the changing nature of warfare. The first uniform ration for the American soldier, set by Congress in November 1775, was issued daily, uncooked. Preparing the meal was left up to the individual soldier. And these rations were not always supplied; Nineteenth Century soldiers often sustained life by foraging the surrounding countryside. But as the armies grew larger, the battlefields more barren, and the battles more often day-into-night affairs, the need for pre-prepared rations intensified.

The canners might be called the first producers of convenience foods — blended, mixed, or combined ingredients to replace comparable products of "home cooking." Canning remains today as an extremely reliable method of long-term preservation of many protein foods. Canned foods had gained some popularity in the late 1840s when canned corn, tomatoes, green peas, and fish guaranteed subsistence to Gold Rush travelers. The Civil War brought canned foods to the battlefield where conditions demanded dependable prepared foods which needed little or no cooking. But canned foods were hardly preferred to "home cooking," for General William Tecumseh Sherman noted that during his famous march to the sea, his men were supplied with all sorts of patent compounds, including "desecrated vegetables and consecrated milk."

But the Civil War did stimulate the American canning industry, for many soldiers and sailors returned to civilian life accustomed to eating canned products. The canning industry expanded in the late 1860s with several new canneries in the Midwest, and in California in the next decade. And, in 1880, California canneries began shipping their goods to England.

The Army's rations in the Spanish-American War differed little from those of the Civil War except the unpopular crackerlike biscuit known as hardtack was finally abolished. But after 1900, emergency rations were issued to those troops on border service and those fighting Indians. These rations included an evaporated, powdered beef, a little sweetened chocolate, and a parched, cooked wheat. This ration remained with the Army into World War I. But the conditions of trench warfare — dampness and toxic gases — spurred work on more reliable containers. The French Army's solution to the problem of getting hot food to the soldiers in the front lines led to the popularization of the vacuum container or Thermos bottle. World War II saw the development of several new rations, the best known being the C-ration (for combat) and the K-ration (for paratroopers). Emphasis, despite widespread joking and griping among military personnel, was on nutrition and palatability while meeting needs for compactness and durability. The canned meat product SPAM is a well known example of the World War II effort.

After World War II, consideration of nuclear age requirements led to the establishment of The Quartermaster Food and Container Institute for the Armed Forces in Chicago, Illinois, in 1945. The Institute coordinated research and development programs of some 80 colleges, universities, and private foundations and about 500 industrial organizations. By 1950, the program had developed foods capable of withstanding long storage, had improved dehydrated, reconstitutable food products, and had studied the effects on foods of long-term storage at extreme temperatures.

One interface between the Army and civilian society is the training of technicians. Here a major checks the work of a private in the 3rd Signal Company, 3rd U.S. Infantry Division, 1954. (USA)

The Army's role as an inspired consumer in the American market for products and inventions bears examination. The telegraph, telephone, radio, and electric power are examples of the Army's adoption of ideas that had already or would soon become commercially successful in this nation. Although the technological reciprocity in these cases is not always obvious, it should be noted that military requirements often demanded greater ruggedness and long-term reliability (e.g., portable radio transmitter-receiver sets) than normal peacetime, civilian needs. Each of these innovations in the Army served to create a body of expert knowledge which then flowed back into civilian society.

The Army and the technical development of the airplane, and also the pioneering efforts Army fliers made in certain peacetime applications for the flying machines, warrant special notice. The dramatic progress of aeronautical design in the half century following the Wright brothers' successful first flight in 1903 can be attributed in part to the willingness of the United States to support the effort for national security reasons and the dedication of the Army officers directly involved.

The Wright brothers made their first sale to the Army Signal Corps in 1909. Subsequently, during World War I the plane developed from an open framework scout to a primitive fighter-bomber. In the following peacetime years, Army fliers engaged in a number of demonstrations that served to test and develop the airplane. They made cross-country flights, set altitude, speed, endurance, and safety records, and made a round-the-world flight in 1924. In 1932, an Army Air Force captain made the first solo flight entirely on instruments. These and other experiments helped develop the airplane to its potentials.

The opportunities offered by the development of the airplane for military purposes were similar to peacetime needs. Size and range are two very important characteristics for bombers, for example. But these same two attributes are also critically important to profitable passenger and cargo operations, to deliver maximum pay loads to faraway destinations.

After World War I, Army fliers found several ways to make themselves useful to peacetime endeavors. Although their part in the early days of the air mail service is fairly well known, other pioneering activities deserve our notice. In 1919, 17 Army planes flew fire patrol missions in California and Oregon, aiding in extinguishing more than 500 fires. In 1921, Lieutenant Alex Pearson made the first aerial survey of the Grand Canyon in Arizona. Subsequently, during World War II, the Army Air Forces Aeronautical Chart Service developed the Trimetrogen system of aerial photography. This system used a method of conic projection, which replaced the time-worn Mercator projection system, and made further

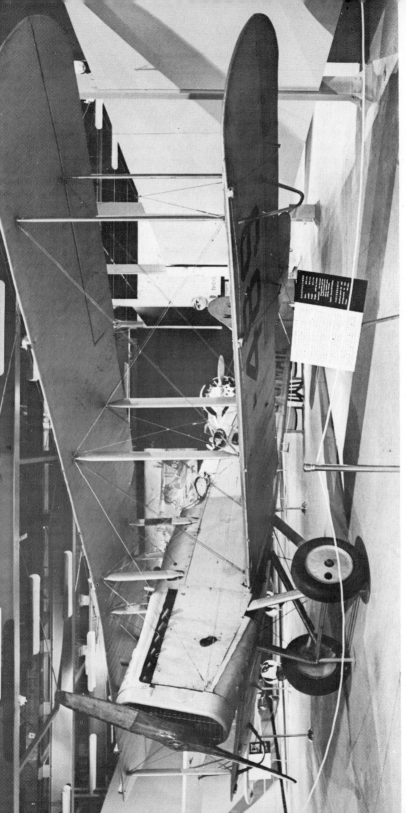

The strides made by aviation in the early days were heavily influenced by Army purchasing power and the demands of the service. Before 1941 the Air Force was part of the United States Army, so it is natural that this surviving DH-4 should be housed in the new Air Force Museum at Wright-Patterson AFB, Ohio. (Air Force Museum)

advances in the entire field of photogrammetry (making maps with photography).

The Army fliers teamed with the Chemical Warfare Service during the 1920s to pioneer agricultural flying in the United States. In 1921, an Army plane treated fruit trees near Dayton, Ohio, which were infested with catalpa sphinx larvae. On 3 May 1923 the Army successfully demonstrated that liquids could be sprayed from a plane, and on 2 June 1924 Congress appropriated $25,000 for the Chemical Warfare Service to destroy boll weevils by spraying American cotton fields. By 1960, agricultural flying in the United States had grown to some 5,000 planes treating 61,000,000 acres of cropland.

Generally speaking, civil aviation moved ahead of military aviation in the late 1920s and early 1930s with the development of the Ford Trimotor and the Martin China Clipper. But World War II and the Cold War eras greatly stimulated the military developments once again. The jet engine, produced late in World War II in the German effort and further developed in England, became the mainstay of the United States aviation effort; after 1959, the traveling public could enjoy the benefits of all-weather flights in comfortable pressurized cabins at rates of speed unthought of 50 years earlier.

The Twentieth Century, with a highly organized military establishment in the United States, has produced "spin-offs" — developments that have been directly adopted for civilian needs. World War II research (jointly between Great Britain and the U.S. Navy) successfully produced radar, which has become the basis for air-traffic control, so essential to air operations of modern high-speed aircraft. The same era produced atomic power, which has yet to prove itself as an unobjectionable source of electric power. Some less spectacular developments, for example servomechanisms (relay devices that operate automatic controls in complex mechanisms), have proven useful in peacetime machines such as computers. Other military innovations may take years to find a niche in civilian life. Such a case is "piggy-back" hauling. The Army's Quartermaster Department, in the 1870s, when transcontinental railroads first began seriously competing with wagon trains as a means of getting supplies to outposts in the West, combined the best features of each by lashing wagons on railroad flatcars — the first such haul.

Another military development, the rugged four-wheel drive Jeep, has proved useful in civilian life. Conceptualized by Colonel Arthur W.S. Herrington who had served in World War I as a transportation officer, the all-wheel drive vehicle was further developed by Captain Robert G. Howie, and demonstrated by Herrington in 1940. The American Bantam Car Company was selected to build the Jeep for the Army, but the demand soon outstripped the small company's capacity, and Ford and Willis-Overland were brought into the picture. After 1945, Willis-Overland (later Kaiser Motors) introduced several models of the jeep for peacetime uses. Another example of Army-developed equipment finding peaceful uses is the modern camping equipment and cold-weather clothing developed through the efforts of the Army. On 4 February 1943, the Quartermaster Climatic Research Laboratory was established at Lawrence, Massachusetts, marking the beginning of continuous scientific study of the relationships between the human body, clothing, and climatic extremes. The laboratory's researches have given American civilians warm, comfortable clothing for camping, hiking, and skiing.

U.S. Army audio-visual instruction, a highly effective teaching method, also has greatly influenced American education. Many audio-visual techniques and materials in use today in American classrooms and industry were developed by the Army in World War II, in response to the challenge of training millions in a very short time. Motion pictures were used as training films, models and diagrams helped personnel understand complex machines, slide projectors flashed silhouettes to teach instant recognition of enemy tanks and planes, etc, and maps and terrain models aided in planning operations and in briefing participants. War games, long used by the military to develop strategies, became management games in 1957 and have proved useful to American business, industry, and local governments. The very size and complexity of some military projects in World War II and the years since have developed in some Army personnel an expertise in planning and managing large-scale projects.

The story of the Army's development of computer technology is interesting in itself. The Army computer was made possible by other developments, some of which were themselves "spin-offs." The first true electronic digital computer was the Electronic Numerical Integrator and Computer (ENIAC), designed and built for the Army under the direction of J. Presper Eckert and John W. Mauchly at the Moore School of Electrical Engineering at the University of Pennsylvania. Finished in 1946, it was installed at Aberdeen Proving Ground in Maryland to perform ballistics calculations. ENIAC could multiply two 10-decimal numbers in less than three-thousandths of a second. Its physical makeup was large and bulky, consuming a room approximately 20 by 40 feet. ENIAC's electronic ancestry includes work in the radio (tubes), the telephone, and, of more recent origins, pulsed circuitry from the research effort that produced radar. ENIAC's successor, installed in 1950, was the first stored-memory computer.

When civilian applications were sought for these "electronic brains," size and cost of manufacture became critical. But the World War II research effort had, in the development of the proximity fuse (an electronic device placed inside explosive shells and bombs which detonated the warhead when within a certain distance of a target), met the drastic needs for compactness with the printed circuit. A system such as in this fuse — cheaper, more uniform and more compact than tubes and wires — proved most useful in adapting electronic computers to peacetime in the 1950s and also became invaluable to space technology.

After 1950, as military research and development projects became more complex and more expensive, more interest was shown in identifying potential civilian uses before the military effort was fully undertaken. Project Plowshare — the Atomic Energy Commission's program exploring peaceful uses of nuclear explosives is a recent example of the national aspiration to effectively harness powerful military technology for peaceful purposes.

Suggestions for Further Research

The metallurgical and chemical research conducted in the Army's arsenals and armories during the Nineteenth and early Twentieth Centuries built up a body of basic knowledge useful in American industry. Not only do the laboratories in the arsenals need to be studied, but also the contact points with various industries. The Ordnance Department regularly assigned inspectors to the DuPont Company's gunpowder works, for example, and some of these inspectors conducted their own research programs, using the company's facilities. Under study, the workings of the armories may yield additional examples of technological contributions to industry. In regard to vehicles, the caterpillar tractor-tank-bulldozer relationship should prove interesting. The Army also developed vehicles for service in snowy regions. Did the "Weasel's" development lead directly to the snowmobile?

The Quartermaster's Department has in its history many examples of useful developments and ideas in the fields of transportation, storage, and distribution. The Corps of Engineers was constantly involved in large-scale projects, many of which demanded unique engineering solutions. The Corps' history should also be examined for the development of management skills. The Army Air Forces' work in developing aerial photography to a high art should also be examined.

In technological history, the scientific principles do not change; rather the context in which they can be applied is the variable. For example, the M-61 Vulcan machine gun developed in the 1960s by General Electric owed much to the study of a museum specimen — the Gatling Gun of the Nineteenth Century. Perhaps useful but less deadly examples might be found in the history of how the United States Army responded to changing needs in various situations.

SOURCES

An excellent survey of research in the government is A. Hunter Dupree, *Science and the Federal Government: A History of Policies and Activities to 1940* (Cambridge, Mass., 1957). "Spin-offs" are treated in Everett M. Rogers, *Diffusion of Innovations* (New York, 1962), and Richard S. Rosenbloom, *Technology Transfer-Process and Policy* (Washington, D.C., 1965).

The impact of the United States Military Academy on American engineering and education is thoroughly discussed in Forest G. Hill, *Roads, Rails and Waterways* (Norman, Okla., 1957).

The most useful general survey of the development of American technology is to be found in Kranzberg and Pursell, eds., *Technology in Western Civilization*, 2 vols. (New York, 1967). Brooke Hindle, *Technology in Early America* (Chapel Hill, N.C., 1966), delivers a first-rate bibliography of military technology and points out the difficulty: "The force of the military impulse can be conveniently dissipated" by scattering its effects among various disciplines, manufacturing techniques, chemical technology, engineering, etc.

The Army's role in developing mass production techniques is drawn from "Interchangeable Mechanism," *United States Census: Report on the Manufactures of the United States* (1880), II (Washington, D.C., 1883), and Robert S. Woodbury's prize-winning article, "The Legend of Eli Whitney and Interchangeable Parts," *Technology and Culture*, I, Summer 1960, 235-253. Another article on the subject is John E. Sawyer, "The Social Basis of the American System of Manufacturing," *Journal of Economic History*, 14, 1954, 361-379. Early fundamental contributions of government armories are presented in *The National Armories: A Review of the System of Superintending, Civil and Military, Particularly with Reference to Economy and General Management at the Springfield Armory* (Springfield, Mass., 1852).

The story of the United States Testing Machine is based on various issues of *Proceedings of the American Society of Civil Engineers*, 1872 to 1906, and *Report of the United States Board Appointed to Test Iron, Steel and Other Metals*, 2 vols. (Washington, D.C., 1881). *Report of the Select Committee on Ordnance and Warships* (Washington, D.C., 1886) provides a view of the American steel industry in the mid 1880s. *Men, Machines and Modern Times* by Elting Morison (Cambridge, Mass., 1966) adds perspective.

The history of the Army Quartermaster effort is treated in Erna Risch, *Quartermaster Support of the Army: A History of the Corps, 1775-1939* (Washington, D.C., 1962).

Two unpublished works detail the labors of two interesting Army officers: Edward C. Ezell, "The Development of Artillery for the United States Land Service Before 1861: With Emphasis on the Rodman Gun," (M.A. Thesis, University of Delaware, 1963), and Stanley L. Falk, "Soldier-Technologist: Major Alfred Mordecai and the Beginnings of Science in the United States Army," (Doctoral Dissertation, Georgetown University, 1959).

Being in the National Guard provides not only pay, but camaraderie and experience. Here Iowa guardsmen undergo ski training at Camp Ripley, Minnesota, in February 1975. (Iowa NG)

Chapter 9

THE ARMY AND THE ECONOMY:
IOWA AS A CASE STUDY

Alvin R. Sunseri

Most Americans probably have little idea of the depths of the Army's relation to the economy and the extent of their dependence on defense expenditures. Indeed, rare is the individual who is not benefiting in some way from his or her involvement, directly or indirectly, with the military establishment.

In determining the *real* impact of defense expenditures on the economy, it is necessary to stop thinking in terms of the Gross National Product (GNP), for although economists have made this concept the fount of all economic truth as a standard of measurement, it conceals the full impact of defense spending upon the economy. For instance, although the percentage of GNP allotted to the Pentagon has decreased, the *amount* of dollars spent has increased.

In order to develop a more penetrating analysis of the impact of the defense organization, and at the same time develop a more effective method of measuring the extent of American reliance on Pentagon dollars, I have designed a more accurate measurement system. This involves microcosmic analysis of restricted regions and has been employed thus far for Colorado, Illinois, Michigan, New Hampshire, Bernalillo County, New Mexico, and Black Hawk County, Iowa. The vague term "the Military-Industrial Complex" is broken down into sectors that interrelate and feed upon each other. Thus the related complexity of the whole and the relationship between the sectors and their dependency on each other can be seen. The following table indicates the various components of what is commonly called the Military-Industrial Complex.

In developing this research project I have chosen to employ the multiple sector concept in Iowa in an effort to determine the impact of defense expenditures on the economy of this state.

MILITARY - INDUSTRIAL COMPLEX

Military	Industrial	Technological	Labor	Academic	Managerial	Political
Regular services Reserves and National Guard Veteran's organizations Veteran's Administration	Direct and indirect (contractors and sub-contractors) Beneficiaries	Research and development personnel Think-tank institutes	Direct and indirect beneficiaries	Research and development Contracts to universities ROTC	Advertising and other specialists Civil Service advisors Defense Supply Agency personnel	President Senators Congressmen Lobbyists Governors

Iowa, with a population of 2,853,000 (1973 estimate), ranks 25th in the nation in size. Fifty-seven percent of that population is classified as urban, whereas forty-three percent (much above the national norm) remains in rural areas. The Gross State Product (GSP) is $14,000,000,000 (1973), ranking it 20th in the nation. Iowa is encouraging industry to move into the state. Forty-seven percent of its economy is based on manufacturing, with the leading products including food processing products, engines, and electrical machinery. Only one percent of the economic activity involves the mining industry. Despite this trend towards industrialization, the state remains the breadbasket of the United States, with fifty-two percent of its economy yet agrarian in nature. The four leading products are beef, hogs, corn, and soybeans. Also, many other lesser dairy and farm products are produced and raised.

Why then did I choose to test my concept in Iowa? The state was chosen because so many people accept the idea that Iowa's economy is basically agrarian and thus cannot be too involved in Military-Industrial Complex operations. Indeed, when in 1972 the Director of the Iowa Development Commission was asked for his estimate of defense expenditures in the state, he described them as being inconsequential — forming less than one percent of Iowa's economy. Consequently, if a significantly greater dependence on defense dollars could be discovered in the state, I reasoned that individuals in other states might be concerned enough to discover the extent of the dependency of their state economies on Army expenditures and what were the benefits (if any) derived from such expenditures.

In Iowa, the military sector of the economy is dominated by the activities of the Army including the following components: 1) the Active

Army; 2) the National Guard and Reserve components; 3) the veterans and veterans' organizations such as the American Legion, Veterans of Foreign Wars, and the Amvets; and 4) the various governmental agencies designed to support the services and assist veterans. Each must be examined separately if one is to discover the relationships between these sectors as well as the impact of the Army on the lives of Iowans.

The number of men on active duty in Iowa has seldom exceeded 400 to 500 in recent years. They are, for the most part, the recruiters stationed in urban centers and advisers to National Guard and Reserve units located throughout the state. In addition, there are ROTC units present on two campuses in Iowa. This last group will be examined as part of the academic sector of the Military-Industrial Complex.

In fiscal 1973, the total active Army payroll in Iowa was $38,092,000. Moreover, $18,598,000 was spent on civilian pay (managerial sector) and "business needs" (rentals, supplies, and utilities) as well as on advertising and other methods employed to recruit individuals into the armed forces. The want-ad pages of all leading newspapers are filled with recruiting ads placed by Reserve and regular components. In all, over $600,000 is allocated for newspaper and billboard advertising in Iowa.

The largest military component in Iowa is the National Guard and inactive Reserve. Here, the federal government acts as a paymaster for a vast number of men in many key areas of the state. Federal funds totaling $18,586,000 were furnished to the National Guard and Reserves during fiscal year 1973. Also added was $28,882,645 allocated for equipment for the Guard. In addition, Iowa's expenditures for fiscal 1973 totalled $1,680,848. These figures do not include the funds appropriated for the construction of armories in Iowa, which is financed by both state (25 percent) and federal (75 percent) funds. Because of legal technicalities, however, the funding averages 35 percent for the state and 65 percent for the federal government. The 64th General Assembly appropriated $480,000 for Army construction and rehabilitation, and the federal government allowed an expenditure of $1,390,000. For the years 1974 and 1978, five armories, costing a total of $4,195,000, are slated for construction in the state. Unfortunately, there are no total dollar-value figures available for the present Army and Air National Guard installations. One officer, however, who is a realtor, suggested a conservative figure of $125,000,000.

The financial impact of the National Guard upon Sioux City and Des Moines is significant, for the total Army and Air National Guard Payrolls in fiscal 1973 were $1,623,000 and $4,175,140, respectively. Moreover, in Iowa 52 communities have 83 100-man units with annual payrolls of

$125,000 each. Thus, a total of $12,298,000 (fiscal 1973 figures) is injected into the economies of these 52 communities.

In the case of the Iowa reserve and Active military sectors, the $56,678,000 that is allowed to float in the state must be multiplied by 1.56 in order to discover the real impact of the outpouring of Pentagon dollars into the state. For in conservatively employing the Charles T. Kindleberger technique, which deals with inter-economy transactions of the multiplier effect, I reached the conclusion that each dollar coming into the state results in $1.56 being generated into the state economy

$$\frac{1}{1-b(1-t)+n} = \frac{1}{1-9(.8)} = .15(9)(.8) = \frac{1}{.64} = 1.56$$

The multiplier refers to the fact that a permanent increase in government expenditures will permanently increase the annual income stream by some multiple of the government increase, as much of the money appropriated is spent again and again in Iowa. For example, in one instance, an Army appropriation of $19,000,000 flowed into the state. Out of each dollar coming to Iowa only 30 cents is to purchase equipment and supplies outside the state; this leaves 70 cents to be spent in the state. Considering that the contractor, as is normal for a service-type business, pays out over 60 percent of his total budget in wages and salaries, this 70 cents appears conservative.

Thus, $1 crosses the state line, and 70 cents goes to Iowa residents and businesses. Then, the federal government calls for about 16 percent of that for income taxes and social security payments. The 70 cents shrinks to 59 cents — the actual added disposable income in the hands of Iowa men and women.

Here again, however, it cannot all be kept in the state. The worker's wife buys sugar grown and processed in Colorado, and the fuel oil used to heat his home and power his car was pumped out of wells half-way around the world. In all, about 70 percent of the disposable income in Iowa is spent on goods and services (management, labor, overhead charges on items imported and handled by local merchants) produced in the state. So the 59 cents is finally down to about 42 cents that really remains to circulate.

Here the story begins to brighten and the figures grow again. The 42 cents circulates and recirculates, being spent and respent. Even though the federal government and the out-of-state producers get their cuts on each transaction, the spending and respending of what is left creates $1.56

in personal income (conservative estimate) for each dollar that originally came in across the state line. This generation of income at each step is recognized by economists and called a "multiplier process."

With the 1.56 figure as the income multiplier, what happens to the original total of $19,000,000 coming into the state? It can be expected to generate personal income for Iowa residents — after allowing for out-of-state purchases and federal taxes.

The veterans in Iowa number 386,000 with the majority having served in the Army. As an organized group with posts in over 500 towns, they represent a potent social force as well as an extremely powerful political grouping. Indeed, the Selective Service System has solicited the support of veterans to insure registration for the draft, and Nixon chose Iowa Legionnaire Donald Johnson to head the Veterans Administration.

More closely related to this paper is the fact that these veterans receive a total of $168,441,126. Moreover, these compensations, pensions, readjustment payments, and loan dollars that are pumped into Iowa by the VA are prime dollars because they are not taxable. Hence, by the application of the multiplier effect, $168,441,126 minus $16,500,000 (money saved by recipients) plus deduction of $75,000,000 spent on imports into the state from other states, results in $76,941,126 added to the economy. One then adds the $75,000,000 spent on construction and hospital administration to arrive at a total sum of $151,941,126 (rounded) that must be multiplied by the 1.56 multiplier. In addition, because the $168,000,000 are prime dollars, they too are added to the total sum. In the end, $405,000,000 annually is added to the Iowa economy by the Veteran's Administration through expenditures on ex-servicemen drawn for the most part from the ranks of Army veterans. Add to that sum the amount spent on the National Guard/Reserves and regular units following the application of the multiplier effect, and the figure now totals $493,886,962, exclusive of state appropriations and the value of defense installations. Finally, the $17,600,000 annually paid to professional retirees in the state must be included in the total spent by the Pentagon on the military in Iowa. When multiplied, this figure reads $27,500,000. As a consequence, when added to the VA and other Department of Defense expenditures, the sum equals $521,500,000, amounting to close to four percent of the Gross State Product of Iowa.

Army dollars are also important to Iowa's industry. Two methods were used to determine the extent of this dependence: interviews and correspondence with industrialists, and qualitative and quantitative analyses of the data that was gathered. One frustration encountered was the discovery that firms with contracts less than $10,000 were not listed by the Department of Defense and could not be included in the survey.

Guardsmen may also enjoy two weeks of summer training as these Iowans are at Camp Dodge in July 1974. (Iowa NG)

Hence, the framework within which the inquiry was conducted includes only larger firms who responded to the questionnaires or agreed to be interviewed. Moreover, the responses were varied and ranged from an attitude of cooperation to a notable reluctance to tell the truth. By April 1974, 52 percent of the firms contacted had responded to the queries addressed to them orally or in written form.

One of the more obvious examples of community dependence on Army expenditures in Iowa is Burlington, the home of the Iowa Army Ammunition Plant. Even before applying the multiplier effect, its Army contracts amounted to nearly $34,000,000 in fiscal 1973. Cedar Rapids and Waterloo are also highly dependent upon Army expenditures. The Chamberlain Manufacturing Corporation of Waterloo received $16,000,000 in Army contracts for the fiscal year 1972, and Collins Radio of Cedar Rapids received $59,000,000. If multiplied by 1.56, the impact on the Iowa economy in these three cities alone is increased to $170,000,000.

In the aftermath of the completion of the industrial sector investigation, I came to the conclusion that 10.5 percent of the revenues of the *responding* firms were based on military expenditures with 8 percent being Army dollars. All firms indicated some percentage of revenue from defense contracts, with the lowest being one-fourth of one percent and the highest 85 percent of total income. Also, the large industries indicated they were more dependent on Pentagon dollars in 1973 than three years before.

When the multiplier effect is employed, it becomes obvious that the economic benefits of Army contracts varies from town to town. The total income generated by the multiplier effect, however, is of such magnitude that its absence would cause economic stagnation and depression not only in the city in which the firm is located, but at the state and regional levels as well. One cannot expect industry to lose over 10 percent of its revenue and the entire state not experience some type of repercussion. Thus, Iowa industry is significantly dependent upon defense contracts. But how important is its dependence? The following suggestion is made. Industries in Iowa that receive Army contracts over a period of time develop a reliance on those contracts as an additional source of revenue. Once established, this source becomes an integral part of the total revenue, and its loss would cause economic hardship. Such a process is not conspiratorial nor is it deliberate. Rather, it is part of a national tendency toward a realization of a rational economic goal — the accumulation of profits and security.

In investigating the impact of Army dollars on the industrial sector in Iowa, it was also possible to discover the significance of the technological sector on the economy of the state. For example, the research and development breakdown reveals that in Waterloo $2,110,000 was spent for research and development by the Army following the standard operating procedure of quantitative production at plants in times of war and qualitative production in times of peace. In Cedar Rapids, Collins Radio was awarded $1,634,000 towards R and D contracts. In addition to these two firms, Iowa industry received an additional $1,407,000 in research and development funds. Before the multiplier effect, a total of $4,151,000 was spent in the state in 1972 by the Army in contracts with firms responding to the questionnaires. After applying the multiplier, however, research and development projects in Iowa accelerated to $6,475,000. The economic spin-offs of such an expenditure on the Iowa economy is obviously quite significant.

Equally relevant to the Military-Industrial Complex project in Iowa are the inquiry results that were concerned with the relations between the Army and labor. As a prerequisite to this examination, an attempt was made to establish some framework for an appraisal of the defense work force. A totally accurate examination of dependence of labor on Army expenditures is not possible — but fairly reliable estimates were developed.

At least one percent of the Iowa work force is *directly* involved with production of defense-contracted products. Those involved in subcontracting among the respondents number approximately two percent. Therefore, at least three percent of Iowa labor is specifically employed in Army-related work. This figure is probably low because the estimate is based on responses from only 52 percent of the firms queried and does not include those with contracts of less than $10,000 per annum. Consequently, the dependence of Iowa labor on defense contracts at the community level looms even larger when one considers the survey is incomplete.

Many individual communities were analyzed in an attempt to determine the specifics of the dependence of workers upon the Army, with the multiplier effect also being utilized in this sector. With the small base population (2.8 million) that Iowa possesses, the relative aspects of the dependence of the community on defense-related contracts is as important as absolute figures. Unfortunately, this category is difficult to estimate for a variety of reasons. For example, Fischer Controls of Marshalltown subcontracts for items designed for both civil and military use. However, the contractors seldom reveal the intended disposal of the products. Consequently, it is suspected that a considerable number of employees in the state do not know if their jobs are in part dependent on Pentagon dollars.

Another facet deserving consideration is the fact that the history of some companies shows the Army contracts may have had such a great influence on production in the past as to form the foundation for the larger labor force of the present in certain areas. This concept is best exemplified by the Firestone Rubber Company of Des Moines. It evolved from the original 100 percent defense-oriented employment to less than two percent today. Because of the original orientation, an economic base of 2,500 jobs was constructed in Des Moines by 1972. The most interesting data was gathered in the studies of the dairies and meat-packing labor forces in Iowa. This information is pertinent when considered in the context of relations between workers employed in the state. For example, Army contractor Wells Blue Bunny Dairy in Le Mars has a market area of 200 miles radius from that town, because of the necessity for processing, transporting, and distributing their goods. Hence, an indeterminate number of jobs are affected by the amount, type, and terms of defense contracts with the dairy.

The most obvious example of nearly complete dependence of a community on Army contracts is Denison, Iowa. There, of the 200 workers employed by World Wide Meats in processing and packing meat, 104 are involved in defense-contract work. Because 22 percent of the manufacturing work in Denison is performed by this company, over 11 percent of the employees in Denison are defense dependent. As with the case of the dairy, when one considers the relation between the activities in the plant to all related activities (feeding, raising, slaughtering, processing, packing, transporting, grading, distributing, and sales management), one only begins to realize the immense negative impact on the regional economy that would result if the World Wide meat-packing plant were closed.

One last example of the dependence of Iowa's economy on the Army involves the migrant workers who harvest vegetables and potato crops in more than a dozen Iowa counties. Thousands of bushels grown in the northern counties and picked by migrant workers are sold only to the Army. Consequently, many of the 3,000 migrants brought to Iowa each year engage in such work.

The conclusions to be drawn from this sector would certainly be more lucid if a greater number of firms had responded to the questionnaires. The evidence, however, clearly shows that a substantial segment of Iowa labor in various communities and rural regions is dependent upon Army contracts. The spin-offs in employment resulting from these contracts are extensive enough to make the state sufficiently dependent upon the Army and other defense contracts to suggest that it would experience serious economic consequences if these contracts were canceled.

Consideration of the academic sector indicates that the University of Iowa, the University of Northern Iowa, Drake University, Iowa State University, and the 25 other private colleges and universities in Iowa receive a variety of military defense funds from the federal government and thus are directly and indirectly involved in the Military-Industrial Complex. Further money is channeled through the following agencies to the campuses: Atomic Energy Commission, Department of Defense, National Aeronautics and Space Administration, Reserve Officer Training Program, and the Veterans Administration. The Reserve Officer Training Corps has Army programs at Iowa State University and the University of Iowa; the former amounts to $172,000, the latter $146,837. Not included in these figures are the salaries paid to the members of the military faculty, which are difficult to estimate because of changes in personnel. The sum is in excess of $500,000 a year, however, at both institutions.

The ROTC programs are important to hundreds of students, and provide scholarships that include tuition, room and board, and books and fees. Also, a significant number of civilian personnel are employed in these activities, whose collective salaries run from $78,000 at the University of Iowa to $50,000 at Iowa State University.

Another source of income to the universities from the Army results from the expenditure of sums of money by the Army Engineers and the Medical Corps on research and development contracts that amount to $1,662,937. Not to be forgotten are the contributions to college income made by Army veterans under the G.I. Bill. On the average, eight percent of the enrollment at these institutions is composed of Army veterans. If these individuals were not on the campuses, heavy faculty and staff cuts of an *extreme* nature undoubtedly would have to take place. The V.A. officer on each campus is entrusted with the responsibility of recruiting veterans (800 at the University of Northern Iowa — 10 percent of the student body) and forestalling the day when there will be a dramatic decline in the number of veterans on campuses.

The Military-Industrial Complex white-collar managerial class in Iowa, based on figures supplied by 60 percent of the firms and offices queried, amounts to approximately eight percent of the total managerial force. Many are employed in government agencies such as research and development sectors of the Small Business Administration, which handles Army contracts amongst others. Also, many are engaged in seeking to develop a more efficient recruiting program for the Armed Forces — both regular and reserve. Finally, not to be forgotten are the Defense Supply Agency personnel, whose salaries, by conservative estimate, total $1,180,000.

When examining the political sector within the state, one fact stands out. Except for ex-Senator Harold Hughes, who earlier announced he was leaving office, all of the responding Senators and Congressmen agreed that expenditures on the Army and other defense sectors should be continued as long as they were not "wasted and were conducive to the development of adequate defenses." Les Aspen, a Congressman from Wisconsin, noted most succinctly, "It is political suicide to do otherwise." Even the liberal Dick Clark, after he was elected Senator in 1972, was proud to announce a new Army contract for Collins Radio. Implications of the situation are obvious: each sector of the Military-Industrial Complex indicates an interdependence on other sectors in which a substantial amount of research has been conducted. What is the final tally in real dollars (multiplier effect dollars) of the money pumped into the Iowa economy by the Army? Speaking roughly, even by conservative estimates, it is possible to calculate that Iowa is much more dependent on Army and other Pentagon dollars than is commonly assumed. The estimates of Army and related expenditures in the state are included below:

Industrial contracts	=	$ 52,869,000
Civilian pay	=	18,598,000
Military active duty pay	=	38,092,000
Construction contracts	=	1,390,000
Research & Development contracts	=	4,151,000
Service contracts	=	33,870,000
Supply contracts	=	114,300,000
Reserve & National Guard pay	=	18,586,000
Retiree pay	=	17,632,000
Contracts of less than $10,000	=	839,000
Veterans Administration	=	168,411,126
Total	=	$468,738,126

Multiply this sum by 1.56, and the total is $731,231,476 — over six percent of the annual Iowa State Product of $14,000,000,000 in 1973.

It must be remembered that this figure is only an estimate based on incomplete evidence. In fact, as an industrialist stated recently, "I am a conservative. However, if people only knew the amount of money spent on defense in Iowa they would be amazed how dependent we are on the armed services."

What of the other states? In 1973 Iowa ranked 34th as a recipient of defense expenditures; over 10 percent of her industrial base and 6 percent of her GSP comes from Pentagon dollars. These figures are more impressive when all of the ramifications are examined. They are even more dramatic when the national spectrum is inspected in an imaginative manner. What scholars must do is cease worshiping the percentage of GNP as the truth in determining the influence of the Military-Industrial Complex on the economy. Instead, they should seek to discover the *dependency* of the nation on Pentagon dollars as I have sought to do in Iowa. Only in the quantitative manner will we arrive at the truth.

In conducting a study such as this, the question naturally arises, "Are the Army units, regular and Reserve, worth the expense?" and, "What does the future hold?"

In response to these questions, it should be pointed out that in addition to economic benefits, Iowans are also dependent on the Reserves for numerous services that are extremely important in their lives. Among the services performed by the National Guard and Reserves since World War II are the following: dispatch of troops to prevent disorder during serious labor disputes, 6 times; utilization of troops to perform search-and-rescue missions in the aftermath of industrial and transportation disasters, 12 times; employment of Guardsmen to aid refugees of disasters that are the result of natural catastrophes such as floods and tornadoes (in Iowa this is a particularly serious matter as the state is located in the tornado belt), 48 instances; security assignments (in 1959 over 1,000 National Guardsmen called up to protect Nikita Khrushchev), 20 instances; control of serious traffic crises (motorcycle rallies, holiday traffic jams), 12 occurrences; miscellaneous — dropping of relief supplies, search missions for prisoners, hauling of water pumps, dam dedications, other formal ceremonies, 6 times. Finally, one of the most significant services of the National Guard consists of airlifting critical patients to places of specialized treatment, i.e., the medical facilities in Iowa City and the Mayo Clinic at Rochester. This service is now accepted as a standard operating procedure by the Reserves.

In addition, one of the finest anti-litter campaigns is conducted annually by the Guard each Spring. Last year the "Make the Scene Green" activity resulted in clean-up projects taking place in every town where a Guard unit was stationed.

In answer to the second question concerning the future of the Reserves, it should be noted that more than ever the Army is relying on the

Reserves in the event of a national emergency. The regular Army is down to 825,000 men and hopes to train enough sufficient Reserve components to provide 48 percent of the force involved in contingency planning — all of which means more money being spent to support a greater number of Reservists. For example, the Iowa National Guard is asking for $15,000,000 to spend on bonuses and tuition grants as a means of inducing guardsmen to reenlist.

The Reserves are older than the United States. They are the essence of the militia concept as accepted by the makers of the Constitution. As long as the nation exists, they, along with the regular army, will be with us as integral parts of both our economy and society — for weal or for woe.

SOURCES

There were no secondary materials employed in the writing of this article. Rather, all of the sources of information were primary in nature and included the following: "Report on Federal Funds Received in Iowa Fiscal Year 1973", *Iowa, Office for Planning and Programming* (1974); *Statistical Abstracts*; "Digest," *Iowa Development Commission* (1974); and several other state publications were utilized. Also, a great deal of information was gathered from the columns of the *Des Moines Register* and the *Waterloo Courier*, and numerous questionnaires were sent and oral interviews conducted with individuals. The University of New Hampshire Public Relations Office provided the outline for discussion of the multiplier effect. In addition, the U.S. Army and Reserve units were very cooperative in providing official data on occasions. Finally, many students in my classes contributed information included in the observations made in this article. In conducting further research activities one should consult the works of Charles T. Kindleberger on methodology and Seymour Melman's books on Pentagon expenditures. Courses in the Principles of Macro-Economics are also helpful.

The first stage of an occupation is the entry of the victors into the vanquished's cities. U.S. troops are shown here entering Pekin at the successful conclusion of the China Relief Expedition in 1900. (NARS 111-SC-88824)

Chapter 10

THE ARMY AND FOREIGN AFFAIRS

Martin & Joan Kyre

War is the most complete method whereby modern states involve themselves in foreign relations. National capitals are shelled and destroyed, and governmental systems are extinguished. Thus automatically armies are recognized as having a wartime influence on foreign affairs—often the ultimate effect. Understandably, America as a nation has traditionally seen its Army's overseas role on actual or potential battlefields as being the primary reason for its existence. Too often neglected has been an appreciation of its many civilian or non-combat activities abroad, especially those in the fields of diplomacy and civil administration, which are the subjects of this chapter.

The Army in peacetime has had a long history of being involved immediately after our wars in military occupations of foreign lands. This started with Winfield Scott's military government in Mexico. Occupation forces were stationed in the Philippines and Cuba after the Spanish-American War, as well as in Germany and Siberia following the First World War. More recently the problems that the Army faced in administering such areas were brought to public consciousness by the post-war German and Japanese operations.

These foreign experiences, and the post-Civil War Reconstruction activities, which lasted until 1877, have had many ramifications for American society, as well as for military traditions. From them, for example, emerged the legal heritages for humane conduct during and after warfare toward all victims, both friend and enemy. They also helped reshape popular attitudes about the wisdom of permitting the Army to have a peacetime voice in delicate matters of international relations and foreign policy. A gradually increasing popular faith that the

The second step is a victory parade in celebration and impression. Here General "Black Jack" Pershing leads American troops from the Arc de Triomphe in Paris in 1919 in celebration of the victory over Germany. (Courtesy B. Franklin Cooling)

Army had no intention of subverting the Founding Fathers' Constitutional dictum on civilian supremacy seems to have paralleled the instances of foreign military occupations. Ultimately there was forged from these epochs a more modern interpretation of the meaning of democratic civil-military relations for the United States.

But the military occupations have also affected the lives of individual Americans, as well as American institutions, in many diverse ways. Staffing a military government has usually required a large contingent of draftees who otherwise would not have been called into service. Upon returning to civilian life these veterans brought home experiences and insights concerning other countries that doubtless influenced their families and friends, and probably helped sway public opinion from isolationism to internationalism. Some returnees acquired foreign brides, resulting in the creation of the bi-cultural households that can be found in virtually every American community. Like the immigrant groups of past generations, the war brides imparted a new vitality to American life.

Sometimes after wars the Army immersed itself in attempts to change an occupied peoples' society into something closer to the American image. This was perhaps most notably illustrated by General MacArthur's efforts in Japan. On other occasions, for example in the World War I Siberian operation, the Army functioned exclusively as a non-political emergency peacekeeping force.

Besides its responsibility for conducting military occupations, the Army has been assigned a variety of additional foreign affairs duties. Many such can be considered under the general heading of military diplomacy. This is logical because the specific tasks which the Army was directed to undertake were determined through diplomatic agreements reached between Washington leadership and embassy officials of other sovereign states. Overseas military assistance projects, military attaché posts, and programs for training foreign officers at U.S. installations have all represented the expanded scope of peacetime demands on Army resources. Their overall significance can be observed not only in the manner by which they affected other nations, but also through recognizing their contribution to the security, welfare, and growth of our domestic life.

Peacetime Military Diplomacy

The Army's emerging role in foreign relations has spawned numerous approaches and organizational schemes; some have been quite innovative whereas others attempted to modernize existing policies and agencies. In the latter category stands the military attaché. Authorized first by Congress in 1888, these posts were established only in major countries having diplomatic relations with Washington. By 1914, 23 were operating, representing as large a number as any European state. By June 1971, 80 overseas delegations were functioning. Originally these had been dominated by Army officers; however, in 1947, the system was broadened and became a tri-service establishment with military, naval, and air representatives working co-operatively within the embassies. In 1965 the three service branches were consolidated into the Defense Attaché System and the new position of Defense Attaché was created to head each overseas post. These evolutionary changes are significant because they reveal one element of a trend toward an expanded peacetime foreign policy role for the military.

Assisted by a staff of fellow officers, the Defense Attaché has numerous responsibilities, aside from the generally recognized one of gathering military intelligence. These duties vary within countries, depending on the international agreements in force. One function is diplomatic. Serving as the representative of the U.S. Armed Forces, the attaché establishes direct communication channels between military elites. The importance of this diplomatic link extends into areas such as negotiating working agreements between armies and rectifying minor misunderstandings that could jeopardize United States intentions.

Military assistance programs constitute another aspect of the Army's overseas actions. Beginning in 1947 and expanding during the cold war era, these were designed to help other states stabilize their internal political environments and prepare modern defenses against external aggression. Part of the task of translating these goals into policy outputs were assigned the Army. A series of new administrative structures was established abroad to accomplish these purposes. Among the more significant in which the Army participated were military assistance advisory groups, specialized functional missions, and country teams, all of which shared foreign aid burdens and were coordinated by the resident U.S. Ambassador and his staff. Extensive projects were undertaken in Greece, Turkey, Thailand, Taiwan, and Korea, and other countries threatened by the communists.

The Army's foreign aid role, however, has included more than in-country training programs. Within the United States, an extensive program for training foreign officers in U.S. Army schools was implemented. One result has been the spreading of United States strategic and tactical doctrine to a significant segment of the international military community.

Foreign aid and attaché activities fall into a distinct category distinguishable by the relative ease with which their consequences can be measured. Thus the success of an attaché's ability to influence local military figures can be appraised partly by the number of personal contacts he is able to establish. Foreign aid also generates direct outputs which, to illustrate, can be calculated in numbers of troops trained, volumes of supplies transferred, and the dollar value of civic action improvements.

However, there is a second group of less definable influences which are difficult to measure precisely, though they sometimes seem more important than the quantifiable items. For instance, it is generally believed that Army units stationed abroad have a behavioral impact on the local society. Base personnel, both soldiers and dependents, possess a capacity to influence popular opinion in ways that either strengthen or weaken political ties between the United States and the host country. This has been a noteworthy source of debate relative to the prolonged operation of our Okinawan bases.

Using simplified alternatives, the Pentagon can choose to establish an enclave-type facility or encourage personnel to live among and mingle freely with the local populace. The Army can decide on a self-contained installation with enforced segregation from the countryside. This occurred to a degree in the Philippines and Okinawa. When such enclaves are used, personal interactions between soldiers and the local people will assume a particular character. However, if the Army chooses to encourage integration, a different tone of relationships may emerge. Soldiers stationed in West Germany frequented local stores, traveled with few restrictions, and often lived off post. Their picture of German life, therefore, was based on relatively wide experience. Whichever choice is made, images about personal values and national traits will inevitably be formed on both sides—the sheer presence of major installations dictates this. An implication for military leaders is how the American people, through its Army, views foreigners, and how foreigners looking at the United States Army will judge America.

Civil Affairs/Military Government

Although it is important that the Army has become integrally immersed in foreign policy through a myriad of different vehicles, historically and concretely its greatest influence has been felt in Civil Affairs/Military Government (CAMG). The most appropriate definition of CAMG is one which is sufficiently broad to incorporate all situations where the United States Army exercises military administration over a

Headquarters Troop, 1st Division, passing through Witlich, Germany, in 1919 as it prepares for the occupation which would keep American troops in Germany for much of the next four years. (FR)

civilian population of a foreign country. Belligerent military occupation following wars is the most frequent and familiar form, as in Germany, Italy, and Japan after World War II.

Basically, the Army is the chief implementing instrument of foreign policy during occupations. In World War II and Korea, the U.S. Army engaged in three different types of foreign policy-related operations, each having a distinctive set of policy goals and a specific administrative approach. The first form, characterized by a civil affairs operation, was used to *reinstall* governments. Stress was placed on the goals of rebuilding facilities and institutions essential for human and social life. The civil affairs sites were those areas which had been overrun and occupied by Germany and Italy. These included Norway, Belgium, The Netherlands, Luxembourg, and France during 1944, and French North Africa from 1942-1944. Both Western Europe and North Africa came under a form of U.S. and Allied administrative jurisdiction which was viewed by the parties involved as humanitarian, emergency, and temporary.

In each instance the Army tried to reinstall governments, rehabilitate urban services, repatriate workers and their families who had been displaced by the war, clear debris blocking the resumption of business, transport seeds and agricultural commodities, and take whatever other steps were feasible to help return the area to its prewar condition.

The administrative approach resembled organizational responses to natural disasters occurring during peacetime. Teams of functional specialists experienced in fields such as agriculture, public safety, health and sanitation, public welfare, education, commerce and industry, and transportation became the administrative focal points. Because local civilians supported the Allied cause and there was an assumption that the Army's stay would be short-lived, little need existed for a detailed set of implementing policy directives allocating authority and responsibilities to various command levels. Teams operated quasi-independently from higher administrative headquarters and did whatever was within their power to meet the immediate human problems with as little bureaucratic fuss as possible. Another important point should be mentioned, however. In both World War II and the Korean Conflict, the most extensive civil affairs undertakings occurred during the final phase of combat operations and the beginning months of the postwar period. Thus, although military government suggested unappealing connotations of military dictatorship, civil affairs appeared to contain few negative implications.

To contend that the Army had complete responsibility for transforming war-devastated regions into habitable communities would be misleading.

Civil affairs activities, for example, were complemented by civilian agencies such as the United Nations Relief and Rehabilitation Administration (UNRRA) and the United Nations Korean Relief Agency (UNKRA). However, the Army retained the dominant voice because it controlled and managed transportation, communications, and logistics, and had an interconnected set of locally staffed offices. In Europe, for example, railroad boxcars for moving civilian supplies were scarce and the priority for their use was set by Army officers. Also, the only practical means whereby UNRRA officials could send requests and messages to Washington was through U.S. Army Signal Corps units. Priorities for unloading military and civilian supplies from ships were determined by Army necessities. Finally, concerning UNRRA's immediate needs for public health and public welfare experts, the only practical place to turn was to the Army's various support units.

Although the term *civil affairs* had been used incidentally in previous wars, World War II popularized it as symbolizing a type of policy distinct from military government. There was no responsible thought, however, that civil affairs would replace military government, which would become the administrative system implanted in the defeated enemy nations. Although military governments' combat phase played an important part in speeding the war's end, the era of postwar administration has had more lasting consequences. The two major enemy states, Germany and Japan, were not placed under the same occupation policy or form of control machinery. Instead, goals were framed separately for each country. Long-range planning cannot entirely be credited for this. Much of what transpired can be ascribed to immediate circumstances, personalities, and expressions of public opinion.

For occupied Germany (1945-1955) and Italy (1943-1947), the policy that President Truman and the State Department expected the Army to implement centered around *reorientation* goals. The prewar units of local government were usually retained. Many of the same officeholders were permitted to continue performing their administrative duties, especially in areas such as public health, fire protection, and public works. Military government officials and their indigenous counterparts were also involved with other civil affairs projects, particularly rebuilding urban facilities.

A distinguishing characteristic of this type policy was its attitude toward *specific* political values held by the occupied. Having goals of eradicating the Nazi mentality and reinforcing the Judeo-Christian principles Hitler had devalued, reorientation programs were implemented. These should be seen as attempted erasures of Nazification.

Re-forming an entirely new governmental system was not visualized. Since Germany had been a Republic at one time, Germans were assumed to understand and appreciate democratic government.

This thinking was illustrated in Washington's initial postwar policy which was sent to the field in April 1945. Officially titled, "Directive to Commander in Chief of United States Forces of Occupation Regarding the Military Government of Germany," it is more popularly known as JCS 1067. Although usually considered a punitive policy which was composed in the heat of war, JCS 1067 was also significant because it included as a long-range goal the "...eventual *reconstruction* of German political life on a democratic basis." The problem of dealing with Fascism in Italy was approached in the same way.

Simultaneously arising with the goal of reorienting Germany and Italy was the choice of a particular administrative system. This emerged from (a) the nature of the overall policy, (b) Eisenhower's leadership style, and (c) the necessity for considering numerous Allies in decision making. A decentralized administrative pattern developed with a multiplicity of country-wide and regional offices, agencies, and lesser staff sections, each having considerable policy interpretation latitude, but all staffed by the Army.

Difficulties unfolded as combat operations gave way to the immediate postwar occupation phase. For example, reports began appearing in both the American and foreign press alleging that certain generals were creating and implementing their own policies. Lieutenant Generals A. M. Patch, commanding the U.S. Seventh Army, and George S. Patton, directing the Third Army, were frequently compared. The criticisms fell primarily on Patton who had often refused to utilize trained military government specialists, relying instead on his combat officers. Increasingly questions were asked about Eisenhower's seeming oversight in allowing this. However, the Supreme Allied Commander saw his own policy as being one of team leadership rather than absoluteness. The record shows his reluctance to interfere with or countermand his field commanders' military government decisions.

Expounding a similar strong reliance on his subordinates, General Lucius B. Clay should receive much credit for his work as Eisenhower's Deputy Commander in Chief for Military Government. During the four tumultuous years beginning in March 1945 he headed the American zone of occupied Germany. Although recognized by his fellow West Point officers for a deep devotion to the Army, as the Military Governor he deliberately appointed a predominantly civilian staff of administrators to oversee the actions of German local governmental officials. His personal attitudes about long-term occupation goals, which also received

Impressing the occupied and staying healthy, a U.S. Army detachment keeps "the Watch on the Rhine," 1919. (Courtesy B. Franklin Cooling)

Secretary of State James F. Byrnes' backing, contributed much to erase the vengeful aspects of the JCS 1067 policy. Clay, the general, also paved the way for a smooth transition from Army control to full civilian control of the occupation machinery. With the appointment of former Assistant Secretary of State John J. McCloy as U.S. High Commissioner for Germany in June 1949, Lucius Clay returned home to a New York ticker tape parade and retirement.

But to appreciate the broad ramifications of Eisenhower's decentralized approach to military occupation matters one must also recognize the contributions made by lower-ranking officers. Many highly inventive colonels and majors were assigned key positions in cities and provinces, and sometimes they seized upon the absence of centralized direction and simply usurped policy-making roles. The most popularly known instance is that of the fictional Major Joppollo in John Hersey's novel *A Bell for Adano*, modelled upon Major Frank E. Toscani and his experiences in Licata, Sicily. From a policy standpoint, however, Lieutenant Colonels Charles M. Spofford and Charles A. Poletti had a much greater impact as cardinal contributors to U.S. and Allied policy.

For instance, Poletti was responsible for formulating the first workable epuration (de-fascistization) policy. It entailed using a questionnaire to determine which local bureaucrats should be fired for political reasons. Only those completed questionnaires submitted by officials holding sensitive posts were scrutinized thoroughly, but the information filed by all workers had to be correct under severe penalty for falsehood. Thus Poletti devised a means for accomplishing fascist purging without impairing the continued functioning of vital governmental bodies, though his methods were in clear defiance of high-level occupation directives which stipulated wholesale dismissals.

The original questionnaire was conceived in 1943 when Poletti was the Military Governor in Palermo. Titled the *Sicily Scheda Personale*, it was eventually transformed into a directive for all of Italy. Later, when the problem of implementing reorientation in Germany arose, Poletti's approach became the pattern for the *Fragebogn* or denazification questionnaire. Despite Poletti's contributions, he was criticized for audacity in ignoring military ranks and command channels. Frequent allusions were made to his personal political clout which seemingly stemmed from friendship with New York Mayor Fiorello LaGuardia and President Roosevelt, plus his association with New York's Italian-American community.

Looking back at World War II occupations in Europe after a quarter-century has elapsed, we believe it is moot to be either overly critical or overly sympathetic with Eisenhower's administrative style. Considering the variety of domestic and foreign pressures for different types of orientation policies, the decentralized method may have been the most advantageous for American interests in Europe, and certainly it appears to have been the most politically astute from Eisenhower's position.

A second type of military government was utilized in postwar Japan. We have termed it reinstitutionalization and note that in the Japanese model there again occurred a high compatibility of policy goals and administrative style. Under the occupier's call for reinstitutionalization, a new constitution was written which represented more than a symbolic change in governmental bodies. Spelling out individual citizens' rights and duties and attempting to alter their political standards, it revolutionized Japanese law. General Douglas MacArthur's Japanese

Armies of occupation often find themselves educating the citizenry. Here a colonel presents diplomas to a girl graduating from a U.S. Army school in Manila, December 1945. (USA)

constitution can be considered a package of Western values imposed on a non-Western state. Military government's ultimate purpose was to establish those principles so firmly within Japanese society that they would remain after MacArthur and the Army departed. A clear direction for this effort was given in the "United States Initial Post-Surrender Policy for Japan," which was the basic occupation directive sent from Washington in August 1945.

The close connection between a reinstitutionalization policy and MacArthur's centralized administrative approach deserves attention. Because of the comprehensive changes in government planned for Japan, as well as Japan's prewar centralized structure, the Supreme Commander's propensity for maintaining control within his headquarters alone became the pattern. He often ignored policy inputs from both Washington and the Allies. With the help of a few trusted aides, notably his intelligence chief Major General Charles A. Willoughby, he guided America's role during the postwar period from his Tokyo headquarters that was isolated from the mainstream of Japanese life. From the start of the occupation, MacArthur disavowed substantial U.S. interference in the communal affairs of individual Japanese. Local officials and social organizations were rarely attacked directly from their political views as they had been in Germany. The reforms, instead, came from the top and filtered down from the constitution and the Supreme Commander through the Japanese bureaucracy.

Yet throughout this period, the occupation Army's daily role was critical in supervising the accomplishment of U.S. policy. It had the major task of inspecting the extent to which the Supreme Commander's orders to the Japanese Government was being carried out on the local level. Where compliance was discovered to be slow or absent, as occasionally happened over land reform and election reform measures, Army investigators reported the facts to their Tokyo headquarters. Staff sections in MacArthur's headquarters would then weigh the significance of the local infractions in light of the intent of overall U.S. policy for Japan and the past performance record of the local officials involved. Serious discrepancies were immediately called to the attention of the Japanese Central Government, usually with orders that it dispatch officials to the scene to correct the situation. However, in most instances the types of infractions encountered were minor, and the Army would request that Japanese leaders undertake a routine investigation and report the results. This administrative pattern persisted until the occupation was finally terminated in 1951.

Even now we can see the reflexive impact within the United States coming from the transformed Japanese society. In the area of trade

The Army abroad needs barracks and housing. Here an American general looks over a contract for housing with a Japanese contractor, Sendai, November 1954. (USA)

alone, both Germany and Japan have emerged as major American trading partners and sometimes competitors. Primarily because of the successful occupation indoctrination, the Japanese are even able and willing today to invest in businesses within the United States. Whether one approves of the practice or not, the Japanese financed factories do provide jobs for American workers. Employment is also generated through the importers and merchants that handle Japanese-made products.

Another economic impact is from the traveling Japanese, both tourists and businessmen, who are now sufficiently affluent to visit and tour the United States. Their expenditures currently represent a large share of the tourist dollars brought into Hawaii, and to a lesser degree contribute to the prosperity of the tourist industry on the mainland.

While trying to survey Army foreign affairs participation via CAMG we must recognize that top-level policy often develops through a series of mistakes and/or defaults. With the enemy's defeat, the Army has historically yielded to civilian agencies of the Executive Branch. Disclaiming responsibility for policy, it has instead attempted to be again exclusively an implementor in the field. This does not always succeed because in reality the Army, like it or not, assumes a duty to rebuild a new government. Sometimes in this role the Army has had the satisfaction of an unimpeded chain of command, where policy directives have been formulated by national leadership and carried successively to command levels through subordinate commanders to operating officials. More often the occupation authorities, operating under vague State Department orders, must make important policy plans. Their decisions are tempered not only by their official mission, but by U.S. public opinion at home and their knowledge of its effect upon the occupied peoples.

The policy process itself also caused difficulties for the Army. Most frequently, problems could be grouped under four headings: (a) directives were imprecise in their goals, (b) directives were the product sometimes of contradictory inputs from different segments of the American policy, (c) directives proved to be unworkable in the field, and (d) directives proved to be unsupportable because of American public opinion.

Although instances of vague policy goals in directives occurred in most U. S. occupations we have examined, the Mexican War and World War I provide classic illustrations. Both were also characterized by the White House's direct involvement with the field commanders who functioned as military governors. First there was the belligerent occupation of Mexican territory, 1846-1848, in the administration of President James Polk. He and Congressional leaders devoted little thought to the civil

During occupations there sometimes is a transfer of technology in connection with the normal peacetime habit of the armed forces of contracting overhaul work to civilian firms or having it done at bases largely manned by civilians. Here Japanese workers under Army supervision install a light airplane engine at the Japan Maintenance Company, Tokyo International Airport, in July 1962. (USA)

affairs problems that would face General Zachary Taylor, the Army's first field commander, and military defeats ensued. Part of Taylor's failures stemmed from the arbitrary behavior of American troops toward Mexican civilian nationals.

General Winfield Scott was sent to replace Taylor, but once again it was a case of an Army commander being dispatched to the front with only a mandate to defeat the enemy and treat the civilian population according to the law of nations. Perceiving the seriousness of the military occupation problem, Scott proceeded on his own to write his General Order # 20 which stipulated a set of specific individual rights and responsibilities binding on both his troops and the Mexicans. This document has great historic significance because it represented America's first comprehensive occupation policy for international wars, as well as providing a precedent for the Civil War's Lieber Code and later Army manuals and standing orders. For Scott's own Mexican War purposes, General Order # 20 guided both wartime and postwar military administration in the continuing absence of meaningful guidance from Washington. Indeed, a broad history of the Army's concern with foreign affairs might well begin with Scott's Mexican experience.

The World War I era shows a greater complexity in the policy process. This was reflected first by President Woodrow Wilson's role in the Siberian intervention. Wilson's *Aide Memoire* to General William S. Graves, who was designated by the White House to conduct the operation, constituted the fundamental directive for the Army's civil administration in Siberia, 1918-1920. Containing little besides a pledge of friendship to the Russian people, it expressed a wish that their legal government could soon re-establish order. Graves read the directive as meaning non-interference in the factional struggles taking place in Siberia. A major controversy between the War and State Departments erupted. The latter's field representative, Roland S. Morris, received a State Department directive ordering Graves officially to recognize one faction, the so-called Kolchak Government. Graves brushed aside the State Department order by indicating that he would continue following his own interpretation of the President's Aide Memoire. Only direct orders by War Department superiors would change his position. He prevailed.

Civilian-military disputes also arose during the Rhineland occupation, 1918-1923. Both Generals John J. Pershing, U.S. commander in Europe, and H. A. Smith, Military Governor for Occupied Germany, were involved. The Army had assumed that it would be in charge of the occupation and that it understood Wilson's goals. These were perceived as Presidential authority to conduct a prolonged occupation using a direct administrative form of military government.

Aid to disaster victims is rendered regardless of race, creed, or sex. A 19th Transportation Company H-37B helicopter brings food and blankets to flood victims at Sunchon, Korea, in August 1962. (USA)

However, in the spring of 1919 Wilson sent Pierrepont B. Noyes to act as his personal civilian representative in negotiating a final Rhineland settlement. Noyes openly opposed the views of Pershing and French Marshal Foch who, he charged, wanted to create a perpetual system of martial law with harsh treatment for German civilians rather than seek a lasting peace. Noyes claimed to reflect Wilson's sentiments, but military leaders questioned both his judgment and his right to speak for the President. Numerous heated exchanges in the Inter-Allied Rhineland Commission and the Supreme War Council apparently persuaded Noyes to write his famous personal letter and appeal to Wilson. In it he proposed a plan for a skeleton indirect administration subordinate to a civilian rather than military commission, which would determine all policy. President Wilson sided with Noyes, and ultimately the civilian-dominated Rhineland High Commission implemented Noyes' basic policy aims.

As the above description intimates, directives are not totally responsible for confused occupation policy. This was especially evident during the Spanish American War's belligerent occupations of Cuba, 1898-1902, and the Philippine Islands, 1898-1901. Present then were a variety of contrary and antagonistic inputs into policy from both governmental bodies and the U.S. civilian sector. One celebrated case of interagency feuding pitted the Post Office Department against the military governor in Cuba, General Leonard Wood. It quickly escalated into a scandal resulting in several post office officials being fired, almost at the cost of Wood's own position.

During the same period, the important policy roles played by Congressional spokesmen, the writings of journalists, and the pressure of public opinion caused a shift in attitudes. Reinforced or perhaps shaped by the Yellow Press, public opinion shifted from calling the Filipinos our "little brown brothers" to the epithets of "Malay bandits" and "Chinese halfbreeds." At first José Rizal was championed as the "George Washington of the Philippines," but then he became a "rebel bandit." And "liberate the people from the Spanish yoke" was a slogan soon replaced by "civilizin' em with a Krag." Churches turned from preaching missionary reform to voicing anti-Catholic prejudice. Congressional views were mirrored accordingly in the idealistic sentiments of Senator McEnery and the imperialist notions of Senator Beveridge. The Army responded to these competing forces by installing successive military governors overseas who, individually and collectively, portrayed through their administrations the differing sides of the mood emanating from the various sectors of American life.

The Army has also suffered from a third dimension of the problem which occurs when the directive, or a part of it, proves to be unworkable in the field. Sometimes the policy is eminently clear but is not operationally feasible. Achievement of one occupation goal may mitigate or even negate another. When this happens, field commanders find means to circumvent or otherwise reject the impractical policy. This gyration is rarely admitted, but what happens is that, as in the case of nonfraternization in post-World War II Germany, Italy, and Japan, the policy is unofficially declared inoperative. Likewise, the punitive emphasis in the original denazification and epuration directives could not be followed without inviting a total breakdown in vital civilian services. Nor could German reorientation be achieved by dismissing every officeholder who had belonged to one of Hitler's numerous political and social organizations.

Civil Affairs During Combat

There is a final question which must be explored to complete the picture of the Army and foreign affairs. Vietnam was the location, and the policy was reminiscent of World War II and Korean civil affairs ventures. However, Vietnam represented a case where both the Washington policy-making authorities and the Army personnel in the field receiving the orders understood each other precisely. Rebuilding societal and governmental institutions, with the Army providing managerial and security support, was the goal.

Complications soon developed because the new civil affairs program was being applied during a period of escalating U.S. combat operations. This situation was opposite to previous circumstances. In World War II civil affairs had been the transitional administration bridging the gap between Axis military occupations and the local peoples' total resumption of sovereign services. For Korea it had supported a friendly but weak regime recovering from a civil war. However, in Vietnam, instead of the American policy becoming progressively less costly and complicated as peace gradually returned, the Army found itself incorporating an ever-expanding array of elements and variables into the policy framework as warfare intensified. Sometimes new names were coined to describe the innovations. Civic action, pacification, and finally Vietnamization became for Americans household terms, often being ballyhooed as secret weapons.

Though many at home were doubtless confused about the differences, for Washington and field commanders these concepts were meaningful.

Yet while the military and civilian agencies had found the will and techniques for cooperating, the American people were withdrawing their support from both the Washington foreign policy establishment and the Army in the field.

As an originally neutral public mood became hostile toward the war, the Army faced the difficult choice of siding with Washington or bowing to public opinion. This was an unorthodox challenge for an Army priding itself on its democratic character. The generals, long accustomed to battling Washington bureaucracy, could cope with most policy wrangles. But fighting public opinion was untenable. Had a professional rather than draftee force borne prime responsibility for implementing the policy, the outcome might have been different.

The evolution of the Vietnamese civilian policy is important for its broader implications, especially when it is viewed against the background of historic debates over earlier military occupation policies. We consistently find the Army balancing, resisting, and eventually forced to formulate foreign policy during military occupations. Trying to balance public opinion, Army traditionalism, and Washington red tape proves difficult. Resisting a role in actually shaping a new governmental entity is impossible. The Army may decry its place in foreign affairs; however, it is deep and permanent.

Suggestions for Further Research

Many areas of Army foreign policy involvement require additional research. These, especially, should be examined: (a) how Army, Navy, and Air Force policies dovetail, overlap, and reinforce each other, and conversely, how they deviate or separate on mission accomplishment; (b) how personnel can or should be selected and trained for current or future overseas assignments; (c) evaluation of coordination between civilian agencies and the military concerning foreign affairs; (d) what resources are available within personal experiences, quantification analysis, and historical documentation that might aid future efforts; (e) how the Army's role in overseas peacetime activities can be justified, accommodated, or disregarded within the theoretical picture of international relations; and, if the present emphasis should be changed, just how would this be accomplished? (f) in what context does the military itself view and evaluate peacetime participation in attaché functions, foreign aid programs, overseas base questions, and civil affairs activities? (g) finally, how do other countries that host U.S. forces perceive the Army's role in their affairs?

Basically, research is needed to explore two dimensions of the Army's involvement in foreign affairs: the theoretical foundations of policy and immediately applicable administrative improvements. This twin emphasis suggests more than dividing research efforts along short- and long-range lines, because ultimately they must be fused to provide guidance in forming a single set of workable policies.

On the theoretical plane we find Professor James N. Rosenau's linkage framework to be particularly useful. He specifies four observable types of policy relationships linking states: penetration, emulation, reaction, and fusion. Among them, penetration is most pertinent because it encompasses an outside army's direct sharing in local transactions—for example, an occupying army administering a defeated country. Through the postwar CAMG policy, Japan was coerced into trying new political and social approaches having lasting benefits for the U.S. Although Army officers learn by practical experience that civilians in a penetrated country tend to react in characteristically predictable behavior patterns, a clear understanding of the psychological and political components entering into the penetrative process is still obscure and requires further research.

Another interconnected aspect of linkage theory is the international system of environments and the matrix which provides a means for charting the interrelationship of U.S. institutions and pressures to their counterpart internal forces in a specific foreign country. Briefly, what is involved is a view of the modern world that is more expansive than the traditional nation-state and balance of power approaches. When planning its foreign role, the military should know where its overseas activities will occur. International environmental settings can be cataloged as contiguous, regional, cold war, resource, racial, or organizational. These, of course, can be combined.

Herein the practical application can mesh with the theoretical. A clear perception of environmental characteristics can aid Army authorities in formulating long-range goals based on the significance of the target country to the future of the United States. Quantitative measurement can also analyze factors such as linked actors, attitudes, institutions, and processes. For instance, instructional programs under foreign aid auspices inevitably export organizational techniques and institutional values creating linkages between American and foreign military elites.

Other avenues for exploring data about Army participation in foreign affairs include the following. First, assemble an extensive collection of oral histories. Experienced officers, whether CAMG officers, attachés, or foreign aid administrators, can contribute helpful insights for preventing future policy bottlenecks. Second, comprehensive case studies of all contemporary military administrations (both U.S. and foreign, i.e., Vietnam, Cyprus, The Dominican Republic, The West Bank, Eastern Europe, and Bangladesh) should be undertaken while the operations are still unfolding. And last, it is time we stopped treating Army foreign affairs as super-secret actions accountable only to military or civilian intelligence agencies.

SOURCES

Excellent accounts of early military occupations are found in Seymour V. Connor and Odie B. Falk, *North America Divided: The Mexican War 1846-1848* (New York: Oxford University, 1971); David F. Healy, *The United States in Cuba* (Madison: University of Wisconsin, 1963); and Human Relations Area Files, *The Philippines*, Vol. I (New Haven: Human Relations Area Files, 1955).

World War I experiences in Germany are recounted by Ernst Frankel, *Military Occupation and the Rule of Law: Occupation Government in the Rhineland, 1918-1923* (New York: Oxford University, 1944); the two most consulted accounts of the Siberian situation are William S. Graves, *America's Siberian Adventure* (New York: Peter Smith, 1941), and Clarence A. Manning, *The Siberian Fiasco* (New York: Literary Publishers, 1932).

Military occupations as a major aspect of Army policy and U.S. foreign policy came of age during and after World War II. The following provide useful surveys: Carl J. Friedrich, et al., *American Experiences in Military Government in World War II* (New York: Rhinehart, 1948); Hajo Holborn, *American Military Government* (Washington: Infantry Journal Press, 1948); and *Military Government* (The Annals of the American Academy of Political and Social Science, January, 1950). Among the particularly useful area studies of that period are Edward H. Litchfield, ed., *Governing Postwar Germany* (Ithaca: Cornell University, 1953); John A. Hearst, Jr., "The Evolution of Allied Military Government in Italy," Ph.D. dissertation (New York: Columbia University, 1960); Russell Brines, *MacArthur's Japan* (New York: Lippincott, 1948); Robert A. Feary, *The Occupation of Japan: Second Phase: 1948-1950* (New York: Macmillan, 1950); Kazuo Kawai, *Japan's American Interlude* (Chicago: University of Chicago, 1960); Edwin M. Martin, *The Allied Occupation of Japan* (Stanford: Stanford University, 1948); and E. Grant Meade, *American Military Government in Korea* (New York: Columbia University, 1951).

The most recent use of American Army forces in the Dominican Republic has generated the following two noteworthy accounts: Theodore

Draper, *The Dominican Revolt* (New York: Commentary, 1968), and Abraham F. Lowenthal, *The Dominican Intervention* (Cambridge: Harvard University, 1972).

Most attempts to deal with the general theme of American military occupation are found in articles. The better ones include Hardy C. Dillard, "Power and Persuasion: The Role of Military Government," *The Yale Review* (December 1952); Ralph H. Gabriel, "American Experience with Military Government," *American Political Science Review* (June 1943); and Malcolm S. MacLean, "Military Government—Fact and Fancy," *Public Administration Review* (Autumn 1947). Two books can be added to this list. Tracing the evolution of occupation policy from the Mexican War to Vietnam is Martin and Joan Kyre, *Military Occupation and National Security* (Washington: Public Affairs Press, 1968). When occupation is viewed as an aspect of diplomatic history, a standard source is Thomas A. Bailey, *A Diplomatic History of the American People*, 4th ed. (New York: Appleton-Century-Crofts, 1950). Military assistance programs are discussed in Samuel P. Hayes, *The Beginning of American Aid to Southeast Asia* (Lexington, Mass.: Lexington Books, 1971), and Gene M. Lyons, *Military Policy and Economic Aid: The Korean Case, 1950-1953* (Columbus: Ohio State University, 1961). For background on the question of military attachés, see Alfred Vagts, *The Military Attaché* (Princeton: Princeton University, 1967).

Insights into Army leadership and command problems concerning military occupation are found in Lucius D. Clay, *Decision in Germany* (Garden City: Doubleday, 1950); Morris Janowitz, *The Professional Soldier: A Social and Political Portrait* (New York: Free Press, 1971); and Robert Murphy, *Diplomat Among Warriors* (Garden City: Doubleday, 1964).

Problems concerning training and assignment of personnel to military occupation units are explored in C. Dale Fuller, *Training of Specialists in International Relations* (Washington: American Council on Education, 1957); John W. Masland and Laurence I. Radway, *Soldiers and Scholars* (Princeton: Princeton University, 1957); and Harold Zink, *American Military Government in Germany* (New York: Macmillan, 1947). A study of field-level administration revealing the difficulties in applying the German JCS 1067 policy is John D. Montgomery, *Forced to be Free* (Chicago: University of Chicago, 1957). Public opinion as it relates to the Army's foreign affairs policies is examined in John E. Mueller, *War, Presidents, and Public Opinion* (New York: Wiley, 1973).

Among the many excellent studies of civil-military relations which stress the impact of the Army peacetime foreign affairs on domestic society are the following: Charles L. Cochran, ed., *Civil-Military*

Relations: Changing Concepts in the Seventies (New York: Free Press, 1974); James Clotfelter, *The Military in American Politics* (New York: Harper & Row, 1973); William L. Hauser, *America's Army in Crisis: A Study in Civil-Military Relations* (Baltimore: Johns Hopkins, 1973); Frank N. Trager and Philip S. Kronenberg, eds., *National Security and American Society: Theory, Process, and Policy* (Lawrence: University Press of Kansas, 1973); and Eugene J. Rosi, ed., *American Defense and Detente: Readings in National Security Policy* (New York: Dodd, Mead & Co., 1973).

The law of war and military occupation is discussed in a pertinent fashion in Doris Appel Graber, *The Development of the Law of Belligerent Occupation: 1863-1914* (New York: Columbia University, 1949); Morris Greenspan, *The Modern Law of Land Warfare* (Berkeley: University of California, 1959); and Gerhard von Glahn, *The Occupation of Enemy Territory*, 2nd ed. (Minneapolis: University of Minnesota, 1970). When used in conjunction with international law books, the following sources of official documents are excellent: Harry L. Coles and Albert K. Weinberg, *Civil Affairs: Soldiers Become Governors* (Washington: U.S. Army Special Studies, Series, 1964), and Beate Ruhm von Oppen, ed., *Documents on Germany Under Occupation, 1945-1954* (New York: Oxford University, 1955).

Possibilities for future research into Army foreign affairs in peacetime are suggested in the following studies: Lincoln P. Bloomfield, *In Search of American Foreign Policy: The Humane Use of Power* (New York: Oxford University, 1974); Frederic J. Brown and Zeb B. Bradford, *The United States Army in Transition* (Los Angeles: Sage, 1974); Frederick H. Hartman, *The Relations of Nations*, 4th ed. (New York: Macmillan, 1973); Klaus Knorr, *Military Power and Potential* (Lexington, Mass.: Heath, 1970); James N. Rosenau, *The Scientific Study of Foreign Policy* (New York: Free Press, 1971); and Jonathan Wilkenfeld, ed., *Conflict Behavior and Linkage Politics* (New York: McKay, 1973).

In the good old days life on post was filled with things like full-dress weddings such as this one in the early Twentieth Century. (LVN)

Chapter 11

THE PEACETIME ARMY: RETROSPECT AND PROSPECT

William L. Hauser

My earliest memory of the Army is a scolding by a stable sergeant when I was five years old. It was 1937, a pleasant Sunday afternoon at Fort Sam Houston, Texas. As was the custom in those parts and times, the officers and ladies of the garrison were at the polo match. And, as was the custom for five-year-olds, I had unconcernedly gone between, behind, and under several high-spirited horses after toddling out of reach of my mother. A stern lecture from the grizzled sergeant was the result.

That was a quaint old Army by today's standards, or even by the standards of its own time. The focus of military life was the horse: an officer's equestrianship was a major measure of his professional competence, and the social schedule of a post was filled with hunts, shows, polo matches, mounted parades, and gymkhanas. The workday was largely taken up with rough soldierly activities, but strict decorum returned during off-duty hours. Each commanding officer had his "at home" evenings, when officers and their ladies, sweating in their dress blues and best frocks, would chat on safe subjects for an obligatory 15 minutes. Calling cards were deposited in a silver tray upon departure — "one for each adult member of the visited household, not to exceed two." It was not a luxurious life, but it offered a profoundly satisfying mixture of wholesomeness, stability, and propriety.

That was for officers, of course. The noncommissioned officer had a very different sort of existence, but it was not an unpleasant life either. The NCO was responsible for the morale, discipline, hygiene, welfare, and performance of the soldiers under his charge. The officers might have titular command, but the NCOs, "the backbone of the Army," had authority over the soldiers and the prestige which that authority con-

Enlisted men may have played baseball, but the Army's elite, the mounted officers, imported polo from India. Here a Saturday match in the 1930s is being played near Camp Forsyth, Fort Riley, KS. (FR)

ferred. As for the private soldier, his work was arduous and unglamorous, and his pay was pitifully small — but it was not such a bad deal for unskilled men in those Depression years.

The Army was small — not even 180,000 officers and men — and scattered about the United States and its territories in a series of regimental posts, arsenals, and Civilian Conservation Corps (CCC) camps. One did not see a general very often, and the annual visit by the Inspector General was an event of much preparation and consternation. The War Department was another world, very far removed from the ken of regimental officers and men.

However idyllic the setting, thoughts of war were ever present in those days. American participation in World War I had lasted only a couple of years, but it had left a deep impression on the peacetime Army. In fact, most of the field-grade officers (majors, lieutenant colonels, and colonels) had served in that conflict. Now both the European and Asian pots were bubbling again. For those with any sense of history, war was coming and the United States would probably become involved.

And war came. Japan invaded China in force in 1937, Germany seized Austria and Czechoslovakia in 1938, and Russia and Germany repartitioned Poland in 1939. If the rearmament of the mid-1930s had not been sufficiently convincing as to Axis goals, these overt acts left no doubt. And then, in rather quick succession, Germany drove the British and French armies from the field in Central Europe, secured the Axis' northern flank in Denmark and Norway and the southern flank in Greece and North Africa, and — turning around — thrust deep into the heartland of her erstwhile ally Russia. On the other side of the world, the Japanese marched southward through China and began making demands for control of the resources of the French and Dutch colonial empires. It was only a matter of time before some precipitating event would involve the United States.

Thus it was that when Pearl Harbor suddenly brought the war to America and America into the war, there was no surprise (other than the event itself) for professional soldiers. They had spent a generation in mental preparation and several years in detailed planning for mobilization. In terms of specific events, they had two and a half years to get ready, between the German drive across France (which made American involvement inevitable) and the landings of Army units on Guadalcanal and the coast of North Africa.

Still, one cannot help but marvel at the ability of that "quaint old Army" of mounted parades and calling cards to expand 50-fold in a handful of years, into the mechanized juggernaut of World War II. True, the world's most powerful and advanced economy performed near-miracles

Riding to hounds endured at Fort Riley at least until 1958 when this picture was taken of the pack trotting past Quarters No. 1, the Commanding General's residence. (FR)

in retooling from peacetime to wartime production, but even more miraculous was the ability of the Army to generate the planners and managers — and the combat leaders — for the mightiest global campaign in all of history.

How was it done? First of all, it should be noted that the senior leaders of the prewar Army did not go on to lead the war effort. Perhaps they would have, at least initially, had not President Roosevelt picked as his wartime chief of staff a little-known brigadier general who had only recently been advanced from colonel — George Marshall. In a matter of months, Marshall carried out a palace revolution in the Army's hierarchy. As the buildup accelerated, a large proportion of the generals and colonels of 1937 found themselves eased into retirement or relegated to peripheral positions. When the conflict ended, it was the lieutenants, captains, and majors of 1937 who commanded the regiments and divisions, staffed the war rooms, and advised high military and civilian leadership.

Postwar Changes

Even more swiftly than it had expanded, the postwar Army precipitously contracted. To the professional soldier, it was a reenactment of the 1920s, but with a major difference. In 1947-1948, as the Army fell to nearly its prewar size and the draft was temporarily allowed to expire, a new enemy arose in the form of Soviet Russia. Army leaders, seeing on the one hand a potentially massive threat and on the other little prospect for maintaining a viable force-in-being, drew on their experience to plan for eventual re-mobilization.

The question that must have been uppermost in their minds, however consciously or unconsciously, was this: Were the successes of World War II, particularly the burgeoning of leadership and managerial talent, the *result of* or *inspite of* that "quaint old Army" of the regimental post? The answer, also perhaps partly unconscious, favored the latter theory. New laws were passed that did away with promotion by seniority, replacing it with accelerated advancement of the best officers and a system of "up or out" for the weaker. If rapid mobilization came again, it presumably would be better handled by men who had reached senior rank while still relatively young and vigorous.

Shortly thereafter came the Korean War, and the Army expanded again — this time not to dwindle afterwards. For a quarter of a century, America was to have what the writers of *The Federalist* termed "a standing army." At the same time, U.S. and Soviet possession of massive nuclear capability rendered general war improbable, but minor conflicts

General George C. Marshall, U.S. Army, 19 January 1945. (USA)

in backward regions more likely. There developed a near-consensus among civilian scholars, particularly Samuel Huntington, Morris Janowitz, and Henry Kissinger, that the day of general conventional war was past. The future role of ground forces, under the umbrella of strategic nuclear balance, would be a combination of deterrence of and rapid response to intervention by an adversary in the affairs of smaller states.

But still the myth of mobilization persisted. The officer corps was allowed to grow until the proportion of officers to soldiers was double that of prewar times, affording a built-in reserve for another great expansion. The officer school system shifted its emphasis upward: the branch courses preapred lieutenants and captains to be field grade officers, the staff college taught majors how to command divisions and corps, and the war college pointed colonels toward the lofty reaches of national security policy and grand strategy. Reserve and National Guard formations were expanded until they were nearly as large as the active Army itself. New weapons were constantly being developed, but tactical and strategic doctrine and organization still pointed toward general war. Perhaps it was not a conscious process, but the Army's actions spoke louder than words: it was preparing to fight a latter-day version of World War II.

There was another phenomenon of the postwar period that must be taken into account if one is to understand what happened later in Vietnam. The better lieutenants and captains of the 1930s found themselves colonels at the end of World War II. Then, like a pendulum pushed in time with its momentum, they were boosted into general officer rank by the Korean War. A sizeable excess of bright and energetic young colonels and generals was created; and in faithful compliance with Parkinson's Law, the Army's headquarters and staffs grew and multiplied to give them work. These officers formed a "Long Generation" which ran the Army for the next 15 years. Seasoned not in the slow pace of the regiment but in the turbulent world of huge armies and high-level staffs, they gradually viewed the military as resources to be managed rather than as soldiers to be led.

It is probably simplistic to stereotype a whole generation in this way, for the strategic situation also had a major impact on military thinking. In earlier times, a post-conflict Army shrank to a tiny fraction of its wartime size and retreated into regimental isolation; after World War II, except for the brief hiatus of the late 1940s, it remained large and visible, sprawled across the world from the Korean DMZ to the Czech border. And, as it had never been before in peacetime, it was ready.

Ready for what? The national strategy was called containment — a circular barrier forged around the communist world. The military component of that strategy was the deterrence of hostile forces moving out of the circle. Manifestations of the strategy included reestablishment of the 38th parallel in Korea, non-intervention in the Hungarian uprising, and brink-of-war mobilizations for the Berlin crisis of 1961 and the Cuban missile crisis of 1962. This Army, long indoctrinated in MacArthur's dictum that "there is no substitute for victory," now had to find its sense of purpose in the maintenance of global stalemate. Although it may look ridiculous in print, the Army's mission was to avoid fighting. Small wonder, then, that the leaders of the Army in the 1950s and 1960s looked back on World War II as "the last real war."

It was perhaps for these reasons that the South Vietnamese Army, organized under the tutelage of American advisers in the late 1950s, consisted of corps and divisions with tanks and supporting artillery, large headquarters, staffs, and even a four-year military academy patterned after West Point. This Vietnamese organization gradually evolved into a regional pattern more suitable for revolutionary warfare; but when American forces were sent to Vietnam in 1965, they came organized essentially for conventional war. Indeed, the mission first assigned to these troops was to engage the "main force" units of the North Vietnamese Army and the Viet Cong, leaving the combating of guerrillas and revolutionary infrastructure to the South Vietnamese.

It is not the purpose of this essay to critique American tactics and strategy in Vietnam. Others have already done so in profusion, from broadly varying levels of expertise. In fact, the Army probably did as well as one might desire or expect, given the professional outlook with which it entered and the combination of pressures and constraints under which it conducted the war.

The Aftermath of Vietnam

The American role in Vietnam ended not a moment too soon, for it was destroying the U.S. Army. The heart and soul of military professionalism lies in its sense of purpose. In a democracy, the purpose of an Army is determined ultimately by the popular will. Thus, when withdrawal of public support — even antipathy in some quarters — combined with the disappointments and the scandals of the war, the Army's sense of purpose was nearly shattered. The crisis, in part reflecting American society in the 1960s, manifested itself in a variety of forms: racial strife, political dissent, indiscipline both on and off the battlefield, drug abuse, and declining rates of recruiting and retention.

The Army responded to these challenges with a threefold program. The first and highest priority task was simply to hold the organization together. A multiplicity of ad hoc programs was launched to address the problems of racial tension, political dissent, indiscipline, and drug abuse. Concurrently, a number of practices were abolished (e.g. reveille formations, rigid restrictions on in-barracks behavior, verbal abuse of junior soldiers by NCOs) which were felt to be harmful to recruitment and retention. There were incentives as well: much higher pay for private soldiers and junior officers, improved barracks and recreational facilities, more variation and adventure in training, and expanded in-service educational opportunities. A multi-million dollar program of advertising spread the news of what the Army had to offer. Finally, in response to the Vietnam-era scandals which had so jarred the professional self-image of the military, a number of officers and NCOs were court-martialed, discharged, or retired.

The second task was to initiate major reform in the career system, both to prevent a recurrence of practices that had contributed to the crisis and to provide for the long-term health of the profession. Both officer and enlisted career systems were overhauled.

The officer system was addressed first. The Chief of Staff, General William Westmoreland, had become convinced in the latter days of the Vietnam War that many problems of adaptability to change, managerial competence, and professional ethics were attributable to an outdated professional ideal. For many years, the model after which ambitious officers patterned their careers was the "generalist" — the jack-of-all trades and master of none. The concept was in part a product of the World War II experience, when it was found that managerial skill rather than specific substantive expertise was in great demand for high-level positions controlling millions of men and billions of dollars. The difficulty arose when the Army institutionalized this ideal, suitable for very high-level positions, into the career management of all officers.

From this hyperbolic extension came the abuses known as "ticket-punching." The key to a successful career became transitoriness: an officer was expected to pack into the first 20 years of his career some four levels of schooling, three levels of command, and a variety of staff jobs with troop units, major field commands, and the General Staff in the Pentagon. Expertise in any particular subject area — such as personnel, logistics, or research-and-development — became something to be avoided, lest the officer narrow his options. The end result was so rapid a movement of officers from command to command and staff to staff that, in the words of Admiral Rickover, "nobody was responsible for anything."

General William C. Westmoreland commanded in Vietnam, the longest and possibly most traumatic war in American history, from which in 1975 the U.S. Army was recovering its balance and readjusting to peacetime. (USA)

Development of the new system, called the Officer Personnel Management System (OPMS), was launched in the fall of 1970. There was intensive study for more than a year, and implementation was begun in 1972. The two principal elements of the system, opposite sides of the same coin, are command selection and increased specialization. Commanders of battalions and brigades (lieutenant colonels and colonels) are selected by boards of officers in the Pentagon, so that command of troops may go to officers most suited to that sort of duty. In sharp contrast to the Vietnam-era practice of rapid rotation through command, these officers are stabilized in their positions for one and a half to two years. As to specialization, all officers are required to choose some specialty (other than simply Infantry Branch, Signal Corps, etc.) at about the time they are promoted to major. The officer can then expect to work in this subject area each time he serves in a staff assignment. For those officers who are not thereafter selected for command, their enhanced competence will provide them ample opportunity for job satisfaction and career success. To ensure that non-selection for command does not spell the end of competitiveness (thereby creating a vicious circle of driving all the good specialists out of the service or causing good men to avoid specialization), selection policies for promotions and high-level appointments are designed to provide "many roads to the top." It is generally understood that the program will take perhaps a decade to be fully integrated into officer attitudes and behavior, but most officers agree that the program of reform is essential.

The counterpart program for the enlisted ranks, initiated in 1973 by Chief of Staff Creighton Abrams, is called the Enlisted Personnel Management System (EPMS). The enlisted problem was entirely different than that of the officers. Since World War II the Army had benefited from Selective Service, which provided a nearly limitless source of talented manpower. Each year's draft call brought in an abundance of high school and college graduates, men easily trained in the complex technology of a modern Army. Only a small proportion reenlisted, but those who did provided a rich pool of talents and skills to the career ranks as well.

Because of this, skill development was concentrated in the first year of service, and career-long professional development went largely unmanaged. The career soldier went from assignment to assignment, gradually gaining through experience the knowledge and skills that he needed as he rose in rank and responsibility. This was the converse of the generalist ideal of the officer corps: the NCO since World War II had become a specialist, narrowly qualified in one of nearly 500 categorized skills. The problem with the system came with increasingly complex

Quarters at some of the famous old posts like Leavenworth have not changed very much. These and the "kindergarten" on the east side of the Leavenworth parade ground are still much the same in 1975 as they were when this picture was taken in 1880. (LVN)

military technology. NCOs in the most senior grades found themselves, after 20 years or so of narrow specialization, unprepared to supervise the broad mixture of soldier skills under their charge. Although a direct cause-and-effect relationship cannot be established, one might speculate that the U.S. Army's unusually high proportion of officers is attributable to this weakness of the NCO corps.

The new system groups soldiers' skills into about 30 career fields. In each field, the soldier begins his career in a rather narrow specialty (but often broader than under the old system, because the number of specialties is being reduced substantially). As he progresses, he is expected to broaden himself in order to better supervise those under him: the number of specialties available at the higher grades will be perhaps one-quarter of those available at the entry level. To assist the NCO in this broadening process, a system of promotion tests and career-long schooling is being instituted. The Army is creating for itself what it has never had before — an integrated system of professional development for its NCO corps.

What is the Army For?

The third great task for the post-Vietnam Army was to redefine its sense of purpose. On the one hand, public reaction to the Vietnam war indicated an unwillingness to intervene in Third World conflicts for the foreseeable future. On the otherhand, Soviet-American detente pointed toward reduced force levels in Europe, while budget pressures made it unlikely that units returned from overseas would be maintained in active status. So the Army was faced with reestablishing its *raison d' être*, to preserve both its share of budgetary resources (thence, its organizational viability) and its functional capability.

The situation is reminiscent of a story from British history. In 1906, the newly appointed War Minister asked the British Imperial General Staff, "What is the Army *for*?" "Silly question!" snorted one old veteran of a dozen campaigns. "As soon ask what the police are for, or the fire department!"

But that was not a silly question for the British then, nor is it for us today. Every army and its political masters must resolve this issue after every war. If we do not know what the Army is supposed to do — in what strategic and tactical situations it is likely to be employed — then we cannot know what sort of Army we need to have.

Perhaps it would be easier to define first what the Army is not for. It is not for ground defense of the continental United States, nor of Hawaii and

Alaska, nor of American territories in the Caribbean and Pacific. Attack on any of these places by a foreign power, other than possibly after the advent of general war, is unthinkable in the nuclear age. Second, it is not for intervention to prop up a faltering regime threatened by insurgency — we shall not pass that way soon again. Finally, it is not for employment in sustained conventional war.

There is hardly unanimity on this last point. The configuration of U.S. ground forces in Germany, and the plans for their reinforcement initially by Stateside active formations and eventually by reserve units, suggests that sustained conventional warfare is considered altogether likely. However, the disposition of these forces is such that a Soviet thrust along the most likely routes might cut them off from their lines of withdrawal; and the readiness of reserves is too low to permit timely reinforcement. This dichotomy between stated mission and strategic capability has provoked intense debate. Those on one side urge withdrawal of a substantial proportion of our troops, arguing that if conventional defense is infeasible — if a "tripwire" is all we've got — then token forces are all we need. Others argue, to the contrary, that redisposition of in-theater forces and reinvigoration of reserve forces are essential to deter or defend against Soviet advance. Both sides agree on the premise that a capability for conventional defense is the preferred goal.

In fact, however, our strategy in Europe is neither that of conventional defense nor of tripwire deterrence. It is what I would call "deterrence by prolonged destructability." That is, our forces in Europe are large enough, in combination with our NATO allies, that their destruction by Soviet forces would be a time-consuming and bloody process. The prolonged spectacle of their engagement would both permit and demand reinforcement from the continental United States. In turn, the act of reinforcing (even if unsuccessful) would inextricably commit U.S. forces to widespread engagement with Soviet forces, a situation likely to trigger general nuclear war. There are, to be sure, arguments that a Soviet-American engagement need not escalate beyond tactical nuclear weapons; but both we and our European allies appear to recognize the hollowness (and, for them, horror) of that line of reasoning.

Of course these arguments are distasteful, which is why they have not been articulated either publicly or internally. Somehow, it is believed that the public tolerates the idea of deterrence by threat of massive retaliation, but finds unpalatable a discussion of what circumstances might trigger such a response. As for internal understanding, policy-makers appear to fear that military morale would suffer if our ground forces in Europe knew that their mission was one of "prolonged destructability" rather than "delay to the Rhine." It does little good to argue that the destruction of ground troops is of far lesser consequence than the holocaust which it would precipitate: the latter appears to be less comprehensible and, therefore, curiously more palatable. It probably will be necessary to continue talking a strategy of conventional defense even though the operative logic (in the minds of the potential enemy, which is where deterrence is applied) is one of "prolonged destructability."

Thus, the question of purpose is answered for a large part of the Army. We need a field army in Europe not substantially smaller than what we have there today, for the ostensible mission of conventional defense. In the continental United States we need another immediately ready force, of the same order of magnitude, to reinforce the first. Neither of these forces can be considered deployable to another part of the world, for if a situation arose which might require deployed ground forces (Huntington's "counterintervention" or Janowitz's "constabulary"), it would probably be accompanied by general international tension of such a nature as to preclude diversion of Europe-committed forces. And thus one might postulate that a third ready force, roughly equivalent in size to the two previously discussed, might be required.

Does the United States intend to intervene with ground forces in any part of the world? No. But if history teaches anything, it is to expect the unexpected. There are places and situations in the world — or if there are not now, there may be someday — where American political leaders may desire to send (or threaten to send) American ground forces.

It would seem, therefore, that the hallmarks of the Army for the foreseeable future must be *flexibility* and *deployability*, and this brings me to the essential point of this essay — we do not and shall not have a "peacetime Army." The fact that the draft has ended and that American troops are not now involved in any conflict anywhere may constitute a peacetime situation; but the need for readiness rules out any near-term prospect for a "peacetime Army."

But if the need is for flexible and immediately deployable forces, while what we have is a mobilization-dependent structure and strategy, is ours a ready Army? If the answer is no — if the "myth of mobilization" still paralyzes our thinking — what chance is there that the situation will change? We cannot wait for another George Marshall at the beginning of a war, for the probable scenario denies us a period of grace in which to clean house. Our hope lies in those who will succeed the "Long Generation" in authority. If they are either conditioned or selected in the image of their predecessors, then the myths of the past will continue to stifle professional reform and stategic innovation. But if they are those who have truly learned the lessons of recent history (as I personally

221

Quarters 24-A was where General and Mrs. Custer were thought to have spent their time at Fort Riley. Only in 1974 was this left half of the residence withdrawn and made into a museum. (FR)

believe will be the case), then the next several years will be a period of major change. As in the 1930s, the talent is there, in undiscovered nuggets and lodes all over the Army. If we are wise, we will bring it to the surface.

Impact on American Life

It would not be proper to end this essay, and this book without returning to the overall subject of *The Army in Peacetime*. What will be the relationship between the Army and civilian society in the era of troubled peace which lies ahead?

First let us look at the reverse side of the coin — the impact of the larger society on the Army. There can be little doubt that domestic factors will tend to shrink and isolate the military. Budgetary pressures will account for much of the shrinkage, as other national needs compete for scarce resources in a period of apparent, however illusory, detente. An even greater cause may be a continuance of relative disinterest in military service by American youth. The effects of this disinterest are perhaps not now apparent, because of the economic recession at the time of this writing. When an economic upturn occurs, however, recruitment is sure to decline to a significant degree. Whether defense leaders accommodate to constrained manpower by reducing force structure or by retaining but skeletonizing a large number of formations (as was done in the 1930s) is not yet foreseeable.

As for the degree of isolation, I would maintain that combat readiness — like war itself — is an apparent anachronism in the modern, urban, post-industrial state. But, anachronistic though it be in civilian eyes, such combat readiness may be crucial to the survival of society in case of armed conflict. So it probably will be necessary for at least the combat formations of the Army (but not its administrative and logistical overhead) to be somewhat secluded from the mainstream of society, in order to maintain discipline and a sense of worth. Isolation should not be allowed to become absolute, of course, for too great a degree of separation could lead to mutual suspicion and hostility. The individual officers and soldiers, and their families, should continue to live within or in close proximity to civilian communities, even though their military activities are confined to training bases of ample size.

There is another phenomenon, little discussed in public, which may possibly contribute to both shrinkage and isolation — race. Optimistic claims by the Gates Commission notwithstanding, the Army's enlisted ranks are becoming increasingly poor and black. There may even come a point at which "tipping" occurs, when some whites might leave out of fear of black predominance — a self-fulfilling prophecy. This would occur more gradually than in the familiar case of civilian residential patterns,

223

If for many long years the professional nucleus of the officer corps came from West Point, the majority of officers came from Officer Candidate Schools (OCS) or from the ROTC. Here in 1949 the Kansas State University detachment in the days of compulsory ROTC marches in review in downtown Manhattan. (KSU Military Science Department)

because of the requirement that soldiers complete their terms of enlistment; but the trend, by the time it was detected, would be hard to reverse.

A related factor, equally serious, is the increasingly complex technology of military equipment and techniques. Soldiers from disadvantaged socio-economic backgrounds — urban ghetto or mountain hollow — are not unintelligent. Given adequate preparation (such as in remedial reading, the use of basic hand tools, and the non-utility of antisocial behavior), they can be trained to operate and maintain modern hardware and to perform complicated military procedures. But at what cost? Within a relatively fixed budget, the Army would have to reduce its size in order to lessen its training overhead.

Political and military leaders, faced with the dangers and difficulties inherent in a non-representative military — one of which would be extreme isolation from society — might well choose to reduce poor/black content by raising educational standards for enlistment. This would reduce the pool of manpower from which to recruit. Thus, an effort to correct isolation would accelerate shrinkage in the size of the Army. Public discussion of this problem will win no prizes for popularity, which probably explains the absence of debate on the subject.

And what of the Army's impact on peacetime society? First one ought to consider a truth seldom addressed in studies on civil-military relations. The Army (any armed force) does not principally serve a productive function in a peacetime society and economy. On the contrary, it is a consumer *par excellence*. It consumes tens of billions of dollars annually in goods and services, not to mention hundreds of thousands of man-years which might otherwise be spent in productive labor. Some observers might disparage this negative contribution to national wealth, or seek to devise some sort of productive role (e.g., "civic actions" projects), but they miss the point. The essential role of the Army is like a term insurance policy, pure protection for a price.

Even though a term insurance policy has no cash surrender value, the prudent family head still wants such protection. There is a finite probability that he may die during the policy's term. Expressing the data in terms of all policyholders of the company, a certain proportion of them *will* die within a given period of time. Transferring the analogy to the subject of this essay, there is a distinct probability (if one reads history) that America will have need of armed forces in the not-distant future. One needs no further justification for maintaining the existence and combat readiness of the Army.

The more useful question, then, might be: how does one enhance the beneficial effects of the Army on society and ameliorate those that are admittedly detrimental? The answer lies generally in three institutional roles: as consumer, as employer, and as social catalyst.

In the consumer role, as in the other two, there are both beneficial and detrimental effects. For beneficial purposes, the government can shift its consumption geographically by enlarging/opening or downgrading/closing military bases, raising or lowering recruiting standards (which, if unacceptable in a direct form, can be accomplished indirectly by tailoring recruiting quotas), or by redirecting research-and-development or purchasing contracts. Contract power could also be used to shift consumption from one corporation to another, affecting both the corporations and the geographic areas from which they draw their labor and materials. It almost goes without saying that the government can use this sort of power also to enforce its laws and social policies. For whatever purpose, the effectiveness of these sorts of measures is limited by political counter-pressure and by long lead-times.

Detrimental consumption effects are currently better known or at least more loudly voiced by critics of the military. That which is consumed by the Army is, *ipso facto*, denied to other sectors of the economy. There is little the Army can do to alter this perception, and thus there probably will be continuing pressures to lessen its magnitude. Proposals may include reduction in the size of forces, a lessening of large-scale training exercises, consolidation of facilities, and simplification of equipment. The military may be expected to resist the last of these vociferously, because of an American conviction that technological superiority on the battlefield can be absolute in its effects.

In the Army's role as employer, a detrimental impact is not currently apparent, because of high civilian unemployment. If and when the economy rebounds to the extent of creating a shortage of skilled labor, the Army will surely be charged with luring scarce skills away from "productive" enterprises. In fact, however, the extent to which the Army, or any of the services, does this is minimal. There is a lateral-entry program by which a proficient worker may enlist, skip skill-acquisition training (although the toughening and socialization process of basic training is still mandatory), and start work as a corporal or junior sergeant. Unfortunately, the monetary and status advantages of these rather junior grades are not likely to lure very many skilled workers from civilian employment — except in those trades in which there is a surplus. Knowing this, Army programs emphasize the *retention* of soldiers with skills acquired through training and experience. There has been considerable success in this effort, except in the case of skills in short supply in the civilian economy; continued success in a revived economy, therefore, is problematical.

The Army is attempting to boost retention through three major programs. The first is the aforementioned Enlisted Personnel Management System, a master plan of professional development for enlisted persons above the private soldier level. The concept behind this system is that self-actualization on the part of more mature soldiers will set an attractive example to their juniors. The program also makes provision for equitable advancement of women in all career fields other than the combat arms. The second program, the "selective reenlistment bonus," pertains more to specific skills. At the end of a soldier's first term of service, usually three years, he is offered a sizeable bonus, the amount determined by the scarcity of his particular skill. The theory behind this practice is simple — the Army is bidding to retain the labor skills in which it has invested so much and for which civilian industry is competing.

Finally, there is a pension-vesting program currently before the Congress. Under its provisions, a soldier completing five years of service would gain a vested interest in the Army's retirement program. Should he wish to leave the service before reaching retired status (currently at 20 years), he would receive a graduated combination of severance pay and deferred annuity. This reform is badly needed by all the services, for the present "no benefits before twenty" practically forces the highly skilled worker out at the three-year point. There was no action on this proposal in the 93rd Congress, but the pension law signed by President Ford on Labor Day 1974 makes enactment of a similar provision for the armed services inevitable.

On balance, then, the Army has a beneficial impact on society in its role as employer. The armed services are, and have been for a long time, major suppliers of labor skills to the civilian economy. That the services would like to lessen the supply is irrelevant — it is a major contribution to the nation's prosperity.

The final role, that of social catalyst, is perhaps the most intangible and, therefore, the most controversial. Is the Army a good place for a young person to mature, to learn to adjust to society — in contemporary terminology, "to get his head screwed on"? Or is it, as some others might attest, a waste of the young person's time or even a corrupter of morals and an inhibitor of psychological adjustment? Either side of the debate has plenty of advocates, many of them more emotional than analytical. In truth, the Army's role is probably like that of "the big city" in Horatio Alger stories: those of strong character are strengthened by its trials; the weak are done in.

What matters most is not which side is correct but which argument the public perceives to be correct. The manning of a large and

History and tradition as well as emotion are personified in the parades of the United States Cadet Corps at West Point passing in review on a sunny day in 1970. (USMA)

technologically modern Army depends greatly on that perception. And that perception ultimately depends on the facts. The post-Vietnam internal reforms discussed earlier should contribute much in this regard, but a restored sense of purpose — which in a democracy originates in the public mind — is also vital. Thus we have a circular paradox: a publicly supported sense of purpose is needed to provide a climate favorable to internal reform, which in turn must occur to produce public support and a sense of purpose. This is but a restatement of an old adage — a democratic society gets the sort of Army it really wants.

Conclusion

We have come a far distance from the polo fields of 1937. And what have we learned along the way?

Surely this. We live in a small and dangerous world, in which, as Plato said, "only the dead have seen the end of war." Civilian society depends on the U.S. Army for its protection in this world; the Army derives its very existence from that society. In their mutual dependence lies the strength of American civil-military relations and the safeguarding of both our domestic liberties and our national security.

Suggestions for Further Research

There are two areas, each complementary to the other, in which research needs to be done. The first is to determine whether military thinking on strategic matters, particularly the *raison d'être* of conventional ground forces, is converging with or diverging from trends in influential civilian thought. A large part of the question will be, of course, how to define and determine each body of thought, if indeed either is unified. Some writers would call this a simple task; I would be wary of stereotypes.

The second area would also lend itself to attitude survey, but vertically — between military generations — rather than horizontally, between military and civilian. If what I have speculated in my paper is true, a distinct shift should be measurable between, for example, a sample of generals and a sample of colonels five to ten years their junior. Then, five years later, one might compare the data pertaining to those earlier colonels with that of the fraction who have since risen to general officer status. The question to be answered is whether the old regime is renewing itself in its own image or if the new breed is a product suited to its own time.

SOURCES

When Robin Higham told the authors of this book to eschew footnotes, I was pleased. A requirement to cite sources keeps writers honest, with themselves as well as with their readers. Unfortunately, it also makes them "cut the suit to fit the cloth," which explains why some of our soundest scholarship makes some of the dullest reading. So I appreciate the liberty which our editor has granted — to brew a mixture of professional experience, borrowed expertise, and intuitive judgment.

But the reader is entitled to at least a guess as to where the ideas come from. The basic source is my own memory and the collective memory of the military family in which I was born and grew up. Equally important are my experiences over plus years of active service, which continues still. Last are books and articles which I have read or consulted in recent years, named last not through preference for my own prejudices but because I confess to finding most insightful those works that synthesize ideas already half-developed in my own mind.

The classic of classics is Samuel P. Huntington's *The Soldier and the State* (1957). Most of us who write in this field show trends from the past to the present; he alone foresaw in the 1950s what the 1960s would reveal. His elitist prescriptions for preserving military professionalism are often derided today, which should tell us something about the mood of post-Vietnam scholarship.

Equally well known is Morris Janowitz's *The Professional Soldier* (1960) and his many essays on the subject since. His approach to reconciling an authoritarian military subculture to a democratic society is opposite to that of Huntington's — that is, he would integrate the two rather than attempt to keep them separate. Two military men who also take sides on the issue are Robert N. Ginsburgh, "The Challenge to Military Professionalism," *Foreign Affairs*, 1964, and Robert G. Gard, "The Military and American Society," *Foreign Affairs*, 1971.

For background reading into the pre-World War II Army, and into the sorts of books that influenced postwar military thought, I recommend the autobiographies of the general officer heroes of that war — Eisenhower, Bradley, MacArthur, Patton, *et al.* — and the superb series on Marshall by Forrest Pogue. Perhaps the book that best sums them up is a work of fiction, Anton Myrer's *Once An Eagle*.

Four excellent journalistic-anecdotal views of the Army are Ward Just, *Military Men* (1970); Peter Barnes, *Pawns: The Plight of the Citizen-Soldier* (1972); Stuart Loory, *Defeated: Inside America's Military Machine* (1973); and Maureen Mylander, *The Generals* (1974). Less readable but more scholarly are Russell Weigley, *History of the United States Army* (1967), and Adam Yarmolinsky, *The Military Establishment*

(1971). Weigley has a tendency (common to military historians) to give short shrift to anything beyond World War II, whereas Yarmolinsky is so busy exposing the interlocking directorates of the Military-Industrial Complex that he neglects the people within the institutions. In this regard, the journalists — for all their lapses into cuteness or moral outrage — may come closer to understanding what motivates today's military leaders.

There are also several valuable books by military officers. Anthony Herbert (*Soldier*, 1973) is a latter-day Baron Munchhausen, and a lot less entertaining than the original because of his bitterness. Another retired lieutenant colonel, Edward L. King, has written a work even more corroded with sour anger at the system which did him wrong (*The Death of the Army*, 1972). Neither book is worthwhile as a source for what happened to the post-World War II Army, for both authors have personal axes to grind. Nonetheless, both are invaluable as evidence that neither of Janowitz's pure archetypes — the heroic leader and the military manager — can make it in a world where success requires functioning in both roles.

Finally, there are two books published in 1973 by officers on active duty: Zeb B. Bradford and Frederic J. Brown, *The United States Army in Transition*, and my own, *America's Army in Crisis*. Both call for extensive reform; the difference in titles portrays the authors' respective views on the consequences of non-action.

MILITARY AFFAIRS/AEROSPACE HISTORIAN
Publishing Series

Order from: MA/AH Publishing Series Eisenhower Hall, Kansas State University, Manhattan, Kansas 66506, USA. Make checks payable to Publishing Series. Standing orders for automatic shipment of new and revised publications will be accepted.

ISBN Number Description

0-89126-000-5   Department of the Army Ad Hoc Committee on the Army Need for the Study of Military History. **Report.** 1971. Volume I, **Report and Recommendations.** $4.50.

0-89126-001-3   Department of the Army Ad Hoc Committee on the Army Need for the Study of Military History. **Report.** 1971. Volume II, **Annexes A-B, D-H.** $7.50.

0-89126-002-1   Department of the Army Ad Hoc Committee on the Army Need for the Study of Military History. **Report.** 1971. Volume III, **Annexes I-N.** $7.50.

0-89126-003-X   Department of the Army Ad Hoc Committee on the Army Need for the Study of Military History. **Report.** 1971. Volume IV, **Annex C, Military History Questionnaire-Evaluation of Results.** $5.50.

All four above volumes for $15.00

0-89126-004-8   Horatio Bond, Ed. **Fire and the Air War.** 1946. $5.50.

0-89126-005-6   W. P. Taylor and F. L. Irvin, comps. **History of the 148th Aero Squadron, Aviation Section, U.S. Army Signal Corps, A.E.F.-B.E.F., 1917-1918.** 1957. $9.50.

0-89126-006-4   Cy Martin. **Men of the Twentieth: The Story of the 20th Aero Squadron.** Foreword by James J. Hudson. 1974. $5.50.

0-89126-007-2   **Technology and Institutional Response: Papers Presented to a Joint Session of the American Military Institute at the Duquesne History Forum,** Pittsburgh, Pennsylvania, November 1, 1972. $4.50.

0-89126-008-0   **Access to Government Documents: Papers Presented to a Session of the American Historical Association, December, 1972.** $4.50.

0-89126-009-9   Fred L. Parrish. **A Yank in the British YMCA in 1917.** $6.50.

0-89126-010-2   John M. Loeblein. **Memoirs of Kelly Field, 1917-1918.** 1974. $4.50.

0-89126-011-0   **Index to Aerospace Historian,** Cumulative, 20 years. 1974. $5.50.

0-89126-012-9   Colonel John F. Whiteley. **Early Army Aviation: The Emerging Air Force.** 1974. $8.50

0-89126-013-7   Marc B. Powe. **The Emergence of the War Department Intelligence Agency: 1885-1918.** 1974. $6.00.

0-89126-014-5   Juliette A. Hennessy. **The United States Army Air Arm: April 1861 to April 1917.** USAF Historical Division, Research Studies Institute, Air University. 1950. USAF Historical Studies No. 98. $8.50

0-89126-015-3   Dr. John C. Warren. **Airborne Operations in World War II, European Theater.** USAF Historical Division Research Studies Institute, Air University. 1956. USAF Historical Studies No. 97. $7.50

0-89126-016-1   Dr. Robert F. Futrell. **Command of Observation Aviation: A Study in Control of Tactical Airpower.** USAF Historical Division, Research Studies Institute Air University. 1956. USAF Historical Studies No. 24. $4.50.

0-89126-017-X   Phyllis and William Bultmann, eds. **Current Research in British Studies.** 1975. $9.00

0-89126-020-X   **Special Operations: AAF Aid to European Resistance Movements 1943-43.** Air Historical Office, Army Air Forces. 1947. $8.50

0-89126-021-8   **The Development of Air Doctrine in the Army Air Arm, 1917-1941.** USAF Historical Division, Research Studies Institute, Air University. 1955. USAF Historical Studies No. 89. $6.50.

0-89126-022-6   Robert F. Stohlman, Jr. **The Powerless Position: The Commanding General of the Army of the United States, 1864-1903.** 1975. $7.00.